MARRIAGE
at the
CROSSROADS

Couples in Conversation About Discipleship,
Gender Roles, Decision Making and Intimacy

Aída Besançon Spencer
William David Spencer
Steven R. Tracy
Celestia G. Tracy

IVP Academic

An imprint of InterVarsity Press
Downers Grove, Illinois

InterVarsity Press
P.O. Box 1400, Downers Grove, IL 60515-1426
World Wide Web: www.ivpress.com
E-mail: email@ivpress.com

InterVarsity Press® *is the book-publishing division of InterVarsity Christian Fellowship/USA*®*, a student movement active on campus at hundreds of universities, colleges and schools of nursing in the United States of America, and a member movement of the International Fellowship of Evangelical Students. For information about local and regional activities, write Public Relations Dept., InterVarsity Christian Fellowship/USA, 6400 Schroeder Rd., P.O. Box 7895, Madison, WI 53707-7895, or visit the IVCF website at <www.intervarsity.org>.*

Design: Cindy Kiple

Images: Robin Cracknell/Getty Images

ISBN 978-0-8308-2890-6

Printed in the United States of America ∞

Library of Congress Cataloging-in-Publication Data

Marriage at the crossroads: couples in conversation about
discipleship, gender roles, decision makeing, and intimacy / Aída
Besançon Spencer . . . [et al.].
      p. cm.
   Includes bibliographical references and index.
   ISBN 978-0-8308-2890-6 (pbk.: alk. paper)
   1. Marriage—Religious aspects—Christianity. I. Spencer, Aída
Besançon.
     BV835.M2355 2009
     248.8'44—dc22

                                                                                    2009000455

P 25 24 23 22 21 20 19 18 17 16 15 14 13 12 11 10 9 8 7 6 5 4 3 2 1

Y 30 29 28 27 26 25 24 23 22 21 20 19 18 17 16 15 14 13 12 11 10 09

Contents

Introduction 9

Chapter 1: Marriage and Being Disciples of Jesus

Aída and Bill Spencer's Viewpoint 17

   Love 18

   Christ Has Priority. 19

   One Flesh 25

   Summary. 31

Steve and Celestia Tracy's Viewpoint 33

   Jesus and Marriage. 33

   Application of Jesus' Teachings 40

   Our Primary Task: Advancing God's Kingdom Together. . 47

Concluding Dialogue 49

Chapter 2: "Headship" and Submission

Steve and Celestia Tracy's Viewpoint 57

   A Trinitarian Model of Headship and Submission 58

   The Foundation of Headship 65

   The Essence of Headship 66

   The Purpose of Headship 70

   An Incarnational Model of Headship and Submission:
   Ephesians 5:21-33 72

Aída and Bill Spencer's Viewpoint 77

Defining Authority 79

Understanding Ephesians 5:21-22: Mutual Submission . . 84

Understanding Ephesians 5:22-33: Head 88

Concluding Dialogue 95

Chapter 3: Marriage Roles and Decision Making

Aída and Bill Spencer's Viewpoint 101

Marriage and Roles 102

Marriage and Decision Making 108

Steve and Celestia Tracy's Viewpoint 117

Innate Gender Differences in Creation 118

The Intersection of Gender Differences and
Gender Roles 120

Additional Evidence for Innate Gender Differences
That Facilitate Gender Roles 127

Designer Love: Crafting the Relationship 131

Designer Work: Building Vocations/Ministries 133

Designer Parenting: Raising Children 134

Concluding Dialogue 138

Chapter 4: Marriage and Intimacy

Steve and Celestia Tracy's Viewpoint 145

Spiritual Foundation 145

Bonding: Three Dimensions 148

Sensate Hour 156

Sex as an Expression of Bondedness 157

Bill and Aída Spencer's Viewpoint 162

Spiritual Intimacy 164

Personal Intimacy 165

Relational Intimacy 167

Emotional Intimacy 174

Physical Intimacy 176

Concluding Dialogue 182

Chapter 5: Responses from Three Couples

**Marriage for a North American Hispanic Couple
(Wanda R. and Robert W. Pazmiño)** 189

**Marriage for a Korean American Couple
(Matthew D. and Sarah S. Kim)** 193

**Marriage for an African American Couple
(Darin and Vicki Poullard)** 198

Conclusion 207

The Spencers' Concluding Reflections 214

The Tracys' Concluding Reflections 215

Contributors 218

Subject Index 223

Scripture Index 229

INTRODUCTION

All of us who marry with honest intentions want our love to last and to be as fresh and endearing as the day we wed. The wise look toward couples whose relationships appear to have deepened and matured with the years to serve as models. Of course, what's really going on in a relationship can certainly turn out to be unexpected, as one visitor discovered who was so impressed at first with a couple of seventy years of wedded bliss, when the husband routinely referred to his wife in the most affectionate terms—"Honey, My Love, Darling, Sweetheart, Pumpkin . . ." and so on. When the wife left the room, the visitor had to comment, "I think it's wonderful that, after all these years, you still call your wife those loving pet names," whereupon the husband shrugged sadly and confessed, "I have to tell you the truth . . . I forgot her name about ten years ago."[1] As with such marital veterans, the bottom line for most of us is we want to be loved—even if our names are eventually forgotten.

This is a book about loving long and loving well, as God intended love to be between one man and one woman in what is often called earth's oldest institution. Genesis, the Hebrew Bible's book of beginnings, says of marriage, "a man leaves his father and his mother and clings to his wife, and they become one flesh" (Gen 2:24). Not surprisingly, Christian couples these days naturally turn to an army of experts to have this verse and its implications explained, but they find they are sometimes assaulted by a fusillade of competing views, all claiming to explain God's precise intentions. Most of the perspectives we've noticed differ with one another by emphasizing varying degrees of submission between husband and wife, ranging from categories of totally mutual submission to complete male authority. They identify themselves under two general categories: egalitarian and complementarian.

---

[1]"The Truth Hurts," #233, *Planet North Shore* (Autumn 2007): 2.

Couples are being asked to choose which model they will adopt and to what degree they will adapt it.

While some couples are selecting between the varying degrees of these models, other couples enter unwittingly into this debate, looking for consensus, wanting to know what positions these views share, asking what are the basic truths that can be identified and applied as the central tenets of godly marriage and how can we live them out together in our homes with God's blessing and a growing experience of mutual, familial love.

This is exactly where this study enters in. Our book is written by two couples with differing views about marriage and gender roles, and emphasizes the essential aspects of Christian marriage upon which all couples can agree while noting the differences that couples need to consider. The book is not set up as a debate, as is the nature of other two- and four-views books. Instead, we recognize each other as devout Christians. We respect each other's home life and see Jesus' ideals alive in each other's relationship. On so many aspects we agree, and on some we disagree. And we lay those aspects out before you, so you will know the core values of Christian marriage we espouse and the variations (not in conflict with those essentials) Christians currently consider.

Why did we write this book? As teachers in seminaries and pastors training called believers to be ministers and as a counselor working to help families find wholeness, we are concerned about promoting healthy Christian marriages. We are dedicated to assisting people who struggle with relationships. Our goal is to correct misinformation and promote mutual understanding. We realize many younger adults have largely given up on marriage, not because they don't believe in it, but because they haven't seen it work.[2] A long-term happy marriage increasingly seems to them a nice but mythical fairy tale. So we want to correct common misperceptions regarding marriage as a viable long-term in-

---

[2] The National Marriage Project notes that the vast majority of high school seniors still want to get married and say that "having a good marriage and family life" is "extremely important" and yet well over half of adolescents approve of "cohabitation" ("The State of Our Unions 2007: The Social Health of Marriage in America, pp. 26-27; this report can be accessed on the National Marriage Project web site at: <http://marriage.rutgers.edu/Publications/SOOU/SOOU2007.pdf>).

stitution by presenting two models of marriage within the Christian worldview that address one of the most debated issues in the evangelical community: the structure of the family. Should it be hierarchical or egalitarian or a position between? Whose calling or career has priority? What are gender roles in marriage? How are decisions made?

Therefore, our goal in this book is to explore the two basic Christian views of marriage with both couples openly discussing each view. Each couple will answer the same set of questions that most believing couples puzzle over. What we are asking is, where are the points of commonality? Where are our similar scriptural views, and where are the issues that divide us? How did each couple arrive at the view each holds, and what is most useful for readers to apply to their own marriages to enrich them and please God?

Our hope is that those contemplating marriage as well as those already married and those helping others prepare for and think about marriage will find in this careful and open, dialogical presentation a treasury of valuable insights we have learned over the years in our own study and practice to help clarify what Christian marriage means for a couple's life together. We aim to lay out helpful ideas for you to apply as you create your own theology and practice of marriage. To do this, each couple wrote a chapter and sent it to the other to read. We took turns writing up the summary of both chapters and identifying the similarities and differences and then we all amended what we wrote as the other couple responded to it and made suggestions. We talked over each response until all four of us were satisfied we had captured as accurately as possible the agreements and variations we discovered. Then, when the draft was finished, we had three couples from different cultural perspectives review the chapters and summaries and respond to them.

In chapter one we centered on the most important aspect of any facet of life for Christians: Jesus' perspective. We asked each other and ourselves, in what way did Jesus speak to the marriage relationship, and how do his teachings serve to guide our views on marriage? Essentially, how do we as a married couple follow Jesus' guidance and advance God's reign?

In chapter two we tackled a knotty issue, the question of what *head* means in Ephesians 5:21-33. This has become at times an acrimonious point of debate, and our goal in this book was to leave the polemics behind and strive to be fair, reasonable and irenic with each other's views. By respecting each other and trying to examine the topic in dialogue, we expanded our focus to discuss the meaning of *submission* and ask how each of our convictions on the proper meaning of *head* and *submission* work out in our daily interaction as spouses. We also looked at the relationships in the Trinity to see what light they shed on the husband and wife relationship. The bottom line, of course, is how our answer affected our marriage, particularly in our understanding of authority.

Chapter three was the natural follow-through of the previous discussion, since the model of authority implemented is most tested out in the making of important decisions that will affect everyone in the home. For example, it will determine how a final decision is made in the case of a deadlock, whose career or calling has priority, in fact, how career choices are made. Our discussion revealed that our understanding of whether the Bible proposes any innate male-female gender differences or roles, or whether such are not innate but learned from fallen cultures, guided the way decision making has come to be practiced in each of our homes. The results were consistent, although, at times, surprising to the other couple!

The final chapter on marriage and intimacy, chapter four, looked in depth at the intimate levels of marriage, including its emotional, physical, relational, personal and spiritual expressions. In it we attempted to explore the deeper levels of human interaction and see how they interrelate with our faith.

Every book, of course, is limited by the experiences and cultural boundaries of its authors (even when an author is bicultural, as is one of ours). Therefore, to break over these borders, in chapter five we invited three couples of Hispanic American, Asian American and African American backgrounds to read and reflect on the manuscript. Their insights are very enlightening and help us put a more multicultural perspective on our findings.

Finally, we summarized key elements that we discovered in our conclusions, and each couple ended with reflections on what we ourselves learned from this dialogue and what we recognized as essential points of agreement we share and disagreement still remaining.

Do doctors take their own medicine to improve their health? We did and prescriptions from both couples are proving very wholesome in our own marriages. We hope you too will find the advice in this book yields the same helpful results in your own godly, intimate, joyful and wholesome marriages. Thank you for dialoguing along with us.

Chapter One

MARRIAGE AND BEING
DISCIPLES OF JESUS

Aída and Bill Spencer's
Viewpoint

W hen we think of the ideal marriage, we often think of such quotations as these:

Marriage is "two friends, two bodies with one soul inspir'd" (*The Iliad of Homer* 16, line 267) or "Two souls with but a single thought, Two hearts that beat as one."[1] The Bible recounts one such couple whose two hearts beat as one. They had a mutual understanding and clear communication. They agreed together to promote their family interests. They stuck together and persevered against all outside pressures. They even died and were buried together. But we have yet to find one person who speaks of them in appreciative terms because they had one major problem—they did not persevere as Jesus' disciples. Who were they? Ananias and Sapphira! The historian Luke tells us Ananias "with his wife's knowledge" sold property pretending to donate all of it to the Christian community while secretly retaining part of the proceeds (Acts 5:2-3). They had "agreed together" to lie to the Holy Spirit (Acts 5:9). Sapphira and Ananias were each individually given the opportunity to rescind their previous marital agreement (to lie to the Holy Spirit and to the Christian community). They were offered the opportunity to be truthful with God (Acts 5:3-4, 8-9). What we learn from this example is that being Jesus' disciple is more important than fulfilling any idyllic idea of marriage. A good marriage involves balancing outward and inward pulls: love toward God and toward spouse; Christ has priority, yet we are limited and need rest; two independent people are interdependent or *one flesh*.

Disciples or followers of Jesus do not cease to follow Jesus in their

---

[1]Friedrich Halm, *Ingomar, the Barbarian* Act II, trans. Maria Lovell (Boston: Walter Baker, 1896), p. 31.

marriage. In what way does Jesus speak to the marriage relationship and how do his teachings serve to guide our views of marriage? In effect, how does being a follower of Jesus affect one's marriage? Jesus has some implicit teachings and practices related to marriage, but he also has some teachings that explicitly relate to marriage.

LOVE

Jesus' second great command is like the first—to love our neighbors as ourselves (Mk 12:29-31).[2] Our love for God is fleshed out in our love for those near us, and our immediate family members are indeed the most near to us (Lk 10:29-37). In this regard, marriage in our experience has been a furnace shaping each of us as gold into a more beautiful jewel. To speak about love is easy. To love another day in, day out is so much harder. Alice Mathews and Gay Hubbard phrase it well in *Marriage Made in Eden*. Marriage is for two fallen people who are reaching out to please Christ together:

> [Marriage involves] living out the intimate connection of two broken image-bearers who are in the process of being restored and who are committed to helping each other in the restoration process. It is about two broken image-bearers forming with one another a community of forgiveness that is an embodiment of the gospel and a living demonstration of God's transforming power.[3]

Jesus (and John the Baptist) preached about repentance for the forgiveness of sins. Repentance precedes belief in the good news and becoming an active member of Christ's kingdom (Mk 1:4-5, 15; 6:12; Lk 24:47). The most moving moments of marriage are times when we seek forgiveness and our spouse graciously grants it, and we are enveloped in God's restorative love.[4] As repentant sinners, we can be sure we will sin (Mk 7:20-23). In that regard, we are no different from sinners Ananias and Sapphira, but our hope is that we will seek to grow by forgiving and being forgiven. As a matter of fact, Margaret Poloma and George Gal-

---

[2]See also Lk 10:27; Mt 22:37-39.
[3]Alice P. Mathews and M. Gay Hubbard, *Marriage Made in Eden: A Pre-Modern Perspective for a Post-Christian World* (Grand Rapids: Baker, 2004), p. 200.
[4]Mt 18:35; 6:12; Lk 6:36-38; 11:4.

lup Jr. found that people who reported that religion was "very important" to them were more likely to respond in positive ways to being hurt
(forgiving, discussing the matter to bring feelings out into the open,
praying for the person) as opposed to negative responses (such as seeking revenge).[5]

CHRIST HAS PRIORITY

Jesus commanded his followers to love one another. In this way, others
will recognize them as followers of Jesus (Jn 13:34-35). Moreover, he
explained that, if we indeed love Jesus, we will obey his command-
ments (Jn 14:15, 21, 23-24). One of Jesus' commands is to proclaim his
kingdom or reign (Lk 10:9). Thus, as a married couple, we see each
other as colaborers in promoting Christ's reign in our world around us.
We pastor each other so that we will each hear God's affirmation:
"Well done, good and faithful servant!" (Mt 25:21, 23 TNIV; Mk 13:32-
37). Our goal as a couple is to follow Jesus and help others follow Jesus
too (Mk 1:17). Kari Torjesen Malcolm explains in *Building Your Family
to Last*: "The more I am united to Christ in deep love, the more I will
love my husband and children, and this life of caring will spill over into
the world. When the kingdom of God is my first concern, my priorities
will be such that my marriage and family will thrive."[6] How do we as a
married couple advance God's kingdom?

When we first met, we did not plan a life of ministry together.
Rather, serving together became a natural outgrowth of our individual
commitment to Jesus as Lord. In various ways, God appeared to bring
us together again and again. For instance, once when Aída missed the
cars leaving for a college retreat and gave up all hope of going, Bill, who
was running the retreat and serving as the last safety net, showed up
with his car ready to transport her. These types of "coincidences" happened again and again.

Becoming one with someone with the same goal in life, to serve Je-

---

[5]George H. Gallup Jr. and Timothy Jones, *The Saints Among Us* (Harrisburg: Morehouse, 1992),
p. 80.
[6]Kari Torjesen Malcolm, *Building Your Family to Last* (Eugene, Ore.: Wipf & Stock, 2006),
pp. 15-16.

sus, is the essential foundation for an effective marriage. At our first hike, we talked at length about the importance of integrity. In our early steps in ministry we encouraged our individual visions for service, taking turns with one leading, while the other helped. We also each tried to look out for the interest of the other. For instance, Bill became motivated to run a coffee house from our home church. Aída helped out but also tried to help Bill pace himself. Aída agreed to develop a course for Hispanic Americans for the local Young Women's Christian Association as part of her work as a community organizer. Bill helped her find the social services resources available. Our challenge was to do ministry, but not ignore our potential spouse in the process. How could we help our future spouse feel included while ministering to others? Quickly, we discovered that weekly we needed to have some time to develop our own relationship with each other. Otherwise, we could easily but inadvertently misunderstand each other.

We were married after completing our masters level theological studies. Bill had developed a ministry as a chaplain at a local college into a part-time call. It took Aída over a year to find a ministry call nearby. Eventually she became a chaplain at another local college. (In the meantime, she taught English as a second language at a maximum security prison, and initiated and ran a Bible study and worship in Spanish at the prison.) The advantage of two separate calls at first was that we each were then free to develop our ministry model as we were led by God, with the helpful advice of the other. In that way, we had more freedom to learn about ourselves and the gifts God gave us. We generally attended the regular group meetings of the other campus group, whenever possible, but we did not take the proactive leadership role when at the other campus, only at our own. Jesus taught his disciples to serve one another (e.g., Mk 9:33-37; 10:45), and in this way we saw ourselves as serving the other. A side benefit of our presence was a reminder to the students that indeed this minister was already married. We clearly wanted to avoid the expectations for unholy sexual liaisons set by our predecessors on both campuses!

The next stage in ministering together came after we married, now that we were "two become one." How were we now "one," yet how were we still "two"? We realized that we should not lose our individuality when we became "one." This dilemma was particularly heightened in our next ministry when we both became organizers of a spinoff college program for training pastors while we were teaching seminary. Now we had one general goal, one vision. We discovered that we would sometimes end up duplicating the same tasks. One of us might feel slighted while the other assumed he or she was in charge. We learned that we needed to clarify our roles, in light of our spiritual gifts and natural interests, so that we could work as one team. Aída became the dean of academics because she enjoyed "organizing" the curricular structure. Bill became the director of personnel since he could handle difficult interpersonal communication, having the gift of "encouragement" (Rom 12:8).

A third stage in ministering together came when we organized a new church. We had learned how to work together, but how do we work as a team of equals with others? Back when we were supervising seminary students in urban college ministry, we discovered two students with unique gifts we did not have. One student as an evangelist could invite strangers forthrightly to visit our prospective campus group. Another student discipled others by being available to be discipled. Nevertheless, we as professors were still in charge. But a more advanced stage now occurred when our new Presbyterian church development joined with an independent church plant. How do we as "two in one flesh" work together with other equal authorities? We spent time again clarifying our roles and gifts in this new group of copastors while clarifying the principles of agreement between us. We each needed to be clear about our strengths, responsible for our area of ministry, while yet willing to help or be inactive when another led. The best leaders make the best followers—we have certainly found this to be true.

It is Jesus' opinion that counts most, not that of others (Mk 2:15-17; Jn 12:42-43). Since we worship a crucified Messiah, our redemption cost Jesus much.[7] Likewise, our marriage as believers costs us at times status and money (Mk 8:34-35; Jn 15:18-21). The three temptations of

---

[7]Mk 10:33-34; Lk 18:32-33; 24:26.

self-glory, sign seeking and materialism can affect a marriage too.[8] Each of us had to decide whether our relationships or our ambitions would take priority. Our relationships with Jesus, each other and then with others as an outflowing of the first two relationships are foundational, and they demand sacrifices or commitment. At times we have had to delay one person's career advancement so that the other person could advance as well. Or, when one person had an attractive career choice, that person sought to find an opportunity for the other. For example, Bill developed a campus chaplaincy position for himself from his seminary internship. When a nearby college had an opening the next year, he recommended Aída.

We have never been called on to act like Ananias and Sapphira should have acted—choosing God over husband or wife. Since we both love God and want to please God that has never been necessary. However, Jesus made it quite clear that obedience to him has more priority—when in conflict—than obedience to one's family member.[9] There is a cost in being a disciple (Lk 9:23). Although a man must cling to his wife, yet his love for Christ must be so great as to be in comparison "hatred" of his wife (Lk 14:26). Christ is the ultimate authority and giver of life. Marriage should not become an idol. Neither husband nor wife can satisfy all one feels called to do with one's life. That is why married couples need to be part of a larger active Christian community. Since "*whoever* does God's will" is our brother and sister and mother (Mk 3:31-35 tniv, italics added; Lk 8:21), we slowly help each other to redefine our concept of self to include first the other as spouse, then any ensuing children and finally the rest of the Christian community as our extended "adopted" family.

Jesus sent his disciples out two by two (Lk 10:1).[10] Paul ministered with a team of men and women. One set of well-known coworkers was Prisca and Aquila, a couple ministering together. They were always mentioned together and always ministering together. They seemed to share all duties, as far as the New Testament records. Both were tentmakers

---

[8]Lk 4:1-12; 9:25; 12:15, 23, 34; 14:33; 16:13-15; 18:22.
[9]Mk 10:29-30; 13:12-13; Lk 12:51-53; 18:29-30; 21:16.
[10]Even the twelve apostles are named in pairs in Mt 10:2-4.

by trade, both offered hospitality to Paul, both were teachers—accurate expounders. Both joined Paul on his trip from Corinth to Ephesus and both stayed there to minister (Acts 18:3, 18, 26). They both send "hearty greetings" from Ephesus to the Corinthians (1 Cor 16:19). Whether in Corinth or in Rome, they organized and offered their home for a church to meet, apparently serving as church overseers (Rom 16:3-5). They developed special relationships wherever they were and had forceful characters. One notices their equality even in the way they are mentioned as a couple. Sometimes one is listed first, sometimes the other (Aquila is cited first in Acts 18:2 and 1 Cor 16:19, and Prisca/Priscilla is cited first in Acts 18:18; Rom 16:3; 2 Tim 4:19). They welded together business interests with ministry goals, offering their time and finances to advance Christ's reign.

When Claudius's decree against the Jews in Rome was lifted after A.D. 54, Prisca and Aquila moved back to Rome after having been in Corinth and Ephesus. Paul describes them as his "co-workers in Christ Jesus" (Rom 16:3 TNIV). Both risked their lives for Paul. Thus, their faith cost them much sacrifice: in behalf of Paul's life, they risked their own "necks" (Rom 16:4). They sacrificed or made themselves vulnerable for someone outside their household—Paul, their brother in Christ. They loved him with a Christlike love. But they also ministered to many. As Jews they made a point to preach the gospel to non-Jews.

Aquila and Priscilla were apt examples of the early church lawyer Tertullian's ideal for marriage:

> How beautiful, then, the marriage of two Christians, two who are one in hope, one in desire, one in the way of life they follow, one in the religion they practice. They are as brother and sister, both servants of the same Master. Nothing divides them, either in flesh or in spirit. They are, in very truth, *two in one flesh*; and where there is but one flesh there is also but one spirit. . . . [He concludes:] Where there are two together, there also (Christ) is present, and where He is, there evil is not.[11]

Jesus taught his disciples not to lead as the nations do—their rulers

---

[11]Tertullian "To His Wife" II.8, *Treatises on Marriage and Remarriage*, trans. William P. LeSaint, Ancient Christian Writers 13 (Westminster, Md.: Newman Press, 1956), p. 35.

lord over one another. Instead, Jesus' followers should serve one another and give their lives for one another (Mk 10:42-45; Lk 22:25-27). Such servant leadership does *not* involve hating oneself more than one loves another, because Jesus has told us to love our neighbor "as yourself" (Mk 12:31). But we do incorporate Jesus' teachings into our marriage leadership style. Formally, neither the husband nor the wife is the ultimate ruler over the other, but should serve the other. Informally, we are tempted in different ways to become an autocratic ruler by not consulting the other in a decision, or assuming the other person agrees. We esteem couples such as Aurelius Patermouthis and Aurelia Tkako of Syene, who, around A.D. 583–584, considered "Christ the Master of all" and stated in their joint will that since they were married they afforded each other "no ordinary peace and comfort, soothing and comforting and serving and obeying and submitting, in no single matter disagreeing but living in all submissiveness."[12] What a beautiful example of mutual appreciation!

Of course, different cultural and gender customs can create misunderstanding at times. We may have different ways to express service. Sometimes our eagerness to get a spouse to participate may be interpreted as oppressive. Instead, we may need to sense when a more quiet person has something to say but cannot break into the conversation. The more outgoing at times may need to curtail excessive speaking. For some, politeness is expressed by waiting to contribute until there is silence. For others, one is expected to break into the conversation at "appropriate" breaks in the conversation.

Further, when it causes no conflict between our allegiance to Jesus and to our spouse or other family member, we are to honor our father and mother.[13] We are to ask Jesus to help our family members, as Peter asked Jesus to heal his mother-in-law (Mk 1:30), as the Syrophoenician mother asked Jesus to heal her daughter (Mk 7:25-30), as Jairus asked Jesus to heal his daughter (Lk 8:41-42), and as the official asked Jesus to heal his son in Capernaum (Jn 4:46-47). We are to do all we can to

---

[12]"A Byzantine Will," *Select Papyri* I, III.86, trans. A. S. Hunt and C. C. Edgar, The Loeb Classical Library (Cambridge: Harvard University Press, 1932), p. 257.
[13]Mk 10:19; Lk 18:20; Jn 19:26-27.

help our family members be in an environment that helps God's Word
become deep and bear fruit and not fall away because of trouble, perse-
cution, cares, wealth and other desires.[14] In the United States, there are
so many ways the lure of wealth can draw us away from being Christ's
followers. For instance, as a couple, we have always tried to live economically—purchasing only one used car at a time, which we coordi-
nate our schedules to share; making our first computer last ten years
before buying a second one; chopping wood for our heating supply;
consulting *Consumer Reports* and watching the sales before making a
major purchase. Our dollars salute before they march out to buy. In
North America our lifestyle appears economically disadvantaged, yet
compared to much of the world, we are quite wealthy.[15] The question is,
who sets our perspective, Christ's mission or our culture's message?
Despite culture's pressure, gain must never replace Christ's mission as
the driving force of a Christian family.

We consider our first priority to advance Christ's reign, yet, at the
same time, we balance our mission in life as a married couple with the
need for rest. Christ as lord of the Sabbath wants us to rest. Jesus ex-
horted the apostles: "Come away to a deserted place all by yourselves
and rest a while" (Mk 6:31-32; 2:27-28). We should serve others, but we
cannot do so if we do not steward our bodies, minds and marriage relationship. We are limited, mortal vessels serving a limitless, immortal
Creator. Since, as ordained ministers, we often serve Sunday mornings
and early afternoon, we try very hard to rest late Sunday afternoons and
evenings and spread the "Sabbath rest" throughout the week: going out
together Friday and Saturday nights. As people in the public eye, we
need breaks from continual scrutiny.

ONE FLESH

Possibly the most explicit teaching Jesus ever gave about marriage is to

---

[14]Mk 4:3-20; 10:21-31; 12:41-44.

[15]Ronald J. Sider reports that "American Christians live in the richest nation on earth and enjoy an average household income of $42,409. The World Bank reports that 1.2 billion of the
world's poorest people try to survive on just one dollar a day." *The Scandal of the Evangelical
Conscience: Why Are Christians Living Just Like the Rest of the World?* (Grand Rapids: Baker,
2005), p. 21.

reinforce God's intentions for it, for a male (and a female) to leave father and mother and for two to become "one flesh" (Mk 10:7-8; Mt 19:5). Jesus taught about becoming *one flesh* at least once, when he was at the Jordan River, near the province of Judea (Mk 10:1-12; Mt 19:1-10). Mark quoted a shortened version of Jesus' lesson, Matthew a more extended version.[16] Some religious leaders (Pharisees) wanted to test Jesus' opinion on a current scholarly debate: Shammai's school said a husband could divorce his wife only for "unchastity," whereas Hillel's school said a husband could divorce his wife for "anything," even if she spoiled a dish for him (*Mishnah* Gittin 9:10). Each school highlighted a different aspect of Deuteronomy 24:1, "Because he has found in her indecency in anything": *indecency* versus *anything*. Jesus attacks the casual approach to terminating marriage for "any cause." Since the Pharisees had already heard Jesus' hard-line pronouncements on marriage and divorce (Mt 5:31-32), his flaunting of the Pharisees' laws on purity,[17] and his self-identification as God incarnate (Mt 9:2-6), they wanted to destroy him. One way to destroy Jesus' popularity was to create a rift between Jesus and the people who were so enthralled with his message and his miracles.[18] Jesus, in his preaching, did not identify with any scholarly school. The Pharisees' strategy may very well have been a divide and conquer one. Jesus may have played into the Pharisees' hands by taking such an unpopular hard line on divorce, but then Jesus expands his reply to continue to fulfill his prophetic mission of speaking forth for the Father and explains God's true intention for a covenantal marital relationship between humans. God's intention is for two seemingly independent people to become totally interdependent. In fact, in God's eyes the two become *one flesh*, a new creature in God's eyes.

Jesus uses a well-known rabbinic law of logic called "Constructing a

---

[16]The older quality manuscripts do not include Mk 10:7, "and be joined to his wife" (codices Sinaiticus and Vaticanus, the oldest [fourth century] Greek manuscripts from the careful Alexandrian text-type, and the oldest Syriac translation [fourth century, from an earlier prototype], which is the oldest Western text-type). Mt 19:3-12 has 184 Greek words, whereas Mk 10:2-12 has 123 words. The footnote in Mark 10 (NRSV) that deletes "and be joined to his wife" should be followed.

[17]Mt 9:11; 12:2, 14; 15:2.

[18]E.g., Mt 19:2; 7:28–8:1; 9:8, 26, 31, 33-34; 12:6; 13:2; 14:13; 15:30-31.

Family from Two Scriptures" (a generalization based on two instances).[19] Jesus builds a chief law by relating two texts together to develop a concluding principle, which can then be applied to other situations. He first quotes Genesis 1:27: "from the beginning a male and a female, he made them" (Mt 19:4b, Aída's trans.) Then, he quotes Genesis 2:24: "for this reason a human will leave the father and the mother and will stay close (will be united, joined) to his wife, and the two will become one flesh" (Mt 19:5, citing the Septuagint). Jesus then concludes "accordingly, no longer are they two but one flesh. Therefore, what God has joined together, let no human separate" (Mt 19:6, Aída's trans.; Mk 10:6-9).

First, we learn that God made humanity into two different kinds. Marriage is made for monogamy in a heterosexual union. God did not take out two ribs or four ribs to create a harem for Adam, but a single one, as Tertullian insists ("God fashioned *one* woman for man, taking only *one* of his ribs, even though he had many," *Monogamy* 4). Nor did he make several males to be companions; therefore, a man leaves his parents and joins his wife to become *one flesh* with her. In the Greek, Jesus uses *proskollaomai*,[20] the same word the apostle Paul will use later (Eph 5:31). However, in the Old Testament (excluding Gen 2:24), it is used for staying close to the Lord or for staying close to humans.[21] It describes the shields of Leviathan that are so closely "joined fast to one another" that air cannot pass between them, nor can they be parted (Job 41:16-17 TNIV). A man is to stay that close or that joined fast to his wife!

---

[19]*Binyan ab mishene kethubim* in Hebrew (*Tosephta* Sanhedrin 7:11) cited by rabbi Hillel who was prominent 30 B.C.–A.D. 10.

[20]Ancient manuscripts differ on whether Jesus used *proskollēthēsetai* or *kollēthēsetai* in Mt 19:5. The two best codices differ (Sinaiticus vs. Vaticanus). However, the external evidence is better slightly for *proskollēthēsetai*. Supporting it are more Alexandrian texts (C, L, Z) and a variety of text types (Alexandrian, Byzantine, Caesarean) and it agrees with the Septuagint text and Eph 5:31. The KJV, instead, translates "cleave to," not "be united to" (TNIV).

[21]Deut 11:22; Josh 23:8; Ps 73 (72):28; Ruth 2:21, 23. See also Sir 6:34; 13:16. If the Greek *proskollaomai* has to do with "staying close" to someone, the original Hebrew *dābaq* (Gen 2:24) was used "to catch up with or pursue," as Laban pursued Jacob and eventually "*caught up* with him" (Gen 31:23), or as the Philistines *pursued* Saul closely (1 Sam 31:2). Ruth decided to "*stay with*" her mother-in-law Naomi (Ruth 1:14). *Dābaq* is an active verb. There is a friend that "clings" or "sticks" closer than a "brother"—that should be one's husband (Prov 18:24)!

At creation, Eve's bodily frame came from Adam's bodily frame and the flesh around her frame was like the flesh around Adam's frame: female was "bone from (male's) bones and flesh from (male's) flesh; . . . (she) was taken" from male (Gen 2:23, Aída's trans.). The woman had already a unity with her man because he was her source of life—that was God's work (Gen 2:21-22). Now the man had to realize his unity with the woman by leaving his own source of life—his parents—and, instead, by force of will, to pursue his wife (Gen 2:24). This is "mutual attraction"! Even though in the ancient Near East the bride would normally leave her own family to go to her husband's household (e.g., Gen 24:58, 67), God actually proposed the opposite. The husband must leave home physically, emotionally and intellectually.[22] The union of husband and wife signifies a new creation symbolically born in God's eyes. Once they were two individuals. Now they come together to form a new entity—the *one-flesh* union that God has joined together. That is why divorce is like committing a murder. The new creation—the *one flesh*—created in God's eyes has been torn asunder. That is why divorce can be so painful and impart a sense of loss. Sometimes we have seen a former spouse grieve a lifetime for the death of a marriage. Theologically, we believe that a person who invades a marriage and alienates the affection of either husband or wife is like a murderer in God's eyes. That one has killed the *one-flesh* creation that God has blessed.

Why does Jesus ignore the opportunity to curry the favor of the crowd, stepping into the obvious trap of the Pharisees? Why does he just go ahead without hesitation and trample his sandals all over the Pharisees and the people's opinions? The reason he takes his unequivocal stand has deep theological significance and some of that can be glimpsed as we look at the word for *one* (Mt 19:5-6; Mk 10:8). 'Eḥād in Hebrew is a flexible word for *one* or unity. It occurs in Genesis 1:5:

---

[22]Herbert Anderson and Robert Cotton Fate, *Becoming Married*, Family Living in Pastoral Perspective (Louisville: Westminster/John Knox, 1993), p. 16, describe "leaving home" emotionally as *"a readiness, willingness, and ability to make one's own decisions, and to make one's way in the world without undue emotional dependence on the home one has come from.* Leaving home is like cleaving in the sense of making one's way by 'cutting or separating' from one's home of origin." Under some circumstances a child can "leave home" but still be in the same household as one's parents (pp. 30-31).

"And there was evening and there was morning—*one* day" (RSV, italics added). *One* refers to a period of time (twenty-four hours or hundreds of years, depending on one's interpretation). God describes the whole earth and its people as "one" because they had one language (Gen 11:1, 6). In other words, diverse people were united, but in this case, not for a good reason. Thus, this *one* flesh allows for plurality within it. In the same way, God is *one*. As Moses reminds the Israelites before entering the Promised Land: "Hear, Israel, the Lord (singular), your Godhead (*Elohim* is plural),[23] the Lord (singular), is *one*" (Deut 6:4, Aída's paraphrase of the Hebrew). The Lord is one God. The Lord has *one* name, but three persons: "the Father and the Son and the Holy Spirit" (Mt 28:19).

A similar singularity and plurality has been present in God's description of humanity since Genesis 1:26-28, where singular and plural language for God and humanity go back and forth, causing the divine and human subjects to reflect each other: "And God (plural) said (singular): Let us make (plural) Adam (singular) in our (plural) image (singular), according to our (plural) likeness (singular) and they will rule over (plural) . . . And God (plural) created (singular) the Adam (singular) in his (singular) image (singular), in the image (singular) of God (plural) he created (singular) him (singular), a male and a female (two singulars) he created (singular) them (plural)" (Gen 1:26, 27, Bill's paraphrase of the Hebrew). In marriage this single male and female become united and reflect again both humanity in its plurality, but unity in God's sight as "one people" God put on the earth. But, in their union, they also reflect a deeper truth about the triune God, who is single, one God and yet is somehow plural and perfectly united.

Marriage is one of God's central teaching tools to tell us about ourselves and about the God who created us. We are who we are because God is who God is. We learn to love the wholly other invisible one God by learning to love the visible other one around us—our spouse. We

---

[23]*Elohim* is an abstract plural when it has a singular verb (e.g., Gen 1:26). It can be translated as "Godhead" because the abstract plural intensifies the idea of God and sums up the several characteristics belonging to God. E. Kautzsch and A. E. Cowley, eds., *Gesenius' Hebrew Grammar*, 2nd ed. (Oxford: Clarendon, 1910), pp. 398-99.

cannot really love God if we do not love people created by God (1 Jn 4:20; Jas 3:9). In the act of union (marriage) we are being schooled in something very deep, very divine, very profound—we are learning something about the nature of the One who created us through a living metaphor that One has given us—union with someone created in the image of God as a gift from the United One.

Becoming *one flesh* is a gift to all flesh, yet its deeper significance is a gift that is not always received. Thus, Ananias and Sapphira were *one flesh* in that they were committed to each other in marriage, they were united companions, but their marriage was horizontal only. By their deceit and lack of truth, justice and loyalty to Jesus, they lacked the vertical aspect. They were disconnected from the deeper theological significance: marriage as a symbol of loyalty to God by being loyal to each other. Prisca and Aquila, in contrast, enjoyed both the vertical and horizontal elements of marriage.

Both the Old Testament and the New Testament use the future of the verb "to be" and the preposition *eis* ("into") to describe "the two will become *into* one flesh" (literally in Gen 2:24 LXX; Mt 19:5; Mk 10:8). On the one hand, the man and woman "are" (present tense) one flesh (Mt 19:6; Mk 10:8) because as soon as they covenant with each other they become a unity in God's eyes.[24] Yet, it takes time for a couple to "become into" *one flesh*.[25] In other words, *one flesh* is both now and not yet. *One flesh* has a beginning, yet it is still "becoming." It is an outline of a possibility and a model in process.

Humility makes marriage work. In the context of Jesus' teachings on

---

[24]The rabbis suggested a "man takes a wife" (Deut 24:1 NKJV) when he declares something like: "Behold, thou art mine, Thou art tied unto me, Thou art singled out for me, Thou art designated unto me, Thou art my help, Thou art meet for me, Thou art gathered in to me, Thou art my rib, Thou art closed in to me, or Thou art taken by me" (*b.* Kiddushin 6a). Such a covenant creates a *one flesh*. The rabbis also saw sexual intercourse and the giving of the bride price or dowry as signs of marriage (*Mishnah* Kiddushin 1:1). See also 1 Cor 6:16 and Tai Ilan, *Jewish Women in Greco-Roman Palestine* (Peabody: Hendrickson, 1996), pp. 88-89.

[25]The preposition *eis* can include this sense of goal or purpose. *Eis* has the sense of motion toward a goal because it takes the accusative case. A. T. Robertson, *A Grammar of the Greek New Testament in the Light of Historical Research* (Nashville: Broadman, 1934), pp. 591, 594-95. The future "will be" or "will become" works together with *eis* to supplement the idea of *one flesh* as a goal. For example, the apostle Paul tells the Corinthians that "having come into *(eis)* Troas for *(eis)* Christ's gospel . . ." (2 Cor 2:12, Aída's trans.).

marriage in Matthew 19 (and Mk 10), the need for humility is mentioned twice: "Whoever becomes humble like this child is the greatest in the kingdom of heaven" and "Let the little children come to me, and do not stop them; for it is to such as these that the kingdom of heaven belongs" (Mt 18:4; 19:13-14). It takes humility to become *one flesh*. It takes humility and a sense of humor and appreciation to see that the very strengths one admires can become weaknesses one detests.

We still need each our own desk, our own space to write and create, our own calling or jobs and our own job descriptions. Yet, we do most everything together. Seeing the havoc distance from each other has created in some marriages, we have decided not to be separated from each other for more than one night (except in extreme emergencies, such as hospitalization or the death of a parent). We are and we strive to be a united entity.

SUMMARY

Some ancient rabbis suggest:

> The Holy One, blessed be He, blesses bridegrooms, adorns brides, and acts as best man. He blesses bridegrooms, as it is written, "And God blessed them"; He adorns brides, as it is written, "And the Lord God built the rib . . . into a woman"; He acts as best man, as it is written, "He brought her to the man."[26]

God, of course, created marriage and performed the marriage ceremony of Adam and Eve, and, as well, is the invisible minister at every wedding. We have a lot to learn from God-among-us, Jesus, in his implicit and explicit teachings on marriage. The same priorities and costs in being Jesus' disciples affect Christians, both single and married. We need to love God and our spouse. Christ has priority in service in our lives but he has also created us to need to steward our lives and relationships. Marriage is a serious venture in which we are and we become one flesh—close to one another yet still plural—reflecting God's unity yet

---

[26]Mt 9:15; paraphrase of Rabbi Simlai, *Midrash Rabbah on Genesis* 8.13 referring to Gen 1:28 and Gen 2:22; Rabbi Simeon ben Yohai 18.1; *Babylonian Talmud* 'Erubin 18b; Rabbi Jeremiah ben Eleazar, *Babylonian Talmud* Berakoth 61a.

plurality. Certainly, we should treat Jesus not only as the best foundation builder and goal setter and significance maker for marriage, but also as the best enabler for marriage. May we ask Jesus, our Creator, to help us as we become *one flesh.*

Steve and Celestia Tracy's Viewpoint

We love to begin a discussion of marriage by looking at the teaching of Jesus because this cuts to the heart of the issue. However, the application of Jesus' teaching to marriage is deceptively complex. We evangelicals rightly place great emphasis on marriage and family since marriage is a divinely ordained institution. Therefore, it is rather surprising to find that Jesus actually had very little to say about marriage, and much of what he did say was quite shocking—to both first and twenty-first-century listeners.

JESUS AND MARRIAGE

Jesus' only direct teaching on the nature of marriage is found in Matthew 19:3-9 and the synoptic parallels.[1] It comes in response to the Pharisees' trial question regarding divorce: "Is it lawful for a man to divorce his wife for any and every reason?" (TNIV). Jesus' response is not a systematic analysis of marriage, but rather a corrective to the dominant first century view (espoused by Rabbi Hillel) that men had the right to divorce their wives for any cause at all.[2] Jesus cites from the creation account to show that marriage was beautifully ordained of God to be an inviolable *one-flesh* union ("they are no longer two, but one"). He notes the sacredness of the marriage covenant by declaring what "God has joined together, let no man separate" (ESV). The concept of marriage being an inviolable sacred union was so radical to Jesus' disciples that they declared

---

[1]Jesus did address the nature of marriage in Mt 22:30, Mk 12:18-27 and Lk 20:27-40 in response to the Sadducees' trap question regarding a woman who married seven different brothers in succession. But this clarifies the nature of marriage in heaven, not on earth.

[2]Joachim Jeremias convincingly argues that, since Philo and Josephus cite only this view, it was apparently the dominant view at the time of Jesus, *Jerusalem in the Time of Jesus: An Investigation into Economic and Social Conditions During the New Testament Period* (Philadelphia: Fortress, 1969), p. 370.

that, if this is the nature of marriage, maybe it would be better never to marry! Given the fact that 40 to 50 percent of American marriages end in divorce, and cohabitation has become universally accepted in the Western world,[3] our own culture certainly does not view marriage as inviolable or sacred. Jesus taught a truly radical view of marriage.

This fundamental model has dramatically affected our own marriage. We married rather young (for our culture at least) at the ages of twenty-one and nineteen. We were madly in love but were rather naïve and in many respects frightfully immature. Further complicating matters we are both stubborn first-borns. (Not surprisingly, of all marital birth order combinations, research suggests that two firstborns have the highest divorce rates.[4]) Many times over our thirty years of marriage, we have experienced the painful post honeymoon reality of living with a fellow sinner! All too often we have failed to meet each other's needs, painfully wounded each other and at best been insensitive regarding understanding our partner's heart. However, never has bailing out been an option for us.

Instead, we began to deliberately study and observe the nature of bonding in marriage. As a result, we began to compile a list of "marital rules" to guide us. We intentionally sought to craft a culture within our marriage to inform the way we would and would not relate to each other. We noted the various biblical principles given by Jesus for relationships and sought to turn these into commitments we made before God to each other. "We will never go to bed with unresolved conflict" (Eph 4:26) is an example of a commitment we had to put into place rather early in our marriage. Clearly, this guideline is predicated on several biblical principles, such as the importance of emotional honesty in relationships (Eph 4:25).

Often, our rules would need modification as we moved from the

---

[3]Pamela J. Smock notes that cohabitation before marriage rose 10 percent in the United States between 1965 and 1974, but it rose to over 50 percent of those marrying between 1990 and 1994 and has not declined since then. "Cohabitation in the United States, An Appraisal of Research Themes, Findings, and Implications," *Annual Review of Sociology* 26 (2000): 3.

[4]Torkild Lynstad, and Vegard Skirbekk, "Does the Combination of Spouses' Birth Order Influence their Divorce Risk? Evidence from a Register Based Study of Norwegian First Marriages" can be viewed on the Web at <http://epc2006.princeton.edu/download.aspx?submissionId=6 0249#search=%>.

ideal into real life. For example, it didn't take us long to discover that fatigue and exhaustion can keep a couple from quality conflict resolution. So we compromised by declaring a truce and making an appointment for the following day to prioritize good resolution that would leave us in a more intimate place with a deepened understanding of this person we had married (knowing and being known), and a heightened sensitivity to our own sinful strategies of self-protection. Why did we put such energy into this seemingly legalistic approach to marriage? We did this because Jesus' teaching on marriage has been a countercultural anchor to secure and guide us. We had very little understanding then of how important this "get to the bottom of it" strategy was for the building of a secure foundation for our love.

There is one other profound marriage principle subtly embedded in Matthew 19:3-9. Notice the indirect but powerful manner in which Jesus challenged Jewish patriarchy and the inequitable treatment of women. In this first-century culture, Jewish women had very limited rights. Under Jewish law they could generally not initiate a divorce,[5] whereas the rabbis taught that a Jewish husband could divorce his wife for any reason, including ruining a meal or finding another woman more attractive.[6] So, when Jesus tells the Pharisees that any man who "divorces his wife, except for marital unfaithfulness, and marries another woman commits adultery" (Mt 19:9, Steve's translation), he is unmistakably elevating the status of women and thoroughly undercutting the entrenched Jewish culture of male superiority. The fact that this is taught in the context of marriage being a *one-flesh* permanent union (Mt 19:5) further strengthens the idea that in marriage the man and the woman are to be intimate equal partners.

The assertion that in Matthew 19:3-9 Jesus undercuts unjust male privilege and superiority and elevates the status of women is reinforced over and over in the gospels by the countercultural manner in which

---

[5]For instance, Josephus, the first-century Jewish historian, states that a woman had no right to divorce her husband for any reason, *Antiquities* 15.7.10.

[6]For the exact rabbinic quotation Git. 9:10, see David W. Chapman, "Marriage and Family in Second Temple Judaism," in *Marriage and Family in the Biblical World*, ed. Ken M. Campbell (Downers Grove, Ill.: InterVarsity Press, 2003), p. 227.

Jesus treats women with respect and dignity as spiritual equals to men.[7] For instance, Jesus invited women to travel with him and the male disciples as he carried out his public ministry (Lk 8:1-3). This counteracts the prevalent ancient Jewish belief that women were spiritually inferior and even dangerous to men. Thus, one ancient Jewish text states, "lots of women, lots of witchcraft."[8] Jesus also allowed women such as Mary to sit at his feet and receive his teaching (Lk 10:38-42). This contradicts the common ancient Jewish belief that women were not to study the Torah as do men. Thus, another ancient Jewish text states, "Whoever teaches Torah to his daughter is as if he teaches her lechery."[9] The fact that in John 4 Jesus talked to a Samaritan woman in public and accepted a drink from her is an enormous statement of female dignity and equality, for the ancient rabbis stated, "Don't talk too much with women."[10] In fact, the ancient rabbis taught that one should not even talk to one's own wife in public, let alone a foreign woman. And perhaps the greatest affirmation of the spiritual equality and worth of women is seen in the fact that women were the first witnesses of Jesus' resurrection and were providentially commissioned to give their testimony to the male disciples (Mt 28:1-10). This took place in a chauvinistic Jewish culture that commonly did not allow women to give testimony in a Jewish court.[11]

We emphasize the manner in which Jesus challenged unjust patriarchy and elevated women as spiritual equals because this teaching has dramatically changed our marriage. While we both enjoyed loving Christian homes, we grew up in traditional, conservative churches. We simply did not challenge the staunchly patriarchal theology we had been given that taught (especially through modeling) that men deserved

---

[7]On first-century Jewish patriarchal views of women, see Tal Ilan, *Jewish Women in Greco-Roman Palestine* (Peabody, Mass.: Hendrickson, 1995), pp. 44, 127-29, 163-67, 204.

[8]Mishnah, Abot 2:7.

[9]Mishnah, Sotah 3.4.

[10]Mishnah, Abot 1:5. This text is describing talking to one's own wife, which makes Jesus' public interaction with an unknown Samaritan woman that much more shocking in its elevation of women.

[11]This was based on Jewish assertions of female inferiority. For instance, Josephus says Jewish women could not give testimony in court due to the "levity and boldness of their sex," *Antiquities* 4.8.15 [219].

the place of privilege. We had absorbed the view that women were made in God's image but really were not spiritually equal with men. Thus, we came into marriage with a deep love for each other but with some unhealthy subconscious perceptions about equality in our relationship. For instance, it took me a long time to feel I had the right to speak up and share my views when they were contrary to Steve's. It was particularly difficult for me to believe it was appropriate to confront Steve when I was concerned about a particular decision he was about to make, even when I believed he was wrong. I basically did not believe my feelings or needs were as important as his. Thankfully, now I understand that it is not only my right, it is my responsibility to seek God's voice of wisdom through his Word and in prayer, and then to communicate honestly and respectfully to Steve my heart's truth.

On the other hand, as much as I loved Celestia, for a long time I really did not treat her as a spiritual equal. If anyone had asked me, I would have vigorously defended Celestia's spiritual equality, but in many subtle ways my behavior belied my gender assertions. I often privately dismissed Celestia's views or concerns by reasoning that she was emotional and tended to look instead, to fellow ministers and male friends for discussions of theology since I didn't see this as Celestia's domain. At times I would prioritize my hobbies and needs over hers since, as the *head*, mine were of greater significance. Thankfully, Jesus' teachings and relational modeling on the true equality of women has dramatically changed our marriage.

Jesus goes on to give us one other shocking perspective on marriage in his scant teaching on the subject. In three different texts Jesus declares that marriage is not the quintessential good. Rather, the kingdom of God is.[12] Hence he validates the choice that some had made to

---

[12]Thus, even such a staunch defender of the traditional family as New Testament scholar Andreas Köstenberger notes that Jesus did not urge his followers to "focus on the family" for "Jesus placed natural kinship ties into the larger context of the kingdom of God." "Marriage and Family in the New Testament," in *Marriage and Family in the Biblical World*, ed. Ken M. Campbell (Downers Grove, Ill.: InterVarsity Press, 2003), p. 247. See also Cynthia Long Westfall, who argues that Jesus relativized the priority of the family in view of the kingdom of God without being antifamily. "Family in the Gospels and Acts," in *Family in the Bible: Exploring Customs, Culture, and Context*, ed. Richard S. Hess and M. Daniel Carroll R. (Grand Rapids: Baker, 2003), p. 134.

renounce marriage for the sake of the kingdom and promises to reward
those who left family members (including spouses) for the sake of the
kingdom (Mt 19:29; Lk 18:29). In fact, Jesus makes it clear that marriage can serve a diabolical purpose—it can inhibit and even prevent
Christian discipleship: "If anyone comes to me and does not hate his
father and mother, his wife and children, his brothers and sisters—yes,
even his own life—he cannot be my disciple" (Lk 14:26 NIV; cf. Mt
10:34-39).[13] Since, as we have already seen Jesus greatly valued marriage and taught that it was a divine institution, he is not here deprecat-
ing marriage or suggesting that spouses need not love each other. He is
using hyperbolic language to shock his first-century Jewish listeners
who placed tremendous value on the family. He wanted to communicate that nothing, even that which you value most on earth (family), is
more important than your relationship with Christ the King. Loyalty
to Christ trumps all other relationships. This is a shocking message to
modern readers for a different reason. Unlike ancient Jews, our ultimate
loyalty and priority is not as much to our biological families as it is to
ourselves (our "own lives" in Jesus' words). So Jesus jolts us by teaching
that the highest good isn't our marital bliss, self-actualization, or happiness, but being a faithful follower of Christ.[14]

For us, the key principle flowing out of Jesus' teaching on marriage
and the kingdom is that marriage should always advance the kingdom
of God. In spite of our early challenges at negotiating conflict, we have
spent three decades being best friends, lovers and soul mates. In fact,
one of the things that drew me to Celestia when I was a wild-eyed adolescent who was quite enamored with the opposite sex in general was

---

[13]Since Jesus only mentions leaving wives, some might draw the hasty conclusion that the primacy of following Christ over family extends only to the husband as the head of the family and
not to the wife. But Jesus need not list every single family member to establish this point. Note
that parallel or similar accounts of this teaching in Mt 10:37-38 and Mk 10:29-30 list various
family members but mention neither husband nor wife; they are assumed.

[14]This is not to say that our happiness and well-being are irrelevant to God. Scripture is replete
with passages that affirm that God desires to bless his children, including giving them joy, the
desires of their heart and "good things" (Ps 37:4; 84:11; Rom 8:31-32; Gal 5:22; Jas 1:17). But
God does not exist to make us temporarily "happy" in the modern trivial sense of the word.
For an excellent discussion of "Christian Hedonism," the concept that God's glory and the
believers' true happiness are not mutually exclusive, see John Piper, *Desiring God: Meditations
of a Christian Hedonist* (Portland, Ore.: Multnomah Press, 1986).

that Celestia and I could talk for hours and never tire of conversing. Somehow she made me "come alive" and understood me in a way that no other girl ever did. And this magical vitality of our relationship has grown exponentially over the years as we have shared so much together (including our three beautiful children). But as joyful and satisfying as our life together has been, this joy is not an end in itself.

Early in our marriage Christ impressed upon us the gospel imperative to let our marriage serve him, not ourselves. I (Celestia) will never forget a defining moment in our first year of marriage when we discovered after entertaining thirty-five boisterous teenagers from our church in our home that one of the adolescents had accidentally gouged three deep scratches into our only nice piece of furniture—an antique maple rocking chair. I had worked very hard to create a beautiful home with our modest income and this was incredibly disappointing. However, this trivial (in hindsight) material loss forced us to clarify the superior purpose for our marriage, home and possessions. Our marriage and all the material goods we jointly possessed were not ultimately ours; God had given us each other to advance his kingdom. That was our joint mandate. This principle has guided our marriage over and over throughout the years. For instance, Celestia has experienced numerous orthopedic surgeries and hospitalizations throughout our thirty years of marriage. This has forced me to come to grips with the reality that God did not give Celestia to be my wife to make me perpetually happy and meet my every need. Rather, I was to consider how in the midst of trials we could glorify Christ and advance his kingdom together. This gave us a focus that was grander than our present personal disappointment and discomfort. We were in it together!

As a man who came into marriage with a moderately patriarchal mindset about gender, I have been heavily influenced by Jesus' teaching that loyalty to him trumps all other loyalties. Early on I tended to see myself as the priest of the family. While I never articulated this out loud, I believed that since I was the husband, God would speak to us through me. Over the years I have come to realize how pointedly unbiblical this is. While we do believe the husband has a unique role as the *head* and has certain spiritual responsibilities to his family (we will develop this concept in the next chapter), Celestia has only one Lord and that is Jesus Christ, not me.

I have gradually learned to respect and listen to Celestia's sense of the Lord's call in her life. For instance, several years ago I (Celestia) felt God's prompting to complete my M.A. in psychology so I could use my gifts as a licensed professional counselor. I knew God had spoken to me in ways that I could not deny. I will never forget Steve's godly and gracious support of this calling and insistence that I obey this divine mandate. While this meant a lot of changes for our family, neither one of us knew then how God would use this training in our lives. Consequently, Steve sacrificed to put me through my counseling program and we all pitched in as a family to make it work. Steve's unwavering support has had an incalculable effect upon our marriage and ministry. It is impossible for me to adequately convey the importance of his belief in me. He supported my mandate not only physically and financially but also emotionally. He learned to love what I loved and I learned to love what he loved—which created a synergistic integration of the social sciences, Scripture and theology. In that sense we were both respectively living out the lordship of Christ in this dimension of our lives.

Looking back almost twenty years after Celestia began her graduate studies, I can see what tragic disobedience it would have been if she had not followed Christ's call into counseling and if I had not supported her. She has been used by God to minister to thousands of individuals, couples and families; she founded Mending the Soul Ministries and is now developing and clinically supervising a new generation of Christian counselors through her clinic. Christ had called Celestia (as his disciple) into this work long before I recognized this as a viable ministry in her life. Thankfully, Celestia takes obedience to Christ very seriously and sees herself first and foremost as his disciple.

APPLICATION OF JESUS' TEACHINGS

We have seen that Christ had very little to say directly about marriage, but his teachings are astoundingly applicable to and essential for marriage. As Douglas Brouwer observes:

The Bible says less about marriage in the sense that there are few places where it tells us exactly how to have a successful, satisfying, and God-honoring marriage . . . We might hope for something much more explicit and direct, but we aren't going to find it . . . So the Bible says *less* about marriage than we want it to. But the Bible also says *more* about marriage than we might sometimes imagine . . . the Bible has many valuable things to say about marriage—but we'll often find them in unexpected places.[15]

We have found these unexpected places exemplified in three dominant themes in the teaching of Christ: (1) grace and forgiveness, (2) the heart and (3) humility and servanthood. These themes have been critically important in our marriage.

1. Grace and forgiveness. Certainly one of the dominant themes of Jesus' ministry was grace and forgiveness. His very mission was one of offering healing and forgiveness to the (morally) sick who didn't deserve them (Mt 9:9-13). He reached out to the most marginalized and unworthy members of society and offered love and forgiveness (Lk 7:36-50; 19:1-9). And he called his followers to forgive seventy times seven (in a limitless fashion) those who sin against them because they themselves had been forgiven by God (Mt 18:21-35). He even goes so far as to say that, if we want God the Father's undeserved forgiveness, we must forgive others who have sinned against us (Mt 18:35).

Before we got married we would have thought it strange to say that Jesus' teaching on grace and forgiveness is central to marriage. After all, we got married because we loved each other and pledged to love each other the rest of our lives. No one gets married planning to divorce a few years later. But it happens all the time. We believe one of the biggest factors in the high divorce rates among believers is that the church has often over romanticized marriage and has not been honest about the hard work and pain marriage creates. Creating and maintaining intimacy in a committed, monogamous marriage is God's crucible for

[15]Douglas J. Brouwer, *Beyond "I Do": What Christians Believe About Marriage* (Grand Rapids: Eerdmans, 2001), pp. 11-12, cited by Mathews and Hubbard, *Marriage Made in Eden*, pp. 159-60.

our sanctification. Alice Mathews and M. Gay Hubbard describe this problem very well:

> In ways that are downright dishonest, Christians sometimes imply, as they talk publicly about Christian marriage, that a marriage license for Christians grants immunity from human sinfulness. It does not. But in an attempt to make their marriage commercials for God, so to speak, Christians sometimes paint a picture of themselves that does not square with the facts. Christians often behave as though they were Brits living in Los Angeles and feeling loyally compelled to deny that London ever has smog.[16]

Marriage does have noxious smog—the ubiquitous smog of human sin. I married Celestia because I was (and still am) dazzled by her many wonderful gifts, character traits and inner beauty. And she says the same about me. But neither of us was really aware of the shadow side of our partner—we were marrying a sinner who could not and would not treat us lovingly all the time. In spite of our best intentions, we would fail and hurt each other. It's not that in marriage we generally commit more grievous sins against each other than do other people. Certainly my enemies have sinned against me in far more outrageous ways than Celestia has. But I expect so much more of Celestia and she does of me. So marriage has a way of "turbo charging" our sins against each other. Even seemingly minor offenses take on a new hue in marriage because our spouse is the one person on the planet we expect will truly love us, understand us and appreciate us one hundred percent of the time.

In other words, the intimacy of marriage brings mixed blessings. The joy of having a *one-flesh* soul mate is glorious, but very risky. Marriage creates a new level of soul vulnerability. No one can lift us up as quickly or wound us as deeply as our spouse. We have been amazed over the years at the silly and stupid things that we have quarreled over, and how painful it can be for us to fight. Often we can't even remember the precipitating issue.

The reality of human sinfulness and the pain it can and will bring in

---

[16]Mathews and Hubbard, *Marriage Made in Eden*, p. 224.

marriage is what makes grace and forgiveness so essential.[17] We have learned that forgiveness is as essential to marriage as love; in fact these are really just two sides of the same coin. We are sinners who fail each other constantly, and only forgiveness not score-keeping will keep our marriage alive. What is particularly helpful is when we cultivate our own sense of spiritual poverty and need of God's grace. That makes it much easier for us to forgive each other. The famous playwright George Bernard Shaw called forgiveness "a beggar's refuge"; he felt it was fit only for the weak. But in a real sense we are spiritual beggars—God graciously forgave us so we could learn to forgive each other. As beggars who have received God's undeserved mercy, we need to grant grace and forgiveness to each other. We have formalized this into another "rule" for our marriage: "We resolve to expend as much time and energy as we must to resolve grievances against each other; we will keep talking until we have forgiven each other. Once we have forgiven our partner, we will never again bring up an old grievance. We cannot use old (forgiven) sins as new ammunition."[18] We find it very interesting that secular marriage experts have documented the destructive effects of failing to offer grace to one's spouse. John Gottman is one of the leading marriage researchers in America. He and his associates have spent thousands of hours analyzing videos of married couples interacting with each other. Through this research Gottman has identified what he calls the "four horsemen of the apocalypse"—the four traits that are most likely to destroy a marriage.[19] Gottman has researched this so thoroughly that he can watch a few hours of video of a couple interacting and predict with over 90 percent accuracy whether or not they will divorce within five years. He bases this prediction on identi-

---

[17]Thus, Walter Wangerin Jr. in his brilliant book on marriage devotes almost one-third of the text to forgiveness: *As for Me and My House: Crafting Your Marriage to Last* (Nashville: Thomas Nelson, 1987).

[18]In time, we did adjust this rule to say that old forgiven grievances can be brought up again in one and only one circumstance—if we believe our partner is developing an unhealthy pattern of behavior evidenced by repeatedly committing the same sin against us. In that case we discuss it for accountability sake, to assess what needs to change to break the pattern.

[19]John Gottman and Julie Schwartz Gottman, *Ten Lessons to Transform Your Marriage* (New York: Random House, 2006). The research basis for Gottman's model is found in his earlier works particularly *What Predicts Divorce: The Relationship Between Marital Processes and Marital Outcomes* (Hillsdale, N.J.: Lea, 1993).

fying one of the "four horsemen," which are contempt, criticism, defensiveness and stone walling. In practical terms, these "four horsemen" that doom marriage are nothing more than descriptions of the failure to offer grace and forgiveness.

2. The heart. Much of the current Christian marriage literature is ultrapragmatic and behavioral. We can purchase the "five key steps to marital happiness" or the "ten foolproof techniques to marital communication" complete with step-by-step workbooks. While we applaud practical marital advice, the danger is that we can easily focus on external behavior and bypass the most essential (and much more challenging) issue, namely, the hidden motives of our heart. It is much easier simply to focus on "doing the right thing" than on tediously assessing the condition and impulses of our inner world. This is the very issue that occupied most of Jesus' conflict with the Pharisees. They did the right thing (praying, fasting, alms giving, witnessing) for the wrong reason (Mt 6:1-18; 23:15). In other words, their observable external religious actions were impeccable but were fatally flawed due to the invisible motives of their heart. So Jesus repeatedly made the hidden motives of the heart the pivotal moral determinant. He taught that sin is committed in the heart (Mt 5:28). Moral defilement does not come from the outside but from the inside—out of the heart come evil thoughts and acts (Mt 15:19). Forgiveness must come from the heart (Mt 18:35). We are to love God with all of our heart (Mt 22:37).

Jesus' focus on the heart is profoundly critical to marriage, especially in our culture that tends to be quite shallow and external. We are not accustomed to looking beneath the surface to probe the heart—especially our own. What can be tricky and deceptive in Christian marriage is that we can seriously undermine our marriage by ostensibly serving God, doing ministry and being a "godly" person. In our second pastorate God drove this point home to us in a painful manner. I (Steve) was an associate pastor in a large vibrant church. God had graciously blessed our ministry to teenagers, singles and families. The students, parents and elders respected and affirmed me. And I gave the church my all. I had developed very effective discipleship ministries with singles, students and parents. I was speaking in public high schools regularly, had developed extensive short-term missions projects and helped produce a nationally distributed movie on abortion. My church groups were bulging, many were coming to Christ, and ministry had never been better. I just accepted the fact that being out of town eight or more weeks a year was the price of serving God. I didn't question the sanity of routinely working twelve-hour-plus days because God was blessing my service for him. Insidiously, menacing cracks began to emerge. I had developed chronic low-grade depression, Celestia could no longer sustain our Spartan regimen (particularly being virtually a single mother with three small children), I was becoming aware of how emotionally and sexually vulnerable I had become, and Celestia and I hardly knew each other any more.

In spite of knowing that God had called me to prioritize my family over ministry, in spite of countless warnings from my own seminary professors about the dangers of overcommitment in ministry, I had fallen into this deadly trap. In retrospect, I realize the culprit was an external focus on my ministry and spiritual life; I had utterly failed to track my heart. Over the course of weeks God began to show me how subtly I had failed Celestia and my children in my zeal to "serve God." In fact, the most painful realization of all was that much of my ministry was not motivated by true love for God but by my own insecurities. For instance, every month I had dozens of early morning and late evening meetings that consistently took me away from my family. I thought I was doing this out of a pure desire to disciple, counsel and witness. However, I came to see that my motives were repulsively mixed. In addition to wanting to share the love of Christ, I was largely but imperceptivity motivated by fleshly pride and raw insecurity. I had fallen into the trap of what T. S. Eliot calls the greatest sin: "The last temptation is the greatest treason: To do the right deed for the wrong reason."[20]

Jesus' teaching on the heart not only creates marital health by arresting subtle patterns of mixed motives, but it helps us identify undiluted, hidden sins against our spouse. This can be particularly essential in the midst of conflict when we are tempted to "maintain the high moral

---

[20]T. S. Eliot, *Murder in the Cathedral* (New York: Harcourt, Brace, and Company, 1935).

ground" by appealing to the purity and propriety of our (external) actions when in fact we are being nothing but odious hypocrites. Celestia and I will never forget counseling a man who poignantly illustrated how searching one's own heart will often reveal flagrant sins against one's spouse. Early in the session Joe shared a breakthrough revelation that God had given him regarding kissing his wife in the morning. Needless to say, this "dark confession" piqued our curiosity, since we often coach Christian men in how to be more physically affectionate to their wives. He explained that as he had prayerfully reflected on his marriage, not just on his external acts but on his motives, the Holy Spirit, with lightening bolt precision, revealed his true heart. He confessed to using that kiss to subtly but powerfully manipulate his wife into giving him what he wanted: sex, compliments and leniency with his faults. He did not kiss her out of love but selfishness. And only Jesus' teaching on the heart can help us ferret out such camouflaged marital sin.

3. Humility and servanthood. Jesus revolutionized the concept of accomplishment and greatness declaring, "If anyone wants to be first, he must be the very last, and the servant of all" (Mk 9:35 NIV). One of Jesus' last acts before his trial and crucifixion was to wash his disciples' feet as a demonstration of the nature of Christian ministry. He taught that true ministry is based on humbly, selflessly serving others (Jn 13:1-17). This concept is eminently applicable to marriage. Being feisty firstborns, we have often struggled wanting to promote our cherished plans and goals. We both like to win. Our culture programs us to see greatness in terms of getting our way, accomplishing our goals and getting others to do what we want. Jesus' radical redefinition of greatness has helped us make serving each other the goal of our marriage.

God taught me to serve Celestia in very practical ways. Three months before I graduated from seminary, while visions of being an all-star preacher were dancing in my head, Celestia suffered a catastrophic orthopedic injury while skiing. She had four major surgeries in the next eighteen months. During this time I needed to bathe her, do her hair and care for our small daughter. Needless to say, this was not the road to ecclesiastical stardom I had envisioned. Instead, I learned that serving my wife in the most mundane ways was in fact exactly what Jesus had called me to do. This was the beginning of the real intimacy we enjoy today. For most of us marital servanthood is not quite as dramatic but no less real.

OUR PRIMARY TASK: ADVANCING GOD'S KINGDOM TOGETHER

There is much we would love to say about this subject in terms of the power of sexual integrity in marriage as a witness to the rule of God,[21] the power of marriage to be a "taste and picture" of the kingdom and the King in a culture that has given up on marriage and knows little or nothing of real love,[22] and the power of marriage to transform us into the image of Christ our King.[23] But here we choose to focus on one very practical concept, namely, that the key to advancing God's kingdom together is to view *one-flesh* union as a sacred call to joint ministry. In other words, marriage is not about Steve's call and gifts separate from Celestia's call and gifts; it is about our collective gifts and our collective call to serve Christ together.

In marriage one set of gifts and calling and history combine with another set of gifts and calling and history to create a new *one-flesh* entity. We view all ministry as "our ministry." Steve does not have one calling and Celestia another. Not that we can perform all ministry together, but all we do is a reflection of our joint commitment and call. This typically involves sacrifice by one of us for the other. A clear example of this is when I (Celestia) chose to change my major two years into my program at the university. I loved space design and architec-

---

[21]See especially Pamela Paul, *Pornified: How Pornography Is Transforming Our Lives, Our Relationships, and Our Families* (New York: Time Books, 2005).

[22]See especially Jillian Straus, *Unhooked Generation: The Truth About Why We're Still Single* (New York: Hyperion, 2006). Strauss as a secular writer argues that a high percentage of singles now opt out of marriage not because they do not value it but just the opposite: they dream of a happy marriage but have never seen one and don't believe they could create one.

[23]On the "transformational" nature of marriage, see Mathews and Hubbard, *Marriage Made in Eden*, pp. 24-25, 219-35; see also Gary Thomas, *Sacred Marriage* (Grand Rapids: Zondervan, 2000). Thomas's thesis is that God designed marriage more to make us holy than to make us happy (p. 13). He develops this in terms of the power of marriage to expose our sin; build character; foster prayer; teach us to serve, forgive, love, respect and persevere; and to make us more aware of God's presence and his calling in our life.

ture, but anticipated this to be a very frustrating career option, as Steve and I had chosen to go into ministry together. Therefore, I transferred into the college of education so I could teach and put Steve through seminary.

Much more recently, after Celestia had gone into the field of counseling and I (Steve) had the opportunity to begin teaching in a seminary, instead of following my field of doctoral research (New Testament), I shifted my academic focus to sexual ethics so that we could more closely minister together. Over the years we have prayerfully asked God to continue to show us how we can maximize our gifts and training together to advance his kingdom. Not only has this been much more powerful in ministry than pursuing separate directions, it has made for a dynamic and fun marriage.

Concluding Dialogue

When we (Steve and Celestia) agreed to this book project, some of our colleagues warned us that it would never work. How could two couples holding distinctly different models on gender roles write a marriage book together? After all, some of the fiercest and most painful debates in the evangelical world center on male/female roles. Making matters worse, all four of us have advanced degrees and have spent years teaching, preaching and counseling on marriage. Each couple has strongly held marital convictions and has carefully chosen these views because each believes they are biblical and are convinced that they lead to the healthiest, most God-honoring marriages. Therefore, we write with a passion to provide a humble, irenic and honest exchange of diverse views on marriage. For us this was a worthy project.

Since each couple's chapters were completed independently, before reading the other couple's chapter, one of the strongest mutual reactions was pleasant surprise at how similar our writings were. We emphasized many of the same points and biblical passages, and even cited several of the same books. Our respective personal illustrations also revealed that God had taught both couples many of the same lessons. This was a tremendous blessing to us. We do have some real differences of conviction. We also come from quite diverse backgrounds (Steve and Celestia both grew up in the West in very conservative families; Aída grew up in the Caribbean in a multidenominational Protestant church, having a Spanish mother and a Dutch father; Bill grew up in a more traditional and private home in the East coast). However, this chapter reveals that far more unites us than separates us. And this is as it should be since we worship the same Lord and are directed by the same Scriptures.

Areas of agreement. Clearly the dominant principle that both couples gave for marriage and being a disciple of Jesus is this: loyalty to Jesus supersedes all other loyalties, including familial. Jesus alone is to be our supreme Lord, master and love. Additionally, both couples placed great emphasis on the fact that in a healthy marriage love for Christ shouldn't compete with love for spouse. Rather, love for Christ becomes the foundation for marital love. As the Spencers stated, "we should treat Jesus not only as the best foundation builder . . . but also as the enabler for marriage."

Both couples emphasized the priority of Christ in marriage not only individually (he is our Lord) but also collectively (in marriage we should jointly advance the kingdom of God). As the Tracys noted, the *one-flesh* union of marriage is a serious call to joint ministry to further God's kingdom. While husbands and wives are two individuals with separate gifts and responsibilities, they have a corporate responsibility to use their *one-flesh* relationship in service to God. Both couples noted how this concept has transformed their ministries and even their career choices.

A closely related theme that both couples noted is that marriage should be transformational. That is, marriage is one of God's most effective instruments to reveal our sin, build godly character and teach us how to love others. This leads us to another theme that both couples strongly emphasized: the importance of humility and servanthood in marriage.

Finally, we should note an area of agreement that will later lead to an area of disagreement. Namely, both couples placed emphasis on the spiritual equality of the husband and the wife. But we will see in chapter two that each couple sees marital equality being lived out in different ways. In this chapter the Spencers stated, "Formally, neither the husband nor the wife is the ultimate ruler over the other but should serve the other." The Tracys agree with this statement and affirm mutual servanthood in marriage based on the ultimate lordship of Christ. However, for the Tracys, affirming these two truths does not preclude affirming that the husband does have some unique marital authority.

Differences. Having noted that we had far more areas of agreement than disagreement, it is still important to note differences in our chapters. We will look at three types of differences: differences of emphasis, apparent differences and real differences. Some of our differences no doubt stem from our differing experiences. For instance, the Spencers were older when they married (both had graduated from seminary) and came into their marriage with a clear individual sense of ministry call. Thus, they experienced a journey of learning to live out their marital oneness. While they were dating, they had two separate ministry calls. Then, when they married, they began the task of learning to become "one" without losing their individuality. Following this, they were challenged in learning to work as a team of equals with others. Finally, they learned to work together as "two in one flesh" with other equal authorities in church ministry. They also came into marriage with egalitarian convictions about gender roles—a conviction they have not changed.

The Tracys, however, were much younger when they married (still in college) and had only one sense of ministry call (Steve's pastoral ministry). Their path was different from the Spencers' as they had to learn over time that God had gifted and called both of them and that, while they were one, Celestia had her own unique gifting and calling from God. Furthermore, the Tracys began marriage as traditional hierarchalists and modified their position in the first several years of marriage to a soft complementarian position.[1]

As would be expected, while we had many areas of agreement, we placed different emphases on various subjects. Both couples noted the need for grace and forgiveness in marriage, however, the Tracys made this one of the three most critical teachings of Jesus for building a strong marriage. They argued that forgiveness is one of the most critical needs in marriage due to the manner in which marriage creates great vulnerability by "turbo charging" our sins against each other.

While both couples noted that, according to Jesus, marriage creates

---

[1] We recognize that all evangelicals are agreed that God made the two genders to complement each other (Gen 2:18). However, in the past decade *complementarian* has taken on a technical meaning that indicates the belief that while husbands and wives are spiritual equals, they have some sort of differing roles based on gender. Hierarchical complementarians see authority and submission at the heart of male-female roles, whereas "soft complementarians" see male headship more as a responsibility to serve than a right to rule. They significantly soften the nature and extent of the husband's authority.

a *one-flesh* relationship, the Spencers put more emphasis on this biblical theme and gave it considerable biblical development, particularly in relating it to the character of God. In particular, they emphasized that "one" allows for plurality, for God is one and yet is a triune being. Thus, husbands and wives are a plurality and yet are one flesh. Marriage ultimately points us to God the creator of marriage for, "union with someone created in the image of God" is a "gift from the United One." Both couples emphasized the danger of loyalty to family over Christ, but in different ways. The Spencers emphasized that husbands and wives cannot meet all of each others' needs, and thus we need a larger Christian community or adopted family. The Tracys, on the other hand, while agreeing that spouses cannot completely meet each others' needs noted that no human being can meet all of our needs (including our adopted spiritual brothers and sisters) which highlights our spiritual poverty and need for God's grace.

A notable difference in the teachings of Jesus as applied to marriage relates to Jesus' teaching on the heart. The Tracys argued that this has been one of the most important themes to shape their marriage, for it helped them get beneath the mere "right behavior" and discern the underlying motive. According to Jesus, the motive of the heart is the real basis for morality and the root of sin. The Spencers did not highlight this theme and understand Jesus' teaching more narrowly as referring primarily to the will as a collective concept that includes the inner motives and passions. For the Spencers, the will reflects one's inner world. For the Tracys the heart describes the emotions and inner motives. *Kardia,* the Greek word that Jesus used, can be translated either as heart or will since it is the "center and source of the whole inner life."[2]

Conclusion. Both couples affirm marriage as a unifying provision from God. God provides a spouse for our own sanctification and the development of our mutual spiritual gifts, with the purpose of encouraging and building up one another in faith and ministry as endowed and empowered by the Holy Spirit.

[2]W. Bauer, F. W. Danker, W. F. Arndt and F. W. Gingrich, *A Greek-English Lexicon of the New Testament and Other Early Christian Literature,* 3rd ed. (Chicago: University of Chicago, 2000), p. 508.

Finally, both couples realized that marriages are also about sacrifice—the sacrifice of one's self—as each spouse has to expand the sense of self to include the other person as the new *one-flesh* entity is born. Therefore, both couples stressed the importance of putting Jesus first in marriage no matter the cost to each individual's sense of self. Marriage can also involve financial sacrifice as two (and more when children are added) do not in reality always manage to live as cheaply as one. Further, sacrifices in ministry also affect one's income, especially when a couple responds to God's call for full-time service. Clearly then, marriage is a tool used by God to help a couple begin to learn personally and economically to "pick up one's cross daily and follow Christ." It is all in one—gift, teaching illustration and blessing from the One who loves us most.

Chapter Two

"Headship" and Submission

STEVE AND CELESTIA TRACY'S
VIEWPOINT

Steve and I thought this would be a fairly straightforward chapter to write. After all, we have taught on this subject for years. I counsel couples daily on marriage and family life, and Steve has researched and written on gender roles, patriarchy and headship/submission.[1] However, as we began to discuss the specifics of the chapter, it led to unexpected frustration and even tears as we agonized to articulate and redeem a biblical and beautiful model of marital roles using biblical language ("head" and "submit"), which has all too often been the source of untold oppression, pain and abuse.[2] It occurred to us that the challenge of explaining the beauty of marital headship/submission is analogous to my frequent counseling objective in which I seek to explain and redeem the beauty of marital sexual intercourse to a woman who has experienced the trauma of rape. In both instances the problem is not with marital sexuality itself (our gender, gender roles or sexual intercourse). These are all given to us as gifts from our loving Creator. Rather, the problem is that every aspect of the exquisite gift of sexuality has been morbidly and painfully twisted by sin, so that the very terms themselves are often fraught with alien baggage that at best clouds the

---

[1]Steven Tracy, "Domestic Violence in the Church and Redemptive Suffering in 1 Peter," *Calvin Theological Journal* 41 (2006): 279-96; "Headship with a Heart: How Biblical Patriarchy Actually Prevents Abuse," *Christianity Today*, February 2003, pp. 50-54; "Patriarchy and Domestic Violence: Challenging Common Misconceptions," *Journal of the Evangelical Theological Society* 50 (2007): 573-94; "What Does 'Submit in Everything' Really Mean? The Nature and Scope of Marital Submission," *Trinity Journal* 29 (2008): 285-312.

[2]On the reality of the historic and present widespread abuse of women and children, which is often rooted in patriarchy, see Steven R. Tracy, "Clergy Responses to Domestic Violence," *Priscilla Papers* 21 (2007): 9-16; "Patriarchy and Domestic Violence." On the specific manner in which male headship and female submission is often used by abusive men, abused women, and ministers to justify and perpetuate abuse, see Tracy, "Domestic Violence in the Church and Redemptive Suffering in 1 Peter."

discussion; at worst it subverts and distorts soul enriching biblical truth. Further compounding the issue, much of the current evangelical discussion of *headship* and *submission* injects notions of male privilege/ power and passive female servility into the very fabric of biblical teaching. We feel this is most unfortunate and highly misleading. So we enter into this discussion gently, with a sober dependence on the Holy Spirit to clarify our words and to do his work to redeem our sexuality where it has been wounded and violated. We sensitively urge the reader to avoid prejudging this subject or these terms as we seek to let Scripture shape, challenge and redeem this highly charged topic. Since the issue of male headship/female submission is so emotionally charged and the arguments numerous and often complex, we will focus in this chapter primarily on explaining our marital model in terms of the biblical data, and in the next chapter we will focus on fleshing this out practically.

A TRINITARIAN MODEL OF HEADSHIP AND SUBMISSION

We are passionate about a strategy that grounds our understanding of marital roles in the relationships and roles within the Godhead. This is a thoroughly biblical strategy in light of 1 Corinthians 11:3 which orders male/female relations based on the Trinity, specifically the Father's headship of the Son. [3] The Trinity also provides a much needed corrective to any discussion of marital roles because a foundational problem with understanding *headship* and *submission* is that these terms are loaded with connotations for all of us based on human relationships. This causes us to make various assumptions, particularly assumptions about power and control. While not all use of power is sinful, much of it is. Our inborn depraved instincts are bent toward self-advancement, and thus we tend to crave power and control in implicit and explicit forms. For this reason Jesus defined greatness in terms of serving others

---

[3]Grounding marital roles in the relationships within the Trinity is also biblical in light of the creation account, which grounds gender and marriage in the Trinity ("let us make . . . in our image," Gen 1:26). We will develop this concept in chapter four when we explain our model of marital intimacy.

instead of overpowering others—in direct antithesis to the way the world defines greatness (Lk 22:25-26). Furthermore, we need the trinitarian example because every moment of our lives we are being profoundly shaped by our relationships, all of which are finite, flawed and tainted by sin or even abuse. Therefore, we must have an external, perfect frame of reference for understanding familiar sounding relational terms. The Trinity is the only possible source for such a cleansing, corrective paradigm.

For sober clarification we would like to share two personal examples that demonstrate an incorrect view of headship and submission. Several years ago our daughter Abby spent a summer in Central America with a well-known evangelical mission organization. As part of their preparation, the teenagers were given classes on various subjects. During one presentation on relationships the teacher gave a traditional hierarchical lecture on male headship and female submission in marriage. Immediately following the session several of the boys made quick and frightening application of the teaching they had just heard. In all seriousness they boldly declared that the girls were to obey them and to do whatever they told them since "boys were the head and girls were to submit." This is a grave example to us of the way *headship* and *submission* can almost instantly turn malignant. As a sequel to this story, Abby is now a junior in college and is currently doing an eight-month internship in Africa. I (Steve) just received an e-mail from her in which she recounted a recent conversation with an African pastor she greatly respects for his wisdom and sacrificial service for Christ. After hearing of Abby's plans to live and minister in Africa after she graduates, this pastor's immediate comment was "then if you come back you will need to learn to kneel before your husband." He meant this quite literally, explaining "God made women inferior to men so in Africa women kneel before their husbands." He went on to explain, "You will need to forget your college training in photojournalism and learn to just serve your husband and keep house. That's how it is." This non sequitur was prompted by Abby's passion and confidence in the use of her gifts to serve Christ in the developing world. Apparently, this respected African pastor felt that her failure to realize her immutable inferiority to men would be the single greatest detriment to her future ministry. Where would a godly Christian leader get such a nonbiblical view of male/female roles? I suspect that it came from his cultural gender preconceptions that were validated and possibly even strengthened when he read about male headship and female submission in Scripture.

Let's now turn to the Trinity to build a specific model of gender roles, beginning with headship. To simplify the discussion, we will focus on the relationship between Christ and God the Father. Let's return to 1 Corinthians 11:3 where, in the beginning of a rather complicated discussion of order in the assembly and male/female relations in the church, Paul addresses headship. He states: "I want you to understand that Christ is the head of every man, and the husband is the head of his wife,[4] and God is the head of Christ." Plainly, headship is to be understood based on the Father's relationship to the Son, but the critical (and vexing) question is, What exactly should we understand by the word *head*? Scholars have felled small forests publishing their arguments over the meaning of this Greek word *(kephalē)*. One complicating factor is that *kephalē* is most often used in a literal manner with an undisputed meaning, that is, as an anatomical reference to the *head*. The challenge is that of the roughly seventy usages of *kephalē* in the New Testament, only a dozen uses are the kind of metaphorical use we have here in 1 Corinthians 11:3, and several of these uses do not have a plain meaning. When *kephalē* is used metaphorically, scholars have given it a range of meanings, including "authority over," "source of provision/nourishment," "source" and "prominent."[5]

---

[4]The Greek phrase translated "the husband is the head of his wife" (κεφαλὴ δὲ γυναικὸς ὁ ἀνήρ) could be translated "the man is the head of the woman" (so KJV, NASB, NIV) but I agree with this NRSV translation (also RSV, ESV) based on the context of the passage which seems to have marital relations largely (though not exclusively) in view. Either way, the principle of human male headship being based on the headship of the Father over the Son is clear.

[5]On the usage of *kephalē* to mean "authority over" see Wayne Grudem, *Evangelical Feminism and Biblical Truth: An Analysis of More than One Hundred Disputed Questions* (Sisters, Ore.: Multnomah, 2004), pp. 544-99; on the meaning of "source," see Catherine Kroeger, "Head," in *Dictionary of Paul and His Letters*, ed. Gerald F. Hawthorne, Ralph P. Martin and Daniel G. Reid (Downers Grove, Ill.: InterVarsity Press, 1993), pp. 375-77; on the meaning "foremost" or "prominent," see A. C. Perriman, "The Head of a Woman: The Meaning of *Kephalē* in 1 Cor 11:3," *Journal of Theological Studies* 45 (1994): 602-22; on the meaning "source of provision" (with a connotation of leader as the one providing the nourishment) see Clinton Arnold, "Jesus Christ Head of the Church," in *Jesus of Nazareth*, ed. Joel Green and Max Turner (Grand

Most of the recent debate has centered on whether *kephalē* denotes any kind of authority (the first two meanings above). The current scholarly discussion on *kephalē* has led to a polarization in which most evangelical scholars argue for one of two opposite positions for the metaphorical use of *kephalē* in the New Testament. One group of scholars (who refer to themselves as *complementarians*) assert that *kephalē* always and emphatically means "authority over." So its use by Paul strongly affirms male authority over women. Which in practical terms leads to models of marriage in which the husband's authority (headship) is said to be so all encompassing and potent that in the words of one of the most influential evangelical gender scholars, "every single decision large or small . . .whether we have reached agreement or not the responsibility [authority/power] to make the decision still rests with me [as the man]." Thus, "male headship makes a difference in every decision that a couple makes every day of their married life."[6] Such an understanding of male headship as all encompassing, strong authority leads numerous (and often very influential) evangelical writers to instruct wives that their husband's headship means a wife must never try to change her husband and should passively accept his sin, must obey him even if it violates her conscience and sense of God's leading, is to follow his mission and dreams (not her own), should be quiet or just say "sure" when she disagrees with him, and should submit even to his sinful behavior that might well lead to her or her children to be sexually abused.[7] On the other hand, many other evangelical scholars (generally called *egalitarians*) assert that there is no sense of authority whatsoever

---

Rapids: Eerdmans, 1994), pp. 346-66.

[6]Wayne Grudem, "Key Issues in the Manhood-Womanhood Controversy, and the Way Forward," in *Biblical Foundations for Manhood and Womanhood*, ed. Wayne Grudem (Wheaton, Ill., Crossway, 2002), p. 38. Grudem encourages husbands to discuss issues with their wives and to be loving, so the point here is not that he endorses an abuse of power (he does not) but that he believes God gives husbands great power (which many argue can and will in many instances lead to abuses).

[7]All of these references plus many more like them are in Steven R. Tracy, "What Does 'Submit in Everything' Really Mean?" Several of these writers reference Grudem's work, they are connected with or promoted by the gender role organization he founded (Council for Biblical Manhood and Womanhood), and apparently believe they are properly applying his authority intensive model of *kephalē*. I am not suggesting, however, that he personally endorses every one of these applications of his teaching but that this is how this kind of model of *kephalē* is often applied.

in Paul's usage of *kephalē*. Paul's teaching on Christ's headship with reference to the church only refers to his servanthood not to any authority he has over the church. So in marriage there is no unique male authority whatsoever, rather, all authority is shared and roles and responsibilities are entirely flexible and fluid depending on individual gifting. Thus, one influential evangelical scholar states, "Imposing an authority structure on this exquisite balance of reciprocity would paganize the marriage relationship."[8]

My (Steve's) own fairly extensive study of *kephalē* and study of the evangelical literature on this subject has led me to conclude that the biblical data is richer than these two opposing models suggest, though both camps of scholars have made helpful and accurate contributions to the discussion. In other words, I believe the current discussion of *kephalē* as applied to marriage is not a "winner takes all" debate after all, since *kephalē* can indicate at least some type of authority,[9] but it has a fairly broad range of meaning. One cannot assume every Pauline usage emphasizes authority; instead, this must be determined from the context.[10] For instance, several of the metaphorical uses of *kephalē* in Colossians and Ephesians convey some sort of authority, particularly when its scope extends beyond the church, but authority does not seem to be emphasized when its primary reference is the church. So the con-

---

[8]Gilbert Bilezikian, *Beyond Sex Roles: What the Bible Says About a Woman's Place in Church and Family*, 3rd ed. (Grand Rapids: Baker, 2006), p. 123.

[9]The Septuagint (the Greek translation of the Hebrew Scriptures), several first-century Greek writers, and all major Greek lexicons note authority as one of several meanings for *kephalē*. I find Wayne Grudem's arguments to be quite convincing in proving that *kephalē* when used metaphorically can mean "authority over" and is used this way in the New Testament, whereas *kephalē* used with reference to persons to mean "source" (with no connotation of authority whatsoever) has slender ancient literary attestation. For instance, all major Greek lexicons give some aspect of "authority" as a metaphorical meaning for *kephalē*, whereas only one major Greek lexicon, the *Liddell-Scott Greek-English Lexicon*, gives "source," as a meaning, and it is not with reference to persons. Having affirmed Grudem's thesis that *kephalē* is used to mean "authority over," and the meaning "source" is not viable, I do believe that Grudem overstates his case by dogmatically attributing a meaning of "authority over" in several instances in which this meaning is far from certain, by failing to note that "authority over" can and does have a very broad range of meanings indicating very different kinds and degrees of authority, and by lumping together every use of *kephalē* in Colossians and Ephesians to mean "strong authority over" without applying the differing contexts to the usages and hence meanings of *kephalē*.

[10]Similarly, Harold W. Hoehner argues that one should not view *kephalē* as inherently denoting authority; this must be determined from its usage in context, *Ephesians: An Exegetical Commentary* (Grand Rapids: Baker Academic, 2002), p. 739.

text is critical for determining what kind of authority, if any, *kephalē* is conveying. Colossians 1:15-20 from start to finish emphasizes Christ's majesty, preexistence, and especially his authority and supremacy over "all things" (vv. 16, 17, 20). This is delineated in terms of Christ's supremacy over rival authorities or powers, both earthly, visible (i.e., human) as well as heavenly, invisible (possibly demonic) powers (vv. 16, 20).[11] Most likely Paul's reference to Christ's supremacy over other powers was promoted by false teachers who had brought a syncretistic religion to the Colossians causing many of the believers to fear these spirits, thinking they had to appease them through various ascetic practices (2:4, 8, 16-23).[12] In this context, then, Christ is said to be the *"kephalē* of the body" with the purpose that "he might come to have first place in everything" (1:18). *Kephalē* here does emphasize his authority over, but the authority is viewed through the lens of his authority over the hostile powers (and hence his being head of the body offers protection). Similarly, in Colossians 2:10 Christ is said to be the *"kephalē* of every ruler and authority," an unmistakable reference to Christ's supremacy and authority over other powers. The most indisputable Pauline usage of *kephalē* that denotes authority is found in Ephesians 1:22 where God is said to have made Christ "the head over all things *for* the church" (italics added). This *headship* is specifically clarified in terms of God putting all "under his feet." We should emphasize that in each of these three passages *kephalē* indicates Christ's authority, but the context highlights not so much Christ's authority over the church but over other powers that might threaten the church.

Three additional christological references to *kephalē* are found in Colossians 2:19, Ephesians 4:15 and Ephesians 5:23. They have a

---

[11]On the language of Col 1:16 being a reference to demonic powers, see Clinton Arnold, *Ephesians Power and Magic: The Concept of Power in Ephesians in Light of Its Historical Setting* (Grand Rapids: Baker, 1989), pp. 49-56. My point here about *kephalē* stands even if one does not see the powers as demonic. Whatever the powers' precise identity, they competed with Christ for the Colossians' devotion, hence Christ being head in this context certainly includes his supremacy (and thus his authority) over the powers (Marianne Meye Thompson, *Colossians and Philemon* [Grand Rapids: Erdmans, 2005], pp. 33-35, 55-56).

[12]For a defense of this understanding of the Colossian opponents, see Clinton Arnold, *The Colossian Syncretism: The Interface Between Christianity and Folk Belief at Colossae* (Grand Rapids: Baker, 1996).

markedly different emphasis, for they all deal with Christ's headship over the church (not hostile powers), and they all focus on Christ's provision of salvation and/or spiritual nourishment. Christ the head is the one from whom the whole body is nourished and held together (Col 2:19). Believers must "grow up in every way into him who is the head" (Eph 4:15). Christ the head is the one who loved the church, gave himself for her, nourishes and cares for her and is perfecting her (Eph 5:23-29). We should not remove *any and all* sense of authority from *kephalē* in these passages, but at best it is greatly deemphasized.[13] The focus, instead, is on Christ the head being the sacrificial servant, the one who cares for and nurtures. To summarize, *kephalē* does often denote some type of authority, but this must be carefully nuanced. When Christ's headship is emphasized as authority, it is for the protection of all believers. When Christ's headship is emphasized over the church, it is expressed in his sacrificial nurturing. This helps us understand 1 Corinthians 11:3, which teaches that the Father and husbands are respectively heads of Christ and women, emphasizing their role in protection and loving support. They have a measure of authority, but based on the texts we've looked at, this authority would be used more toward other individuals or forces that might threaten, than it would be used over Christ or wives.

Let's return to the Trinity to develop a model of marital headship. We believe this is best done in an *incarnational* model. By *incarnational* we mean the nature of the Father's relationship with the Son during the Son's earthly life. Thankfully, we have much data, particularly from the Gospel of John, about this relationship. We believe that headship is incarnational in its *foundation, essence and purpose*. Let's break this down.

---

[13]For instance, the affirmation of Christ's authority in terms of his lordship and ascension (Eph 4:7-8) sets up the next paragraph in which Christ is said to give gifts to build up and nurture his body, of which he is the head (Eph 4:11-16). Similarly, while Col 2:19 emphasizes his nourishment of the body not Christ's authority, the immediately preceding paragraph highlights his disarmament and triumph over the demonic spirits through the cross (Col 2:14-15), so Christ's authority is not entirely absent from Col 2:19, but it is not the emphasis. If one understands the commands in Col 2:16-23 to relate to ascetic appeasement of the demonic spirits, this link is even tighter. Clinton Arnold has particularly shown in an evaluation of ancient medical literature that *kephalē* was used to mean "source of nourishment" and he also argues that this use denotes some sense of authority, "Jesus Christ Head of the Church."

THE FOUNDATION OF HEADSHIP

The *foundation* of male headship is the Father's headship over the Son. This is another way of saying we must not import our human experiences into the term *head*. More specifically, any authority denoted in *kephalē* must be determined by the nature of the Father's headship. What kind of authority do we see the Father exercising over the Son? Is it the type of power intensive, top-down hierarchical authority that is assumed and asserted by many Christian writers?[14] This is hardly the case. However, we do see some type of authority in the Father-Son relationship since the Son does what the Father commands (Jn 15:10), does the Father's will (Jn 6:38), and does nothing on his own authority (Jn 8:28-29). But upon further investigation, we see that even these statements do not denote a power intensive, rigidly hierarchical type of authority structure for the Father shares with the Son and their work is amazingly mutual and interconnected.[15] For instance, while the Son does carry out the Father's commands, the Father in turn gives the Son *all* authority in heaven and earth (Mt 28:18; cf. Jn 17:2). The Father gives all to the Son so that all that are the Father's are the Son's (Jn 3:35; 16:15; 17:10). While the Son was sent by the Father and does the Father's works, the Father sanctified the Son, empowered him and did miraculous works through him (Jn 10:36-38). Christ did teach his disciples to pray for the Father's kingdom to come (Mt 6:9-10). At the same time, the Father placed the Son on David's throne so that the Son's kingdom will never end (Lk 1:32-33). Furthermore, after the Son's obedience on the cross, the Father exalted him to the highest position of authority and honor and will someday force every created being to worship the Son and affirm his lordship (Phil 2:8-11). Thus,

---

[14]On the specific writings of fundamentalists and conservative evangelicals, which understand male headship in terms of all encompassing, authority, see Tracy, "What Does 'Submit in Everything' Really Mean?"

[15]One of the best biblical surveys of the Trinity that gives several hundred different biblical texts that show the overlap and mutuality in the Old Testament/New Testament descriptions, actions and ministries of the Father and Son is Edward Bickersteth, *The Trinity: Scripture Testimony to the One Eternal Godhead of the Father, and of the Son, and of the Holy Spirit* (Grand Rapids: Kregel, 1959). This is a reprint of a nineteenth-century work by a English minister who was responding to an increasingly popular Unitarianism, which denied the Son was divine and equal to the Father in his being and attributes.

male authority being foundationally incarnational greatly qualifies the husband's headship, deemphasizing its authority, instead emphasizing mutuality and empowerment. So in marriage a husband is to use his headship to lift up and empower his wife so that they might work together as one.

THE ESSENCE OF HEADSHIP

The *essence* of male headship involves initiation, protection/provision and honoring/empowering in the unbroken context of oneness and love. Thus, Celestia likes to refer to this headship as "an authority of love," not "an authority of power." Some may assert that this is really not authority but an egalitarian marriage model in disguise. On the contrary, we affirm that the Father's and Son's roles are not entirely reversible. Though they work in union with each other and enjoy rich, mutual and overlapping activity in many of their works, during the incarnation the Father initiates, protects and provides for the Son in ways the Son does not for the Father. The Son then, joyfully responds to the Father's initiation, protection and provision, which is where submission comes in. (We will develop this concept in the next section.)

I (Celestia) think of this surrendered response of a wife to her husband as a "receiving well" his initiations of support, protection and care. Men have a vulnerable (although this is hard for many to admit) and relational dependence upon their wives for respect and affirmation. I find this to be particularly true in our modern culture. It is often difficult and intimidating for men to initiate relationally within their marriage. Isn't it interesting that God has mandated men to initiate love and care to their wives, knowing that this kind of intentional loving would often not come naturally to them? Rather, it would necessitate a dependence upon God for courage and strength, and it would necessitate a surrender and vulnerability to one's wife for the "coaching" he would need to love her well. Scripture commands *wives to respect* their husbands and *husbands to love* their wives (Eph 5:33).

Let's briefly break down the essence of male headship seen in the Trinity:

1. *Initiation of love.* The Father is the ultimate creator of everything, and Christ is the agent of creation (1 Cor 8:6). The Father is the one who planned and initiated redemption by sending Christ to secure our salvation (Jn 8:42; 10:36). The Father planned and initiates various redemptive acts.[16] Husbands are to use their headship to lovingly initiate for the sake of their family. While all too often husbands are sinfully aggressive, using their physical and social power to dominate their wives, in our culture husbands often go to the other extreme by becoming harmfully passive.[17] This may be connected with the common masculine need to be in control and to be right. Thus, when men are not certain of the best course of action, they often do nothing, leaving their wives and children to take care of themselves. In our own marriage, this has been one of the bigger areas of conflict and frustration. All too often, particularly when our children were young, I was passive in the face of our children's misbehavior or needs. I saw my headship primarily in terms of final decision making and not in terms of daily, strategic and proactive initiating designed to meet my family's needs, whether by initiating family devotions, stepping in quickly when the children were struggling, or prayerfully and carefully assessing Celestia's daily concerns and initiating action to meet those needs.

Allow me (Celestia) to share another example. In the evening, when the house is quiet and dark, Steve will slip into bed and roll toward me. He uses his big, strong hands to deeply massage my back, shoulder and arm. I am weak there. I have pain and am vulnerable there. (I have had over fifteen orthopedic surgeries and live with chronic back and shoulder pain.) As he works the lotion into my back we share our day. He knows my body intimately and can feel the tension release. He knows when he is done by his attuned response to my body. He then wraps his bulky arm around me and cradles my head upon his shoulder and prays—he prays for all that burdens my heart, our children, our work and our world. He knows how to pray for me because he knows me. Today he knows me

---

[16]The Father chose believers for salvation (Eph 1:4; 2 Thess 2:13-14; 1 Pet 1:2), sent the Holy Spirit to indwell believers (Jn 14:16, 26), and judges, disciplines and sanctifies believers (Jn 15:1-2; 17:17).

[17]Larry Crabb cogently argues that, beginning with the first human sin recorded in Gen 3:1-13, males are inclined to be sinfully silent when they should take the risk and initiate, that is, speak: *The Silence of Adam* (Grand Rapids: Zondervan, 1995).

better than I know myself. In the beginning, it was hard for me to receive this consistent, powerful and intentional loving. I felt I owed him something in return. In an odd way, his intentional loving of me surfaced my shame—which was my deep-seated belief in my unworthiness of this kind of love. He would not let me put him off but would respond, "Here Celestia, let me do that for you." He just kept on loving and in time melted my resistance and healed my wounded heart. What has been my spontaneous feminine response? To love him like he has never been loved before. This is the fruit of his initiating love in our home.

2. *Protection and provision.* In Scripture we find the Father's protection of the Son to be a strong theme, particularly in Messianic Psalms such as Psalm 2 and 110. We also see the Father's provision for the Son in terms of giving him a position of honor. For instance, in Psalm 110:1, a text cited frequently in the New Testament, God promises to give Christ a position of honor and to defeat his enemies (making them his footstool). In Psalm 2:1-13, in the context of rebellious human rulers, the Father empowers the Son and warns earthly rebels to honor the Son or face destruction. Thus, following this example of the protective headship of God the Father, a husband should use all of his resources (including his physical strength and stamina, which is most often considerably greater than his wife's) to protect and provide for her. While this certainly means protecting one's wife from any hostile physical threats, in the Western world this is much less frequent than the myriad of more subtle but essential expressions of protection and provision. These include actions such as a husband giving his wife the more reliable car to drive; responding quickly and assertively to men who demean, slander or harass her; teaching and requiring their children to honor and respect her; and as much as possible, using the bulk of his income (instead of hers) for fixed monthly family expenses.[18]

Protection also encompasses taking responsibility for the protection

---

[18]Even in cases where a wife makes as much or more than her husband (which is not problematic in our model), we believe that when a husband strategizes to use the bulk of his income for fixed family expenses, he protects and loves his wife by lifting some of the psychological pressure from her. In Scripture males are repeatedly commanded to use their power and resources in the home and society to care for and protect women and children (Deut 25:5-10; Jer 22:1-3, 15-16; Mic 2:8-9; 3:1-12; 1 Tim 5:8).

of his sexual purity, so that their sexual intimacy will be nourished and protected. Some examples include Steve being proactive by purchasing Covenant Eyes for Internet accountability (not only for his computer but also for our son's), teaching our children the importance of purity and the dangers and lies of our sexualized culture, and asking me if there are any changes he needs to make to help me to feel more loved and protected emotionally and sexually. His initiating protection makes me feel more loved than any woman in the world. Because our present culture often desensitizes men to issues of sexual purity, it would be difficult to overstate the powerful effect of a husband's responsiveness and initiation in this area, on the heart of his wife.

3. *Honoring and empowering.* Our human experience teaches us that those in positions of headship or authority receive the greatest honor and have the greatest power. *The Trinity teaches us otherwise.* Jesus scandalized the Jewish leaders in John 5:23 by declaring that the Father had given all judgment to the Son "so that all may honor the Son just as they honor the Father."[19] John is saying that the Father gives the Son authority to judge with the strategic purpose that the Son would be honored to the same extent that he the Father is honored.[20] Therefore, husbands exercise incarnational headship when they deliberately strategize to lift up their wives, empower them and see that they receive more honor. In fact, God threatens not to answer a man's prayer if he does not learn how to honor his wife (1 Pet 3:7).

I would like to personalize this concept in our own marriage. I was young when Steve and I married and not yet fully developed in my sense of identity or confidence in who God had made me to be. Steve's interest in my ideas—attention to my undulations of emotion (believe me these

---

[19]The Greek word καθώς translated here "just as" is used of comparison meaning "just as" (Mt 21:6; Lk 17:26; 2 Cor 1:5) and of extent to which indicating "to the degree that" (Acts 11:29; 1 Cor 12:11; 1 Pet 4:10), BDAG, s.v. "καθώς." The latter meaning is probably in view here.

[20]The grammar of the passage clearly indicates purpose (the use of the conjunction ἵνα with the subjunctive verb τιμῶσι). Other Scripture passages such as Phil 2:9-11 develop the theme of the Father lifting up Christ, giving him power and authority, and decisively working so that all created beings would honor him. On the Father giving the Son authority (a concept that many gender traditionalists seem to deny), we should note that the Father gives the Son "all authority in heaven and earth" (Mt 28:18), and the Son is repeatedly called "God Almighty" (ὁ παντοκράτωρ) the all powerful, authoritative One who rules and judges and is to be worshiped (Rev 1:8; 15:3; 16:14).

were great) and his focus on listening to me—were instrumental in helping me discover my particular original design by God. This in turn
helped me discover my call and life's work. Steve valued my walk with the
Lord and spent time listening to my heart's expression, allowing himself
to be influenced and changed by me. This was profound.

Today, as we look back over thirty years of marriage, it is a joy to see
how God has honored and blessed us because of Steve's obedience to a
headship that was focused on not just his own growth and development,
but on mine also. We grew together—alongside of each other. What
have been God's blessings to us? Today, we write, speak and minister
together around the world. Steve helped me start a nonprofit ministry
that was the explosion of vision God had given me. Steve took that vision and call seriously and supported me in the development of Mending the Soul Ministries. Today, we partner in the leadership of MTS—
each focusing on our particular areas of strength and passion. We
delight in sitting under each other's teaching, allowing ourselves to be
influenced and changed by the other. With each year that passes, I am
more fully aware of the difference Steve's strategic emphasis on my empowerment and development has made in my life, in our lives and for
the kingdom. Conversely, I have enjoyed supporting Steve's gifts and
passion to research, write and teach at Phoenix Seminary. Much of the
evolving and dynamic intimacy we share today comes out of our mutual
support of each other's goals and dreams.

THE PURPOSE OF HEADSHIP

The *purpose* of male headship is to glorify God by giving the world a
glimpse of the character of God, particularly the nature of his love. For
instance, in the clear context of headship, four different times in Ephesians 5:25-33 Paul commands husbands to love their wives. This love is
to be patterned after the sacrificial love of Christ for his church. However, headship not only reflects the love of God through the redemptive
work of Christ for sinners, but also reflects the eternal relationship of
the Father and the Son. From eternity past the Father's headship over
the Son reveals not domination or "power over" but a headship of love,
unity and intimacy. Such love and intimacy is repeatedly described in

the gospels, for we read that the Father loves the Son and give all things to him (Jn 3:35); is well pleased with his "beloved" Son (Mt 3:17); is in the Son and the Son in him (Jn 14:10); is with the Son (Jn 16:32).[21] Throughout Scripture, the Father and Son work together in incredible unity and mutuality in creation and redemption.[22] Such unity sends a powerful message to the world about the character of God and the truthfulness of the gospel. Thus, Christ prayed that believers would experience unity and love based on the unity and love he had with the Father, for this unity would show the world the gospel was true and that the Father loved the Son (Jn 17:11, 21-23).

When headship is focused on a husband's power and authority over another, this central aspect of the Trinity is tragically lost.[23] Clearly then, husband-wife relationships should be characterized first and foremost by love and intimacy, which flow out of unity and mutuality of purpose and work. When this happens, the world gets a powerful message that such love and unity ultimately come from God. For example, in my office I have a picture of Steve and me. It is a candid snapshot of Steve's arms cradling me with his head bent toward mine. We are laughing. Needless to say, it is my favorite picture because it captures the essence of his protective love for me and the loving intimacy it has

---

[21]This verse is significant, for in the context of imminent abandonment by the disciples, Christ carried out his difficult redemptive mission not based on subjection to the greater authority of the Father but based on unity with the Father.

[22]For instance, the church is in God the Father and the Lord Jesus Christ (1 Thess 1:1). Paul was an apostle sent by Christ and sent by the Father (Gal 1:1). Grace and peace come from a knowledge of the Father and a knowledge of Jesus (2 Pet 1:2). The grace of God brings salvation (Tit 2:11); the grace of Christ brings salvation (Acts 15:11). The Lord God corrects the one he loves (Prov 3:12); Christ corrects the one he loves (Rev 3:19). God satisfies the weary soul (Jer 31:25); Christ gives rest to the weary soul (Mt 11:28-29). The mutuality of the Trinity is also seen in the manner in which their names appear together describing their united redemptive work with their names sometimes reversed; the Father does not always appear first in the list (1 Cor 12:4-6; 2 Thess 2:16-17; 1 Pet 1:2; Jude 20-21).

[23]Sadly, some influential evangelicals have recently misconstrued the biblical data, declaring the most definitive characteristic of the Father/Son relationship is not mutuality, love and intimacy but an eternal authority-submission structure in which the Father must be obeyed by the Son and the Spirit because he is supreme. This is then made the basis for an eternal (fixed) authority-submission structure in which men have relational primacy and authority over women: Wayne Grudem, "Key Issues in the Manhood-Womanhood Controversy and the Way Forward," in *Biblical Foundations for Manhood and Womanhood*, ed. Wayne Grudem (Wheaton, Ill.: Crossway, 2002), p. 51; Bruce Ware, *Father, Son and Holy Spirit: Relationships, Roles, and Relevance* (Wheaton, Ill.: Crossway, 2005), pp. 46, 73, 132-51.

created in our relationship. Just last week, one of my clients noticed this picture and said, "That is the color of love." She went on to describe her history of abuse and, hence, how she did not have an accurate script for the love of God for herself. She then declared, "Your relationship puts it [God's love] in color."

AN INCARNATIONAL MODEL OF
HEADSHIP AND SUBMISSION: EPHESIANS 5:21-33

We have devoted the bulk of this chapter to clarifying headship in terms of the Father/Son relationship. We are convinced that looking to the Trinity not to human relationships to understand marriage gives us the purest and safest model to follow. Now to complete our biblical examination of marital relationships, particularly submission, we want to survey Ephesians 5:21-33 briefly. This passage gives an astounding picture of marital roles that harmonizes beautifully with the incarnational model of headship we just described. This model emphasizes unity, love and mutuality while still encompassing some gender differentiation. It is essential that we maintain the tension of the dual emphases in the trinitarian model—intimacy and mutuality but not (role) sameness—as we examine this passage. For instance, the passage begins and ends with mutuality and intimacy (mutual submission in v. 21, *one-flesh* intimacy in vv. 31-32). But within the "bookends" of mutuality and loving intimacy, Paul encompasses gender role differentiation (the submission of wives and the sacrificial, nurturing headship of husbands in vv. 23-30).

In terms of mutuality, we affirm that verse 21 is a command to mutual submission of husbands and wives to each other ("be subject to one another"). Such mutual submission is in keeping with other passages that direct believers to serve and defer to each other's needs (Phil 2:1-4; Gal 5:13; cf. Eph 4:2; Gal 6:2). Mutual submission is particularly harmonious with Paul's statements in 1 Corinthians 7:4 that explain marital sexual rights and authority over one's body in terms of mutuality.[24]

---

[24]"The wife does not have authority over her own body, but the husband does; likewise the husband does not have authority over his own body, but the wife does." What is particularly significant about the marital mutuality described in this verse is that this is the only time in

This mutual submission qualifies male authority but does not negate all gender differentiation. We believe there is both mutual submission pictured here (v. 21) as well as a wife's unique, appropriate submission to her husband (v. 22, 24).[25] It is important that both aspects of submission are recognized, for mutual submission is the foundation for a strong, biblical marriage. In other words, it does not detract from our unique male/female roles but is essential for understanding them. Dan Allender and Tremper Longman clarify this point well:

> Mutual submission does not compromise the headship of the husband; it enhances it. Indeed, mutual submission is the only workable path to a strong marriage. After all, what is submission? Submission is the giving up of one's own will and agenda for life for the benefit of another person. It is putting oneself in alignment to the greater good of the other. Submission is not obeying another; it is putting oneself under the other to serve the good of God for that person's life.[26]

As far as the specific meaning of *submit*, the verb used here indicates a willingness to yield to, defer or follow another.[27] We will significantly develop female submission in this chapter, but will give it greater development, particularly in terms of life examples, in the next chapter. We would briefly note, however, that we are quite convinced that the strong clarification of male headship (as we have sought to provide in this chapter) makes a detailed discussion of submission much less necessary, for it clarifies the nature of the husband's authority. Loving, empower-

---

the Pauline literature the primary Greek word for authority (ἐξουσία) is used of marriage, and it is not used here to assert male, but mutual authority.

[25]So Andrew Lincoln, *Ephesians* (Dallas: Word, 1990), p. 366. We mean "unique" in the sense that husbands are never specifically commanded to submit to their wives (Col 3:18; Tit 2:5; 1 Pet 3:1-2). This is a very important biblical fact that should not be overlooked. We see this multifaceted view of submission elsewhere in early Christian literature, particularly in 1 Clement where the same verb (ὑποτάσσω) is used of mutual submission (1.3; 37.5) but also of the unique submission of believers to Christ (34.5) and of church members to ecclesiastical leaders (57.1).

[26]Dan Allender and Tremper Longman, *Intimate Allies: Rediscovering God's Design for Marriage and Becoming Soul Mates for Life* (Wheaton, Ill.: Tyndale House, 1995), p. 118.

[27]For instance, in the New Testament ὑποτάσσω is used of the submission of all believers to the governing authorities (Rom 13:1), the spirits of the prophets being subject to the prophets (1 Cor 14:32), all things being made subject to God (1 Cor 15:28), of holy women being submissive to their husbands (1 Pet 3:5), and of the future subjection of the world to come to Christ (Heb 2:5-8).

ing headship patterned after the Trinity also makes her submission more natural and straightforward. So what is female marital submission? We believe it involves a wife first and foremost submitting to her only Lord and Savior, Jesus Christ, by responding to, respecting and yielding to the leadership of the husband God has given her. This is not to be done passively ("whatever you say dear") but actively, as a wife boldly, graciously and persistently states her perspective and sense of what is wise, and as she gives her husband accountability—confronting him when he sins. It is essential to note that this submission command to wives does not reflect the type of powerful male patriarchy seen in first-century secular writings on the family for the command is to submit not to obey;[28] the command is given to the wife (she voluntarily submits; he is given no authority whatsoever to make her submit); the context places the greatest responsibility on the husband to serve his wife sacrificially (even to the point of death).

Trust deepens in a marriage when a husband consistently cherishes his wife, loving her like Christ loved the church. A wife's respectful yielding to her husband is not a right to be demanded or controlled by any man. It is a *gift* given by a wife who can trust in the heart of her husband. It is my greatest joy to submit to and support God's movement in Steve's heart and life. He has taught me that I can trust him. In fact, Steve's unselfish love for me has helped me better understand and experience God's unconditional love for me. My husband's love is an echo of my Abba Father's love.

In terms of the specific meaning of the word "submit" in Ephesians 5:22, it is very similar to other uses in the New Testament indicating "voluntary yielding to another in love."[29] To underscore this submission command to wives, Paul says they are to submit to their husbands "in everything" just as the church submits to Christ. This is an often misconstrued verse that in and of itself could appear to give husbands unlimited power. Many other Scripture passages clearly limit a husband's

---

[28]The verb here is ὑποτάσσω, whereas Paul uses ὑπακούω of children and slaves (Eph 6:1, 5; Col 3:20, 22). The latter verb is best translated "obey," BDAG, s.v. "ὑπακούω."

[29]This is precisely the lexical definition given for the use of ὑποτάσσω in 1 Cor 16:16; Eph 5:21; and 1 Pet 5:5; 1 Clem 38.1, BDAG, s.v. "ὑποτάσσω."

authority, so "in everything" here does not mean she must obey every single command but that she is to yield to her husband in love in every category of life.[30] Furthermore, husbands are not being identified with Christ for wives have only one Lord and master and it is Christ. Rather, the point here is simply that marital submission is appropriate, logical and Christian. This analogy reveals that submission is based on a love relationship in which one party yields to another who uses his position to sacrifice on her behalf. At this point we should also note the logic of a wife's submission in light of our explanation of incarnational headship. God does give a husband some authority as the head, and this is to be used to nurture, protect and serve his wife. If a wife refuses to yield to her husband in love, then his ability to care for and protect her can be significantly compromised. We will give some specific illustrations of this principle from our own marriage in the next chapter.

Another observation we should make about Ephesians 5:21-33 is that the primary focus of the passage is *not* on the woman's submission to her husband, but rather on the husband's sacrificial headship patterned after the sacrifice of Christ for the church.[31] The husband is to love, nourish and tenderly care for her regardless of how costly an enterprise this turns out to be. Paul sets the bar as high as he possibly could here, for the husband is to love his wife and attend to her well-being and growth as sacrificially and vigorously as Christ attends to the well-being of the church. Finally, just as we saw with the Father/Son relationship, while there is an authority structure here, this is not the essence of the relationship. Rather, the relationship centers on love and intimacy (being *one flesh*). It is an "authority of love."

We have covered a lot of ground on a difficult subject. We have seen that, based on the Trinity, there are unique and differing roles for hus-

---

[30]In "What Does 'Submit in Everything' Really Mean?" I give six specific categories (with biblical support) to govern times a wife should not submit (yield) to her husband. They include circumstances in which submission would violate a biblical principle (not just a direct biblical command), compromise her relationship with Christ, violate her conscience, compromise the care and protection of the children, enable her husband's sin, and entail submitting to any type of abuse.

[31]For instance, Paul's admonition to husbands is over three times as long as his admonition to wives (143 words versus 47 words in the United Bible Society, 4th ed. of the Greek New Testament).

bands and wives, but these differences must not be overemphasized. God the Father and husbands do have a *headship* role that involves some authority but that is not the central focus. The overriding emphasis in the Father/Son relationship is mutuality and intimacy. So in marriage, husbands are called to an incarnational headship, which involves initiation, protection/provision and honoring/empowering in the unbroken context of oneness and love.

Aída and Bill Spencer's
Viewpoint

The United States has more marriages and divorces than any other country studied by the United States Census Bureau. In 2002 there were 11.7 marriages and 6 divorces per 1,000 people in the United States. Denmark is a close second with 10.4 marriages and 4.3 divorces per 1,000 people. In other Western countries many children are born to unmarried women. In 2002 in Sweden 56 percent of all live births were to unmarried women, in Denmark and France 44 percent, in the United Kingdom 40 percent, in the United States 34 percent, whereas in Italy 10 percent and in Japan 2 percent. Single parent households have been steadily increasing in almost all countries, but most especially in the United States (28 percent of all households with children in 2003).[1] But despite such great cultural change, we Christians cherish marriage because it is commanded in the Bible. Yet, we wonder, what model of marriage will work in such a culturally changing world? Today, finding *the* model for everyone that God will honor is not so clear. Let's consider, for example, the model of King Ahasuerus and Queen Vashti versus the model of the Shunammite and her husband.

The movie *One Night with the King* reminds us of the first example. King Ahasuerus (Xerxes I) reigned in Susa over Persia and Media during 486–465 B.C. In the third year of his reign for six months he celebrated and boasted about the splendor and pomp of the majesty of his reign. He concluded with a week-long party for men of all classes with no limits on drinking (Esther 1:1-9). Queen Vashti, his wife, had her own party for the women. On the last day of the banquet, when Aha-

---

[1]The divorce rate has been going down in the last 25 years in the United States. It remains highest in states such as Nevada, Arkansas, Idaho and Wyoming (5-6 per 1000 people). Tables 117, 1319, 1320, 1321, *Statistical Abstract of the United States: 2006* (Washington, D.C.: U.S. Census Bureau, 2005), pp. 93, 869.

suerus was really drunk, he commanded his wife to come in and show herself off. She refused (Esther 1:10-12). The Bible text does not tell us why she refused. However, the context is quite clear about the setting she would walk into: one in which there would be many men who had been heavily drinking over many days! Ahasuerus was not thinking about his wife at all. He was displaying her like an exotic dancer in a brothel, not with the dignity and decency she deserved as queen.[2] But what emerged from her refusal as most important to him and his male colleagues was King Ahasuerus's power, honor and authority, foremost in his home and second as a standard for all husbands to emulate in Persia and Media (Esther 1:17-18). Therefore, they decided that Vashti would no longer be queen so that "all women will give honor to their husbands, high and low alike" (Esther 1:20). In a time when the men feared for their own authority, they responded with a hierarchical and cavalier decree.

However, another biblical model appeared earlier in 852–841 B.C. when both Israel and Judah had become steeped in paganism. A woman living in Shunem, on her own, urged the prophet Elisha to dine regularly at her house, thereby supporting his ministry. Discerning Elisha was God's holy representative, she urged her husband to join her in building guest lodging exclusively for the prophet (2 Kings 4:8-10). Elisha showed his appreciation not by acknowledging the husband as figurative representative of the home, but addressing only the "Shunammite

---

[2]Scholars have posited reasons why Xerxes commanded Vashti's presence and why she may not have come: Xerxes may have been rallying support for his military campaign against the Greeks in the war council of 483 B.C. to which Vashti, wearing her royal diadem, was a living trophy of Xerxes' power and glory. She was his greatest status symbol to honor the king and elicit political support. E.g. Karen H. Jobes, *Esther: The NIV Application Commentary* (Grand Rapids: Zondervan, 1999), pp. 60-61, 67; Joyce G. Baldwin, *Esther: An Introduction and Commentary* (Downers Grove, Ill.: InterVarsity Press, 1984), p. 57; Timothy S. Laniak, *Shame and Honor in the Book of Esther, SBL Dissertation Series 165* (Atlanta: Scholars Press, 1998), pp. 36, 41, 56; *New International Biblical Commentary: Ezra, Nehemiah, Esther* (Peabody: Hendrickson, 2003), p. 199. Linda M. Day simply says the king was motivated by voyeurism since he was drunk (*Esther*, Abingdon Old Testament Commentaries [Nashville: Abingdon Press, 2005], p. 32. Some have posited Vashti may have had to appear naked or unveiled (Mervin Breneman, *The New American Commentary 10: Ezra, Nehemiah, Esther* (Nashville: Broadman & Holman Publishers, 1993), pp. 307-8). She might have been in the late stage of her pregnancy (Jobes, *Esther*, p. 74) or she was simply too busy with her own party (Johanna W. H. Van Wijk-Bos, *Ezra, Nehemiah, and Esther*, Westminster Bible Companion (Louisville: Westminster John Knox Press, 1998), p. 109.

woman" (2 Kings 4:12). He wanted to thank *her*. Elisha and his servant
Gehazi explained God would also thank her by allowing her to conceive
a child. The husband too recognized the wife's capabilities because,
when the child was older and suddenly had head distress, he sent him to
his mother to be doctored. But, the child died. The Shunammite woman
determined to petition Elisha to resurrect the child. She commanded
her husband (though older than she) to send her a servant and a donkey
so she could visit Elisha. She did not choose to explain to her husband
why she went. She then commanded the servant to drive the donkey,
making their trip as quick as possible. She insisted on talking directly to
Elisha and demanded that only he, Elisha, must come (his prophet's
staff, the sign of his office, as carried by his servant Gehazi was not
enough). Elisha was not insulted at all, but came personally. Responding
to Elisha's personal petitions, God resurrected the young man. Later,
when a famine was to occur, Elisha warned the woman, not the husband, to bring her household to live outside Israel for seven years (2
Kings 4:13-37; 8:1). In a time of great difficulties in Judah and Israel, the
Shunammite and the prophet Elisha responded with obedience to God
without regard to patriarchal conventions of authority.

These two accounts show us two ways to run a marriage. In the first
the man is in charge, in the second, the woman is. However, the Bible
is more interested in whether the family serves the Lord than who calls
the shots. In this chapter we will examine whether authority is gender
based or gift based. Then we will look in more detail at Ephesians 5
and suggest some practical ramifications for marriage.

DEFINING AUTHORITY

What is *authority* anyway? According to *Webster's Dictionary*, *authority*
is "the power or a right to command, act; enforce obedience, or make
final decisions; jurisdiction."[3] It comes from the Latin *auctor*, "author"
or "originator." *Auctoritas* is "origination, source, cause."[4] Thus, an *au-*

---

[3]Noah Webster, *Webster's Unabridged Dictionary*, 2d ed. (New York: Simon & Schuster, 1983),
p. 126.
[4]Ibid.; John C. Traupman, *The New College Latin & English Dictionary* (New York: Bantam
Books, 1966), p. 25.

thority is the source or origin of power. *Power* (which comes from the Latin *posse*, "to be able") is the "ability to do; capacity to act; capability of performing or producing."[5] Some Bible interpreters understand 1 Timothy 2:12 as good authority: "I permit no woman to teach or *to have authority over* a man; she is to keep silent" (NRSV, italics added) (also translated as "to assume authority over" [TNIV], "dictate to" [REB], "to usurp authority over" [KJV], and "dominate" [New Living Translation (Tyndale, 1990)]. Therefore, some Christians might conclude that women never have the power or right to command men or make final decisions. They do not have any jurisdiction over men.[6] However, this Greek verb *(authenteō)* occurs nowhere else in the Bible. We do discover the noun cognate used by contemporary Jewish writers. Josephus uses *authentēs* to render "assassins" (murderers of Galilean Jew(s) on their way to a festival in Jerusalem, *War* 2.12.5 [240]). He describes Antipater, Herod's son, as an *authentēs* because he was accused of killing his family members (*War* 1.30.1 [582]). Philo describes the person who has tried to destroy the virtues as his "own murderer" (*The Worse Attacks the Better* 21 [78]). The Wisdom of Solomon describes bad parents as *authentai* who "*kill* defenseless souls by their own hands" (12:6). In the first century *authenteō/authentēs* clearly had negative connotations.[7]

Why would Paul use *authenteō*, a verb that most likely means "to

---

[5]*Webster's Dictionary*, p. 1412.

[6]In other words, women may not govern or have authority in the church or home, for example, Wayne Grudem, *Systematic Theology* (Grand Rapids: Zondervan, 1994), pp. 459-66, 915, 937-44. Harold Hoehner describes husbands as having "positional power," "a power by virtue of one's position." *Ephesians: An Exegetical Commentary* (Grand Rapids: Baker, 2002), p. 740.

[7]Contemporary historian Appian (A.D. 95-165) used *authentēs* for "murderer." *Roman History*, Civil Wars I.7.61; III.13.115; IV.17.134. Diodorus of Sicily, writing a century earlier, also used *authentēs* in negative contexts: "the *perpetrators* of the sacrilege"; "the *author* of these crimes." *History* XVI.61.1; XVI.5.4. *Authenteō* is similar to the negative type of leadership Jesus portrays for the Gentile rulers (*archōn*). Their leadership is described in two words *katakyrieuō* and *katexousiazō* (Mt 20:25), formed from the root preposition "under" (*kata*), which vividly describes the position of the person being ruled. *Katakyrieuō* signifies "to exercise complete dominion." Henry Liddell and Robert Scott, *A Greek-English Lexicon*, 9th ed. (Oxford: Clarendon, 1968), p. 896. *Katakyrieuō* literally means to make oneself "lord over." *Katexousiazō* literally means to wield "authority over" or "tyrannize over someone." BDAG, p. 531. Both verbs, as does *authenteō*, take the genitive case for the person "over" whom one rules. *Katakyrieuō* is used of the demons who "overpower" the Jewish exorcists so that they are left naked and wounded (Acts 19:16).

have absolute destructive power over"[8] persons (or at best is an obscure word) to describe the normal relationship between men and women? The reference in 1 Timothy 2:12 is probably a public setting since it suggests a context of public prayer (1 Tim 2:8-10) and the men mentioned are *not* described as "*her* man" or "husband."[9] Paul could have used any one of at least twelve Greek word families with positive connotations denoting authority that are used elsewhere in the New Testament. Instead, he used the rare word *authenteō*, which is most likely a negative word.

What were Paul's alternative choices? *Exousiazō/exousia* has positive or neutral connotations. Its authority refers to governance. As Paul explains in Romans 13, human government has God-given power to function judicially, to judge, discipline, forgive, punish with the ultimate goal of promoting good conduct.[10] This type of authority also includes the power to make decisions or complete work in one's jurisdiction. For example, Jesus compares our current situation where we expect his imminent return to slaves whose master has given them *power* or *authority (exousia)* to do their own work (Mk 13:34).

Are women ever described as having such *authority* or *power*? Yes, women ought to have such "authority" on their "heads," according to 1 Corinthians 11:10. Wives exercise this kind of authority *(exousiazō)* over their husbands' bodies, even as husbands exercise this same authority over their wife's bodies (1 Cor 7:4). Jesus gave authority or power to the apostles to cast out unclean spirits and to heal illnesses (Mt 10:1).

---

[8]See also Aída Besançon Spencer, *Beyond the Curse: Women Called to Ministry* (Peabody, Mass.: Hendrickson, 1985), pp. 86-88.

[9]Jerome agrees that the pronoun delineates marriage. *Commentary on Eph 5:25-7* in Ronald E. Heine, *The Commentaries of Origen and Jerome on St Paul's Epistle to the Ephesians*, The Oxford Early Christian Studies (Oxford: Oxford University Press, 2002), p. 236.

[10]E.g. Rom 13:1-7; Lk 23:7; Jn 19:10-11; Acts 9:14. *Exousia* comes from *exesti*, "it is proper, permitted or lawful." Joseph Henry Thayer, *Thayer's Greek-English Lexicon of the New Testament* (Marshallton, Del.: National Foundation for Christian Education, 1889), p. 225. It can refer to the authority (or power) of God or Jesus (God: Lk 12:5; Acts 1:7; Rom 9:21; 13:1; Jude 25; Rev 16:9); (Jesus: Mt 7:29; 9:6; 21:23; 28:18; Mk 1:27; Jn 5:27; 10:18; 17:2; Rev 12:10); the devil or the demonic (Lk 4:6; 22:53; Acts 26:18; Eph 2:2; 3:10; 6:12; Col 1:13; 2:15; Rev 11:6; 13:2, 4, 5, 7); death (Rev 6:8); angel (Rev 18:1) and human rulers, such as governor Herod, are called "authorities" (Lk 12:11; 20:20; 23:7; Eph 1:21). To everyone who "conquers and continues to do" Jesus' works to the end will be given this *"authority (exousiazō)* over the nations" and to *pastor (poimainō)* them (Rev 2:26-27).

One woman apostle is Junia, who is "prominent among the apostles" (Rom 16:7). The main qualifications for apostles are: (a) to have been with Jesus and have witnessed his resurrection and (b) to have been specifically commissioned by Christ to preach. All of these qualifications were also fulfilled by Mary Magdalene, Salome and other women (Mt 28:10; Jn 20:17). Jesus said, "Keep on going, proclaim to my brothers and sisters that they should go into Galilee, there they will see me" (Mt 28:10, Aída's trans.). There is no reason to suppose that women were *not* included in the seventy-two or the "more than five hundred" believers or the larger group of "all the apostles" who were witnesses to the resurrection (1 Cor 15:6-7).[11]

Proistēmi primarily means "to exercise a position of leadership, *rule, direct.*"[12] Paul writes that one of the gifts of the Spirit is this kind of leading (Rom 12:8). He tells the Thessalonians to pay proper respect to the ones working among them and leading them in the Lord and instructing them (1 Thess 5:12). This same verb describes elders and deacons in 1 Timothy itself (1 Tim 3:4-5, 12; 5:17). The noun form *(prostatis)* of this verb is used to describe "sister" Phoebe who "has been a *leader* over many" (Aída's trans.) and even of Paul (Rom 16:1-2, "overseer" [*New Testament in Modern English,* trans. Helen Barrett Montgomery]). Phoebe is an explicit, commendable example of a woman set in authority over a man, namely the apostle Paul himself.[13]

One word family that clearly has to do with having authority over the household is *oikodespoteō/oikodespotēs.* It is a composite word made up of *oikos* ("house" or "household") and *despotēs* ("lord" or "master").

---

[11]See further Aída Besançon Spencer, "Jesus' Treatment of Women in the Gospels," in *Discovering Biblical Equality: Complementarity Without Hierarchy,* ed. Ronald Pierce and Rebecca Merrill Groothuis, (Downers Grove, Ill.: InterVarsity Press, 2004), pp. 137-38; *Beyond the Curse,* p. 62.

[12]Frederick William Danker, ed., *A Greek-English Lexicon of the New Testament,* 3rd ed. (Chicago: University of Chicago, 2000), p. 870. Liddell and Scott, *Lexicon,* p. 1526, indicate that the noun *prostatēs* is part of the same word family as *proistēmi.* William D. Mounce agrees *proistēmi* means "to lead, govern." *Pastoral Epistles,* Word Biblical Commentary 46 (Nashville: Thomas Nelson, 2000), p. 178.

[13]See also Spencer, *Beyond the Curse,* pp. 115-17. George and Dora Winston also conclude in chap. 3 of *Recovering Biblical Ministry by Women: An Exegetical Response to Traditionalism and Feminism* (Longwood, Fla.: Xulon Press, 2003) that they "see no biblical evidence for reducing the essence of maleness to the exercise of authority over women and the essence of femaleness to submissiveness to men" (p. 41).

A *despotēs* is someone "who has legal control and authority over persons," thus an *oikodespotēs* is a "master of the house."[14] In the gospels, masters of the house are landowners, farmers, and builders who hire and pay laborers.[15] Thus, it is significant that Paul commands married women to "be master (or head) of a house, to rule a household."[16] A synonym for *master* of the house was "lord" of the house.[17] Sarah called Abraham, her husband, "lord" (*kyrios*, 1 Pet 3:6), a respectful or deferential term similar to "sir,"[18] but women leaders were also called "lord" (*kyria*, e.g., 2 Jn 1, 5). Candace was called "ruler" *(basilissa)* and "sovereign" (*dynastēs*, Acts 8:27).

In 1 Timothy 2:12 Paul could have used many other positive synonyms for leading in the church, such as *episkopeō/episkopē/episkopos* ("to oversee"),[19] *poimainō/poimēn* ("to shepherd"),[20] *hēgeomai/hēgemōn* ("to lead"),[21] *archō/archōn* ("to rule"),[22] *epitassō/epitagē*, the one whose command will be obeyed,[23] *hyperochē/hyperechō*, "to have power over,"[24] or *basileuō/basileus/basilissa* ("to rule").[25] Together all Christians are described as "a kingdom" *(basileia)* who "rule" (*basileuō*, Rev 5:10).

---

[14]BDAG, pp. 220, 695. *Despotēs* is used to refer to slave masters (1 Tim 6:1; Tit 2:9; 1 Pet 2:18).

[15]Mt 20:1; 21:33; Mk 14:14.

[16]*Thayer's*, p. 439; 1 Tim 5:14. The "capable wife" of Proverbs 31 provides food and clothing for her household, and as well works as a business woman and farmer (31:14-24).

[17]Gal 4:1; Eph 6:5, 9; Col 4:1; Liddell & Scott, *Lexicon*, p. 1013.

[18]E.g. Mt 8:6; Jn 12:21; 20:15; Liddell & Scott, *Lexicon*, p. 1013.

[19]The noun forms *episkopē* and *episkopos* for elder occur in 1 Tim 3:1, 2; Acts 20:28; Phil 1:1; Tit 1:7.

[20]Eph 4:11; what elders are to do (Acts 20:28; 1 Pet 5:2).

[21]The noun *hēgemōn* refers to governors Pilate (Mt 27:2), Felix (Acts 23:24), Festus (Acts 26:25, 30), Joseph (Acts 7:10) who have derivative power from the emperor (or Pharaoh) (1 Pet 2:13-14; Acts 7:10). The verb (*hēgeomai)* is used for leaders in general (Lk 22:26; Heb 13:7, 17, 24) such as Judas Barsabbas and Silas (Acts 15:22).

[22]The noun *archōn* can refer to a leader of a synagogue (Mt 9:18, 23; Lk 8:41), leader of the Pharisees (Lk 14:1), ruler or members of the Sanhedrin, such as Nicodemus (Jn 3:1). It is a synonym for *exousia*, Rom 13:1-3.

[23]*Epitagē* refers to "command" in the New Testament, not to "commander." The verb *epitassō* means "to enjoin upon" or "to command" (Mk 1:27; 9:25; Lk 8:25; 14:22; Philem 8). Titus is told to "exhort and reprove with all *authority*" (*epitagē*, Tit 2:15).

[24]BDAG, p. 1033. *Hyperochē* and *hyperechō* are synonyms for *basileus* and *exousia* (Rom 13:1; 1 Tim 2:2; 1 Pet 2:13). Literally, *hyperechō* is "to have or hold over" (cf. Phil 2:3; *Thayer's*, p. 640).

[25]Archilaus and Agrippa are examples of rulers (*basileuō*, Mt 2:22; *basileus*, Acts 26:2), as were David (Mt 1:6), Herod (Mt 2:1), Pharaoh (Acts 7:10), the queen of Sheba (*basilissa*, Mt 12:42), and Candace, queen of the Ethiopians (Acts 8:27).

Our example is Jesus, who instead modeled servant leadership. Jesus Christ our Lord has complete power and authority as God incarnate ("Emmanuel," Mt 1:23), and, significantly, almost every positive synonym for *authority* is used of Jesus: *exousia* (Mt 28:18), *archōn* (Rev 1:5), *episkopos, poimēn*,[26] *hēgeomai* (Mt 2:6), *despotēs* (Jude 4). Jesus Christ is "the blessed and only Sovereign *(dynastēs),* the King *(basileus)* of kings and Lord *(kyrios)* of lords" (1 Tim 6:15), but Jesus uses his power to serve others (Mk 10:45). Jesus assumes he is the apostles' teacher and lord, but he leads by washing their feet as a slave might (Jn 13:3-17). Even for the church, Peter admonishes elders not "to lord it over" the flock but to be examples to them (1 Pet 5:3). Leadership that overpowers and destroys is never approved by Christ for either men or women.[27] What is true for the church is true for the home.

UNDERSTANDING EPHESIANS 5:21-22: MUTUAL SUBMISSION

Christ's love for us is a model for the church and for married couples as well. When studying Ephesians 5:21-33, we sometimes forget the introductory verses in chapter five: "Therefore be imitators of God, as beloved children, and live in love, as Christ loved us and gave himself up for us, a fragrant offering and sacrifice to God" (Eph 5:1-2). In the church and in all our relationships including marriage, we are to "walk in love" (KJV). "Walk" brings out the step-by-step actions that make up our life. Because we are heirs of God's gracious calling, we need to live lives worthy of that calling (Eph 1:5, 18; 4:1).

How does the church "walk in love"? The church needs to be wise, investing its time well, understanding God's will, being filled with the Spirit (Eph 5:15-18). Paul then explains further how to become filled with the Holy Spirit by using five participles. The church, and members of it, become filled with the Spirit by (1) "*speaking* to one another in psalms and hymns and spiritual songs, (2) *singing* and (3) *making*

---

[26]1 Pet 2:25; Mt 26:31; Jn 10:11, 14; Heb 13:20; Rev 7:17; 19:15. *Archēgos* ("author, chief leader, furnishing the first cause"), *archipoimēn* ("chief shepherd"), and *archiereus* ("chief priest" forever) in the New Testament are used only of Jesus (Acts 3:15; 5:31; Heb 2:10; 6:20; 12:2; 1 Pet 5:4).

[27]Mk 10:43; Lk 22:26; 2 Cor 1:24.

melody in your heart to the Lord, (4) *thanking* God the Father always for all in the name of our Lord Jesus Christ, (5) *being subject* (or "subjecting yourselves") to one another in fear of Christ" (Eph 5:19-21, Aída's trans.). In addition to praising and thanking God, in the church Christians need to be subject to one another as a means of becoming Spirit filled. This mutual submission applies also to the home, to women's relationship to their husbands (Eph 5:22-24, 33) and to men's relationship to their wives (Eph 5:25-33). The earlier and better ancient Greek manuscripts omit the verb "be subject" in verse 22,[28] thereby showing that a woman's submission to her husband (5:22) is one application of mutual submission in the church (5:21).

What does the apostle Paul teach us about mutual submission? Submission is not subjection of another. No church leader or husband ever makes another submit. Submission is not about taking power over another. "Being subject" is in the middle or passive voice ("subjecting oneself" or "being subject"), not the active voice ("subject"). It is the only one of the five participles *not* in the active voice ("speaking," "singing," "making melody" and "thanking"). The church chooses to be subject to Christ (Eph 5:24), Christ does not force the church to be subject to himself.

"To submit" (*hypotassō*, literally, "to place or arrange under") may be categorized in three ways in the New Testament depending on the object: (1) to submit to God, (2) to submit to human rulers, (3) to submit to one another. All humans, and especially believers, are commanded to submit to God, God's law, God's righteousness, as James tells his readers: "Submit yourselves therefore to God" (Jas 4:7).[29] Human ruling authorities have derivative power from God, so Peter commands believers: "Submit yourselves to every human creation on account of the Lord, whether a king as the one ruling or governor as through him be-

---

[28]The oldest Greek manuscript (p[46], A.D. 80-200) has no verb in 5:22, as does the authoritative codex Vaticanus (A.D. 4th century). In the fifth century Jerome said he knew of no Greek manuscripts with the verb, since the ellipsis of the verb refers back to v. 21. *Commentary on Ephesians.* 5:22-3a, Ronald Heine, *The Commentaries of Origin and Jerome on St Paul's Epistle to the Ephesians*, p. 233; Archibald Thomas Robertson, *Word Pictures in the New Testament IV* (Nashville: Broadman, 1931), p. 544. In the third century, at least once, Clement of Alexandria cites Eph 5:22 without the verb. *Stromata* 4.8.64.

[29]See also Rom 8:7; 10:3; Eph 5:24; Heb 12:9.

ing commissioned" (1 Pet 2:13-14, Aída's trans.).[30] Mutual submission,
then, is two ruling authorities bowing (or submitting) to each other.
Christians mutually submit because they bow (or submit) to a greater
authority: Christ (Eph 5:21, holding "reverence" or "respect" [phobos]
for Christ"). So, in marriage wife and husband see each other as joint
authorities with Christ over both. To be submissive to someone else is
to become a supportive presence in actions and words because of a more
important reason—out of respect for Christ. For instance, the noun
form hypotaxis refers to the lightly armed infantry that drew up behind
to protect the phalanx, the "Foot Companions."[31] The ancient Mace-
donian battle order was formed as a V-shaped wedge with the general
and part of the cavalry ("the Companions") in front, next to the phalanx, those soldiers who were heavily armed, followed by the hypotaxis,
soldiers who were lightly armed, followed by the rest of the cavalry.
The cavalry, phalanx and hypotaxis would rotate roles. The Macedo-
nians won many fights because of their flexibility, mobility and individual skill.[32] In the same way, in the home wives (and husbands too)
should become supportive of and cooperative with and even protective
of each other.

The New Testament has several other examples of mutual submission. For instance, "The spirits of prophets are subject to the prophets"
(1 Cor 14:32). At Corinth prophets were to speak and then listen to one
another. One prophet should not monopolize the whole time, but they
should take turns so that all learn and encourage and evaluate one another (1 Cor 14:29-31). Thus, mutual submission is cooperation with
others so that those others can exercise their roles with effectiveness. It
is mutual deference and mutual understanding. Another example may
be found in the relationship between a family and a church. Stephana's[33] household appointed itself to minister to the Christians at

---

[30]See also Rom 13:1; Heb 2:8; Ps 8:6.
[31]Liddell & Scott, Lexicon, p. 1897.
[32]Lesley Adkins and Roy A. Adkins, Handbook to Life in Ancient Greece (New York: Facts on File,
    1997), pp. 89, 91, 97-98; Guy Thompson Griffith, "Phalanx," The Oxford Classical Dictionary,
    ed. N. G. L. Hammond and H. H. Scullard, 2nd ed. (Oxford: Clarendon, 1970), p. 809.
[33]See Aída Besançon Spencer, "El Hogar as Ministry Team: Stephana(s) Household," Hispanic
    Christian Thought at the Dawn of the 21st Century: Apuntes in Honor of Justo L. Gonzalez, ed. Al-
    vin Padilla, Roberto Goizueta and Eldin Villafañe (Nashville: Abingdon, 2005), pp. 70-77.

Corinth. Because its members did this, Paul tells the Corinthians to subject themselves to them (1 Cor 16:15-18). Synonyms for *submit* are "respect" or "honor." We saw this already in Ephesians 5:21 ("being subject to one another in *fear* of Christ" [Aída's trans.]). Ephesians 5:33 summarizes the relationship of the wife to her husband as "respect" *(phobeomai)*. Peter also uses "respect" *(phobeomai)* as a synonym for "submit" *(hypotassō*, 1 Pet 2:13,17).

Thus, if mutual submission is cooperation toward a shared goal— each person exercising his/her strengths, being supportive of the other in actions and words, listening, learning, teaching, encouraging and being encouraged, and being deferent—how do we (especially Aída) apply that to our marriage?

1. Aída notes: It is tempting to try to make my spouse submit to my desires, especially when I think they are good. But, I am never successful. We are each too strong willed ever to submit to what we do not want. Furthermore, what we have learned through the years is, if we do not pressure each other, we will do what we think is best out of love. Sometimes each of us has to learn for him/herself. And, at other times, we are simply wrong. When we are stressed out, we have tried to control the world by controlling each other. But Paul commands us to "Put away from you all bitterness and wrath and anger and wrangling" (Eph 4:31). Over the years, we have learned to center on being thankful when trying to control and dissipate stress (Eph 5:4, 20). A positive approach puts things into perspective and helps us cope more effectively.

2. We, Bill and Aída, are indeed both strong willed and opinionated. We are both professors used to lecturing! But we both deeply believe in the necessity and wholesomeness of having Christ as our joint authority. Mutual submission does not mean no leadership. It means revolving leadership by gifting, ability or responsibility. For example, when Bill is asked to speak, Aída goes to support him. Aída will drive the car both ways so Bill can rest. She will handle the book sales and pass out any handouts. She will be there to be supportive in whatever way possible. If Aída speaks, Bill then takes the active supportive roles. When we both are responsible for a job, such as writing this book, we divide up the responsibilities, deciding who will write the first draft of

each chapter, then the other will edit and add additional ideas, which is exactly what we did.

3. When we were first married, upon finding out that we practiced "mutual submission," one pastor asked us, "Who then speaks first at the end of the workday?" This was his concern! What do we do? We informally try to rotate turns unless one of us clearly has undergone a more exciting or traumatic experience. Then that person goes first. One of us does not monopolize the whole time but pauses and asks the other to share too about his/her day.

4. Respect is important, and it is easy at times not to respect the person you know well. Aída tries to respect and honor Bill by taking seriously all his suggestions. She tries to speak positively of Bill in public. Planning ahead so neither is embarrassed in public is also important as a way to show respect. Bill does the same.

5. Since mutual submission is done "in reverence for Christ" and "as to the Lord," focusing on Christ is crucial for Christian mutual submission. One way to focus on Christ is to pray and another way is to study the Bible, God's revelation, as the basis for action. When we cannot agree what is God's will for an important decision, together we first bow down on our knees and ask God for help. Thanking God for God's blessings is an excellent way to invoke God's perspective for our lives.

UNDERSTANDING EPHESIANS 5:22-33: HEAD

If mutual submission is the overarching theme for Ephesians 5:21-24, how would it relate to the husband as "the head of the wife" (Eph 5:23)? If all Christians are to be mutually submissive to one another in reverence *(phobos)* for Christ (Eph 5:21), then, more specifically, wives are to be submissive to their own husbands "since a man is head of his wife," which is analogous to the way "Christ is also head of the church, Savior himself of the body" (Eph 5:23, Aída's trans.). *Head* now describes the husband's role that is further defined in Ephesians 5:25-33.

Head for many of us has become a dead metaphor. Its metaphorical quality is lost and we take its meaning as a fixed literal meaning. To us *head* of the school or *head* of the business is the president who has the power or right to command, enforce obedience, and make final decisions. The *head* has ultimate jurisdiction. In other words, a *head* symbolizes thought. But does *head* necessarily have the same figurative meaning for Paul? Providentially, in this passage, Paul defines the metaphor *head* with the appositive (the clarifying phrase) "Savior himself of the body" as part of an extended simile. He did not define the *head* as the "ruler" *(archōn)* or "decision maker" or "judge" *(kritēs)* or "mind" *(nous)* of the body. A "savior" is a "deliverer" or "preserver."[34] Thus, to be a *head* is to give life to another. Paul extensively developed the meaning of *head (kephalē)* in Ephesians as an image for growth:

> We should grow into him, the all, who is the head, Christ, from whom all the body, being brought together and being held together by every ligament that serves to give support according to the proportionate activity of each individual part, makes the growth of the body for the building up of itself in love. (Eph 4:15-16, Aída's trans.)

The head is the source of growth of the bones, even as Christ is the source of spiritual growth for the church. This is an apt image since the pituitary gland which causes bone growth is in the brain. Lack of growth results in spiritual immaturity (Eph 4:14). Similarly, Christ as *head* fills the body by nourishing it and knitting it together and thereby causing growth (Eph 1:22-23). Again, the head provides life to the body.

How exactly does the husband become a *head* like Jesus?[35] He loves his wife (Eph 5:25, 33) as "Christ loved the church and gave himself up for her in order to make her holy" (Eph 5:25-26). Paul uses two extended similes (Eph 5:25-27, 28-30) to describe what it means for a husband to become a *head* who saves like Jesus. Earlier we learned that Jesus loved us by giving himself up for us as a fragrant offering and sacrifice to God (Eph 5:2). Now, the husband too gives himself over to helping his wife become the very best disciple of Jesus she could be: to "make her holy" in order to "present" her honored "without a spot or wrinkle . . . so that she may be holy and without blemish" (Eph 5:25-

---

[34]Liddell & Scott, *Lexicon*, p. 1751; e.g., Lk 23:35-39.

[35]Notice that the wife is *not* compared to Jesus, and neither is the husband compared to the Father. Such a comparison would suggest a Platonic eternally hierarchical view of the Trinity as a model for (what we believe to be) a nonbiblical hierarchical view of marriage. We imitate the Father who loves us as Christ loves us and fills us with the Spirit (Eph 5:1-2, 18).

27).[36] The husband needs to follow the example of what Jesus did for the church. Jesus' love for the church resulted in him giving himself up for her as "a fragrant offering and sacrifice to God" (Eph 5:2, 25). Jesus' goal at the crucifixion completed God the Father's goal before the foundation of the world, that we be "holy" and "blameless (unblemished, *amōmos*) before him in love" (Eph 1:4). To be "blameless" or "unblemished" was first modeled by the Old Testament sacrifices, only animals were to be sacrificed who had no physical infirmities (e.g., Ex 29:1, 38). King David transferred this literal use of "unblemished" to a metaphorical one, to describe a person living without disobedience to God's will (2 Kings 22:24, 33 LXX). Cleansing preceded sanctification (e.g., Ex 29:36-37). If in the Old Testament temple, "cleansing" was literal, Jesus' blood offering of himself was intended spiritually to "cleanse" the church (Tit 2:13-14). But, now the "cleansing" comes not from literal water but through the preaching and receiving of the message about Jesus (Eph 5:26). Jesus' main goal was for the church to become "holy," by having been a holy offering himself (Eph 5:2, 25-26). The husband is to help the wife become a holy, unblemished, wonderful, spotless, wrinkle-free offering to God.

Being made "holy" was language used for the temple, the temple animals, and the temple priests themselves. God wanted Moses to sanctify Aaron and his sons so they could serve the Lord in the priesthood (Ex 29:1, 21, 44-45). They were washed with water (Ex 29:4; Eph 5:26), their head anointed with oil, wearing holy apparel of honor and glory (Ex 28:2-8; Eph 5:27). The priests themselves were to have no

---

[36]*Endoxos* was primarily used in the Old Testament for persons of nobility and status (e.g., Num 23:21; Josh 4:4; 1 Kings 9:6; 18:23), but it was also used to describe God's actions and the temple itself ("the house I [Solomon] am about to build must be great and *wonderful*" (2 Chron 2:9). God promises Moses "I will perform *marvels*, such as have not been performed in all the earth" (Ex 34:10). In like manner, Jesus, God incarnate, did *"wonderful* things" (Lk 13:17). Thus, the church as God's creation is "in splendor": noble and of high status, wonderful, unblemished—to be a perfect sacrifice, like Jesus. (See also Rom 12:1; 15:16.) A creation by God has no "spot or wrinkle" (Eph 5:27). *Spilos* and *rhytis* are rare nouns. They are synonyms (a pleonasm). *Spilos* is a type of sin that contaminates and spreads. James describes the tongue, a small thing, that yet can "stain" the whole body and Jude, his brother, describes the body that can "stain" the tunic which covers it (*spiloō*, Jas 3:6; Jude 23). In the same way, a painter can spread diverse colors over a *painting* (Wis 15:4). *Rhytis* may come from *rhyō*, *"to draw together, contract." Thayer's*, p. 564. Thus, it is a "pucker" or "wrinkle." Liddell & Scott, *Lexicon*, p. 1578.

skin blemishes, such as leprosy (Lev 21:17-20). They then laid their hands on the head of the animals as part of the offering before the Lord (Ex 29:10, 15, 24). To compare a wife to an aspect of the temple is not new to the Bible. God compared Ezekiel's wife to the temple in Jerusalem, both were "the delight of your eyes," "your heart's desire," a "stronghold," "joy and glory," "heart's affection" (Ezek 24:16, 21, 25). Being made holy precedes being sent out into the world (e.g., Jn 10:36). One is set apart for the purpose of glorifying God.[37] In the same way, the husband offers himself as an acceptable offering to God in order to help his wife become an acceptable offering to God so that together they can be set apart as God's holy priesthood (1 Pet 2:9; Rev 1:6; 5:10). The husband needs to help his wife avoid sin, become a person of nobility and status, and actualize her God-given vocation in ministry.

The second extended simile (Eph 5:28-30) continues the imagery of a Savior who preserves life and cares for it, now referring to his own body. Men should love and nourish and take care of their wives as they do their own bodies. To "nourish" one's own body is to nourish it to maturity,[38] to help it grow. Husbands are to give the same extended care to their wives. They are to include their wives in their definition of who they are because they are "one flesh" (Eph 5:31). A husband who loves his wife as much as he loves himself and gives himself for her sake is in effect becoming subject to or servant to her.

If mutual submission covers both wife and husband, should wives also love their husbands and help them become holy? Of course, yes. Christ is a model of love for all Christians. We all, husbands, wives and singles, need to "live in love, as Christ loved us and gave himself up for us, a fragrant offering and sacrifice to God" (Eph 5:2). The New Testament also cites wives as examples of sacrificial love. Sarah obeyed Abraham, calling him "lord," because she was willing vicariously po-

---

[37]E.g., the seventh day (Gen 2:2-3; Ex 20:8, 11) and the first born (Ex 13:2, 12) were set apart for God.

[38]*Thayer's*, p. 200. *Ektrephō* ("nourish") can refer to physical provision (Gen 45:7, 11; Ps 22:2; Ezek 31:4) and to the whole process of rearing a child (1 Kings 11:20; 12:8, 10; Is 23:4; 49:21; Hos 9:12; Zech 10:9), including a father's rearing of children (Prov 23:24). *Thalpō* ("tenderly care for") can refer to a mother nursing an infant, the way Paul, Silvanus, and Timothy cared for the Thessalonians (1 Thess 1:1; 2:7). It can also refer to a mother bird's warming of its young (Deut 22:6; Job 39:14).

tentially to suffer for him. She was a Christ type (1 Pet 2:20-24) when she agreed to tell the Egyptian Pharaoh that she was Abraham's "sister" so the Egyptians would not kill Abraham (1 Pet 3:6; Gen 12:11-20). This was her choice to agree to Abraham's request. God, though, protected her.[39] Also, elsewhere Paul tells Titus to encourage wives "to love their husbands" (Tit 2:4). Husbands also need to respect their wives by bestowing "honor" on them as "coheirs" of God's life-giving grace (1 Pet 3:7, Aída's trans.). All Christians need to respect one another (Rom 12:10; 1 Pet 2:17). Paul has not given us two contrasting roles for wives and husbands (submission and respect for the wife, love and self sacrifice for the husband), but two roads toward a larger unity. Mutual submission and love are both the overarching themes and, as well, the overarching goals for marriage. This is the way some in the early church understood the passage. Jerome states that the general notion of mutual submission in Ephesians 5:21 "is divided and distributed in the words which follow" (5:22-6:5) so that "not only is a wife subject to her husband, and children to their parents, and servants to their masters, but also husbands are to be subject to their wives according to the duty which is commanded, and fathers to children so that they do not provoke them to wrath, and masters to servants that they may abstain from threats" (*Commentary on Ephesians* 5:21).[40]

So, in summary, to be someone's *head* is to help save, deliver, give life, help mature, love, sacrifice for, sanctify, honor, care for, nourish, serve that person as Jesus did. This type of love is totally committed. There is no room for abandonment. How does this affect our own marriage (especially Bill)?

1. We try to do all we can to help each other develop our gifts so that we can better serve Jesus. We try never to compete with each other (1 Cor 12:26). For instance, Bill was the first one of us to attend seminary. He used to tell Aída about his courses and she would reply, "Wow!

---

[39]See Aída Besançon Spencer, "From Poet to Judge: What Does Ephesians 5 Teach About Male-Female Roles?" *Priscilla Papers* 4 (Summer 1990): 10-16; "Peter's Pedagogical Method in 1 Peter 3:6," *Bulletin for Biblical Research* 10, no. 1 (2000): 107-19.

[40]Also, Clement of Alexandria, in the third century, concludes his study of Eph 5: "Let them, then, love one another, they who are joined together, 'as they love their own bodies'" (*Christ the Educator* 3.12.94).

That sounds like fun!" He then encouraged her to come to study with him. Not only did he encourage her to study, he helped make it possible for her to get a scholarship. One evening he brought her to Philadelphia to find the home of the president of the seminary in order to ask for financial help. Bill did not call ahead. But to the president's amazement, together we found the home among a row of town houses when the president and his wife had come for only an hour from a month of traveling. (Aída did receive a scholarship!) In addition, later, when an adviser discouraged Aída from studying New Testament Greek, Bill offered to teach her Greek one hour a week in addition to all their other graduate studies. Bill communicated his own love for Greek so well and was so encouraging of Aída's studies, she ended up getting a doctorate in New Testament studies and became a professor of New Testament. No human encouraged Aída's spiritual maturity as much as her husband Bill.

2. Bill is always ready to sacrifice for his wife. For instance, when Aída took a semester off to recuperate from an operation, in addition to taking care of her, cleaning, draining, and dressing her wounds, Bill made room in his schedule so she could heal physically and mentally once a month at some beach. Being in New England, the ocean is quite frigid in the fall, so we traveled to Bermuda, Puerto Rico and the Dominican Republic. The salt sea was very restorative. These travels were inconvenient for Bill since he was in the midst of his busy semester, but he came along (carrying stacks of student papers to grade) in order to love his wife, as God loved her. He was totally concerned for her welfare.

This type of sacrificial love is a model for children too. After Aída's operation, our son Steve, a chef, brought dinners for us and helped in any way he could. We are always amazed as to how loving and sacrificing our son can be when it is necessary. Our church also provided meals and encouragement, rounding out the full picture of mutual care.

In all times, but particularly in a time of marriage crisis when fear abounds, serving God needs to take priority. Assuming control over others is not the answer. Actually it may cause problems. According to research by John Gottman, "husbands who share power and control within their marriages are less likely to divorce than men who resist their wives' influence. When husbands aren't willing to share power—in theological terms, to practice mutual submission—81 percent of those marriages end in divorce."[41] We have concluded that the Bible does not explicitly teach that in the home only men have final authority. Moreover, whatever derivative authority any human has should be used to serve others by loving them, not taking control over them. Mutual respect and flexibility and creativity are what we need today (and always). We do need to cooperate with and support and protect one another, to encourage and be encouraged, to be thankful in a time of thanklessness. In a time of less and less commitments, we need to imitate the total commitment of Christ's sacrificial maturing love. God, the Trinity, can be our help.

---

[41]Douglas J. Brouwer, *Beyond "I Do": What Christians Believe About Marriage* (Grand Rapids: Eerdmans, 2001), p. 113.

CONCLUDING DIALOGUE

Jesus asks the church if he will find faith on earth when he returns (Lk 18:8). Meanwhile, the church argues, "I belong to Christians for Biblical Equality" or "I belong to the Council for Biblical Manhood and Womanhood" or "I belong to neither" or "I belong to both!" Has Christ been divided (see 1 Cor 1:12-13)? Yet, will we proclaim the gospel?

We were most curious to discover on the oft divisive issue of what does head and mutual submission mean in marriage, Can we find important points of agreement as evangelical Christians? Why and where exactly do we disagree? How do our similarities and differences relate to God's nature?

Areas of agreement. John wrote that "whoever does not love does not know God, for God is love" (1 Jn 4:8). Here is where we find our basic similarity. Because God is love and both couples "know God," therefore we emphasize the importance of love. For a husband to be "the *head* of the wife just as Christ" (Eph 5:23) means he loves her, sacrifices for her, honors her, and nurtures her. The husband should lift up and empower the wife so that the couple might work as one. Love is the essence of the marriage relationship, which mirrors the love, mutuality, intimacy and unity of the Trinity. Both couples affirm mutual submission and agree that submission is never forced subjection. Mutual submission is the voluntary yielding to another because of *respect* for Christ. It is built on mutual respect and cooperation toward a shared goal.

Jesus' teachings and model are crucial for defining leadership and authority. Both couples caution against the misuse of authority. In fact, both couples agree that the *one-flesh* relationship centers not on authority, but on love and intimacy. Authority should never be used for control or power over another, but to be a servant leader who sacrificially loves. The husband does not have authority to make the wife submit (nor vice versa). Authority should be used to nurture, protect and serve, in other words, love the other. Both couples also valued each spouse honoring and teaching the other spouse. The husband should encourage the wife, and the wife should honor the husband.

Jesus taught his disciples that, if they loved one another, everyone would know that they were indeed his disciples (Jn 13:34-35). Thus, both as couples and as Christians we can witness to a watching world that we are Jesus' disciples who teach about the importance of love, a key essence of God's nature.

Areas of disagreement. The Tracys highlight that, as women and men, we uniquely reflect God, male and female flowing from and reflecting God in the divine image. On the other hand, the Spencers assume that personhood reflects God, seeing gender as strictly material, God's teaching tool to instruct humans to love someone other, so that we might learn to love the Wholly Other (though as an image not an allegory since God is in three Persons and humanity is in two). While both couples affirm the key centrality of God as love revealed in the complete unity and mutual work of the Father and the Son, they emphasize different aspects of the Trinity. The Spencers highlight Christ as a model, emphasizing God's unity (e.g., see chap. one, Deut 6:4), whereas the Tracys highlight the differences between the persons of the Godhead (1 Cor 11:3). Thus, the Tracys focus on the Father's relationship to the Son (during the incarnation) as a model for the husband's relationship to the wife. As the Father initiated love, care/protection, and honor/empowerment with the Son, so too the husband should initiate love, care/protection, and honor/empowerment with the wife in a relationship of authority-love, not one of authority-submission. Thus, the husband as male has a unique authority different from the wife's as female. The husband's role is to love, the wife's role is to respond and respect. Therefore, they affirm some gender-based role differentiation and are wary of "role sameness." The metaphor of *head* can refer to authority but most often the New Testament emphasis is provider-nurturer.

The Spencers do not mention differences within the Trinity. Christ's love of the church as Savior is a model for all Christians (husband and wife included) to honor, love, care, cooperate with and protect one another. Even though Paul begins his exhortation in Ephesians for husbands to love and wives to respect, his teachings in this one passage do not encompass all the possible roles husbands and wives should have. Love and respect are not two contrasting roles (they cite Tit 2:4; 1 Pet 3:7). Rather, in the home (and church) leadership should be revolving leadership based on giftedness, abilities or mutually agreed responsibilities.

Authority is not gender based in the home or the church. The metaphor of *head* does not refer to authority, especially in Ephesians, but to source of life. Thus, even as the husband can (and should) protect the wife, the wife might also protect the husband, as Sarah intended to protect Abraham from Pharaoh. Thus, the Spencers are wary of role conformity.

In effect, the Spencers looked at the metaphor *head* through the lens of mutual submission, while the Tracys looked at mutual submission through the lens of *headship*. Thus, for the Tracys mutual submission does not negate gender role differences. The Tracys began their chapter by explaining *headship*, while the Spencers began their chapter by defining *authority*.

The difference between the two couples' approaches was in their hermeneutics or philosophical frameworks that guided their exegesis. In methodology, the Spencers thought the Tracys used more of a biblical theological approach by drawing from a broad overview of the Father's relationship to the Son during the incarnation as the basis for marriage, relying heavily on selected lexicons, while the Spencers thought they did a closer literary reading of Ephesians 5, using the immediate literary context to understand the words in the passage. In contrast, the Tracys thought the Spencers more broadly used several biblical texts that dealt with women in ministry and biblical examples to support their gender model, while the Tracys thought they focused more on biblical texts that directly addressed marital submission/headship and marriage. Although both couples dealt in-depth with Ephesians 5:21-33, only the Tracys referred to 1 Corinthians 11:3. The Spencers did not see that as a marriage text, but rather as ecclesiastical only.

Even though we all agree that Christ's sacrificial love is a model for husband and wife, the Spencers emphasize that mutual submission and love between equals in marriage allows for flexibility of roles, whereas the Tracys emphasize that mutual submission and love (between equals) in marriage can have role differentiation. For the Tracys, the responsibility and mandate to husbands is one of sacrificial love; he has an authority of love. A wife is created by God to respond intuitively to her husband's loving initiation. For the Spencers, the burden on the husband is as great as the burden on the wife. It is a mutual burden. Thus, prayer is emphasized as a way to rely on Christ, the source of life. Both are thankful to Christ and to one another. Both are God's holy priests.

In addition to teaching about the importance of love for evangelism, Jesus prayed that all his disciples would be "one," as God is one, "so that the world may believe" that the Father sent Jesus into the world and that the Father loved the world even as the Father loved Jesus (Jn 17:21-23). What does it mean to be *one?* Can we differ on gender-based roles yet still be *one?* We certainly are *one* in agreeing that love is key, and authority should never overpower another. These are great shared convictions that should not be undermined by the differences.

Chapter Three

MARRIAGE ROLES AND DECISION MAKING

Aída and Bill Spencer's
Viewpoint

In chapters one and two we drew out some biblical principles that affect roles and decision making in marriage. From chapter one we learned that being Jesus' disciple as an individual and as a family unit has top priority. This will entail both literal and metaphorical cost. Being *one flesh* implies singularity and plurality. It is both a statement of what is true and a description of what is becoming. From chapter two we learned that mutual submission is two ruling authorities bowing or submitting to each other because they bow to a greater authority: Christ the Lord. It is cooperation with others so they can exercise their roles with effectiveness. The *head* is the source of growth of the body. Thus, leadership in the home may be revolving or it may be mutually agreed designation of areas of jurisdiction. Walking or living in love entails step-by-step actions that make up our life.

In the fourth century, John Chrysostom ably stated what we think marriage is *not:* a benevolent monarchy. Chrysostom thought that Paul "places the one in subjection, and the other in authority, that there may be peace; for where there is equality of ranks there can never be peace; neither where a house is a democracy, nor where all are rulers; but the ruling power must of necessity be one" *(Homily 20 on Ephesians 5:33).* For Chrysostom the wife is second in authority, not equal to the husband, who is first in authority. This is also the view of the esteemed (but non-Christian) philosopher Aristotle: "Authority and subordination are conditions not only inevitable but also expedient; in some cases things are marked out from the moment of birth to rule or to be ruled ... as between the sexes, the male is by nature superior and the female inferior, the male ruler and the female subject ... and the government of a household is monarchy (since every house is governed by a single ruler)" (*Politics* 1.2.8, 12, 21). We agree that there must be one ruler, but that ruler is *Christ*: Christ should be the ruler of the household. In the second century, Irenaeus, unlike Chrysostom, thought Eve was "a helper equal and the peer and the like of Adam" (*Proof of the Apostolic Preaching*, 13). Consequently, the husband and wife both are first in authority; only underage children would be second in authority.

Do we have any biblical example of such mutual submission? We have already mentioned Prisca and Aquila, Stephana's household, the Shunammite and her husband. Another example is Achsah and Othniel. Achsah is Caleb's daughter. Caleb, son of Jephunneh, along with Joshua, was one of the two spies who was not intimidated by the inhabitants of Canaan and thus was allowed to enter Canaan eventually (Num 14:30). Seeking a husband who could trust the Lord in battle, Caleb offered his daughter Achsah as wife to whoever conquered Kiriathsepher (Debir). Othniel, son of Kenaz, accepted the challenge and conquered Kiriathsepher. Achsah, of the same mindset as Othniel (and Caleb her father), urged Othniel to ask Caleb for a field, then she herself asked Caleb for a wedding present of springs of water. And Caleb in appreciation generously gave Achsah the upper and the lower springs (Upper Gulloth and Lower Gulloth) (Josh 15:13-19; Judg 1:11-15). Here both Othniel and Achsah work toward one goal—acquiring valuable land—each in their own way, while they advance God's conquest in the process. Both Caleb and daughter Achsah set out challenges to others and Othniel fights. Neither Achsah nor Othniel are first in authority, governing the other, but each appear proactive in their own way.[1]

MARRIAGE AND ROLES

In shared leadership, husband and wife lead from the basis of their spiritual gifts, their strengths, where Christ is the only ruling high

---

[1]Miriam Peskowitz and S. Treggiari and others find that in ancient Jewish communities in Roman Palestine "husbands and wives often worked at the same trade, as indicated by inscriptional evidence," "'Family/ies' in Antiquity: Evidence from Tannaitic Literature and Roman Galilean Architecture," *The Jewish Family in Antiquity*, ed. Shaye J. D. Cohen, Brown Judaic Studies 289 (Atlanta: Scholars Press, 1993), p.32.

priest.[2] Shared leadership began in Genesis, where Adam and Eve, who represent all humanity, are given the same command, to rule over the earth, to work, serve and protect the earth as equals (Gen 1:26-28). Many people are like the Israelites who wanted a king over them, a ruler in whom all power is subsumed. God considered that a rejection of God as the ruler over the people (1 Sam 8:4-20). Sometimes even today people want one human to take care of everything for them, but no human is capable of doing that well. Even Moses could not be a judge by himself, so he needed to distribute his power (Ex 18:13-26; Num 11:11-17, 24-28). And when the Holy Spirit fell on two elders who were out in the camp, Moses replied: "Would that all the LORD's people were prophets, and that the LORD would put his spirit on them!" (Num 11:29). At Pentecost, God's Spirit was poured out upon all, male and female, young and old, poor and wealthy, so that all could prophesy (Acts 2:4, 17-18). Thus, both in the church and in the home, leadership should be chosen by spiritual gifts and natural gifting and education and godly characteristics. Couples should not settle on society's roles or the Christian culture's roles for themselves. *Both* the right and the left have politically dictated roles. Instead, a couple should work on clarifying its roles with God's help in dialogue with one another. Paul tells the church at Rome not to be "conformed to this world" (Rom 12:2). This also applies to marriage.

Thus, in our marriage, division of roles (tasks or functions) comes from five basic principles: (1) spiritual gifts, (2) natural or learned abilities (part of which may be physical strength or physical distinctiveness or physical health at the moment), (3) equal division when certain roles are necessary but either unpleasant to both or pleasant to both,[3] (4) consequences of jointly agreed areas of responsibilities outside the home, and (5) division by time periods or time availability. One example relating to spiritual gifts is when we travel, for leisure and business. After we together choose a place, Aída, who has the gift of organization, tends to make the specific plans. On the other hand, when

---

[2]Heb 3:1; 6:20; 7:26-27; 8:1-2; 9:11-12.

[3]For helpful suggestions, see G. Wade Rowatt Jr. and Mary Jo Rowatt, *The Two-Career Marriage* (Philadelphia: Westminster Press, 1980), pp. 64-71.

there is a misunderstanding in the church, Bill, who has the gift of encouragement (which includes discipline), will tend to call close Christian brothers or sisters and solve the difficulties. Another example regards natural abilities in which Aída tends to handle paying bills. Like her father, who was a comptroller, she has the organizational ability to make sure all is paid. But her talent in organization is not determined by her gender. It is given variously to women and men.

The apostle Peter mentions that frequently men are physically stronger than women (1 Pet 3:7). This should result in more consideration and honor, not physical abuse or disrespect by men. Bill uses his superior physical strength to chop wood for our home heating. For him this is also a way to maintain his health while he contributes toward the household. But the strength to chop or not chop wood is not the definer of masculinity. Men with back problems may not be able to chop wood or shovel snow but their masculinity is not thereby diminished. But, for our household, chopping wood is an example of how more physical strength (and interest) affects our roles. Both of us shovel snow. Aída normally cuts the lawn and does the gardening because Bill is more talented (and trained) at household repairs. Examples regarding equal divisions would be when neither of us is particularly gifted or interested in taking out the garbage or cleaning the bathrooms, so these tasks may be done by either of us. We both like to drive so we have agreed to divide driving. Aída usually drives to a place, while Bill drives back. Since Bill normally rests in the afternoon, and Aída dozes in the late evening, we try to accommodate each other. Thus, Aída will tend to drive in the late afternoon and Bill in the late evening. We have jointly agreed both to work to fulfill our ministry calling. Work outside the home also has consequences in the home. For instance, when Bill discusses editorial details with the graphic artist, Aída will serve refreshments but not remain. Or, when Aída has a group of students over for dessert, Bill will not take charge of running the meeting, but he will remain present and be helpful when possible.

Dividing roles by time period was especially important when child rearing. We discovered that we each had strong but distinctive ideas about child rearing when our son was young. At times Bill was more protective, while Aída allowed more freedom. When a decision had to be made quickly, one person had to decide. These were not long-range foundational decisions, but decisions as to whether to pull the child from bouncing on the sofa or let him keep jumping. Because Aída was studying for her doctorate during the day, and Bill was teaching adult education at night, Bill took charge of rearing our son from morning until 3 p.m., and Aída took charge from 3 p.m. on. We still had to watch out not to meddle in the other person's time, to stay away or to keep silent when we disagreed. Even now our adult son, Steve, will come to one parent for one need and another parent for another need. For example, Bill and Steve go out periodically to trade and purchase CDs, records and videos. Aída will help Steve with his tax forms (and then Steve helps his friends with their tax forms!). And now Steve, a chef for many years and a self-taught music producer, advises us, his parents, about cooking and food sanitation, and helps his dad produce demonstration recordings.[4]

Sometimes a church group might invite both of us to speak over a weekend. If both of us or either one of us could speak on the proposed topic, then time availability could be a factor. For example, a group asked us to speak during Aída's sabbatical. Bill wanted to accommodate the group. We agreed to speak on our own agreed condition that Bill take the major preparation.

We would not recommend everyone specifically divide tasks as we have done. Rather, we would recommend that couples divide their roles

---

[4]See further on shared parenting: William David Spencer, "Equaling Eden: A Practical Male Afterword," in *Beyond the Curse: Women Called to Ministry* by Aída Besançon Spencer (Peabody, Mass.: Hendrickson, 1985), pp. 154-67. The afterword was updated in *Lydian Network* (Winter 2001): 8-9. Judith Balswick and Jack Balswick's description of sons who were coparented certainly seems true of our son. They say sons who were coparented were "able to display empathy, affection and nurturing behavior; they thought highly of the way they were parented and . . . were more nurturing and rational." "Marriage as a Partnership of Equals," *Discovering Biblical Equality: Complementarity Without Hierarchy*, ed. Ronald W. Pierce and Rebecca Merrill Groothuis (Downers Grove, Ill.: InterVarsity Press, 2004), pp. 454-55. Mary Stewart Van Leeuwen affirms the value of nurturant and gender role flexible fathers' high involvement in child rearing. Their sons "have the most secure sense of masculinity." *Gender and Grace: Love, Work and Parenting in a Changing World* (Downers Grove, Ill.: InterVarsity Press, 1990), p. 161. She reiterates the importance of nurturing fathers during children's early years, for example, in *My Brother's Keeper: What the Social Sciences Do (and Don't) Tell Us About Masculinity* (Downers Grove, Ill.: InterVarsity Press, 2002), pp. 116-17, 207-8.

from the basis of the five principles we have suggested.[5]

Who, then, is the priest of the family? In ancient Roman days the father (or the eldest male in the family) as the *paterfamilias* would be the chief priest of the pagan family who performed the religious rituals of his family and whose power legally dispensed life or death to all household members.[6] In ancient Israelite days a tribe was designated to make the offerings. Priests functioned often like butchers: slaughtering the animals, draining and dashing the blood against the altar, cutting up the animal, arranging the offering correctly, washing the entrails, burning the offering, figuring out what part of the offering was burnt and what part could be eaten, keeping the fire burning and arranging the wood for the sanctuary. They also laid their hands on the offering, placed the bread of the Presence on the table, examined lepers, valued things devoted to God and bore the ark.[7] Certainly many of those roles were assisted by physical strength. But those tasks were all eliminated by Jesus who, by becoming the perfect sacrifice and perfect high priest, replaced these daily imperfect sacrifices (Heb 7:26-27). But not all priestly functions have ended. There still is some consistency between the new and the old covenant. Priests (or ordained ministers) today, as then, pronounce the benediction, teach the Scriptures, supervise tithing, call the congregation to worship, invoke the Lord, encourage the people for spiritual battle, designate other priests, officiate and act as magistrates.[8]

---

[5]Judith Lingenfelter and Sherwood Lingenfelter discern four "prototype social games" in different cultures, which also affect roles and decision making in marriage: authoritarian (status/role differences), hierarchist (insider/outsider), individualist (personal autonomy), and egalitarian (insider/outsider). The individualist and egalitarian social games do not emphasize roles, while the authoritarian and hierarchist social games emphasize differentiation of status and role. *Teaching Cross-Culturally: An Incarnational Model for Learning and Teaching* (Grand Rapids: Baker, 2003), pp. 75-76. A couple can have the same tensions as any two people from different cultures about time, judgment, handling crisis, goals, self-worth, and vulnerability. Sherwood Lingenfelter and Marvin Mayers, *Ministering Cross-Culturally: An Incarnational Model for Personal Relationships* (Grand Rapids: Baker, 1986).

[6]Sarah Pomeroy, *Goddesses, Whores, Wives, and Slaves: Women in Classical Antiquity* (New York: Schocken, 1975), pp. 150-54, 159; James S. Jeffers, *The Greco-Roman World of the New Testament Era: Exploring the Background of Early Christianity* (Downers Grove, Ill.: InterVarsity Press, 1999), p. 92.

[7]Ex 27:20-21; 30:7; Lev 1:3-17; 6:12, 16-18; 13:1-44; 24:5-9; 27:8; Josh 4:15-17; 1 Sam 2:12-17; Heb 10:11.

[8]Lev 10:10-11; 6:22-26; 8:11-14; 10:8-10; 18:1-5; Deut 20:2-4; 2 Kings 12:9-10; Neh 10:38. See "Priest," ed. Edward Viening, *The Zondervan Topical Bible* (Grand Rapids: Zondervan, 1969),

However, forms of all these continuing functions are now also des-ignated to the priesthood of *all* believers, male and female.[9] Thus, in the home as well, these priestly tasks can be divided according to our five principles. When our son was relatively young, he suggested that each one of us, son, father, and mother give grace at a different meal each day. We also have whoever has prepared the meal give grace. Also, when our son was young, Bill and Aída together planned family devo-tions, done once a week, each leading a different week. Now that our son lives in his own home, though we pray often together, we tend to have only individual devotions, except when we go on vacation. Since both of us spouses are Christians and theologically trained, we jointly function as the priesthood of the family.

What should you do if one spouse is not a Christian or is limited by being addicted or being ill? Even fourth-century scholar Jerome, who thinks a wife "has been made for a secondary rank and with a baser substance," questions whether wives should be ruled by husbands worse than themselves: "Wives are frequently found who are much better than their husbands. They rule over them, manage the household, edu-cate the children, and maintain the discipline of the family while the husbands revel and run around with harlots" *(Commentary on Ephesians 5:33)*. If one spouse is not a Christian, the other cannot have a complete Christian marriage. Nevertheless, the Bible exhorts such a Christian to try to win over the unbelieving spouse.[10] Further, if an addiction is in-volved, the addicted spouse has become a slave to another master than the living Lord (2 Pet 2:19). If one is intoxicated, one cannot be filled with the Holy Spirit (Eph 5:18). Jerome agrees: "Just as we cannot serve two lords, God and mammon, so we cannot be filled with the Spirit and with wine at the same time. One who is filled with the Spirit pos-sesses wisdom, meekness, shame, and purity, but one who is filled with wine possesses foolishness, rage, shamelessness, and lust" *(Commentary on Ephesians 5:18)*. Then the Spirit-filled spouse needs to do all that one

---

pp. 806-7. See also chap. 14, Victor Matthews and Don Benjamin, *Social World of Ancient Israel 1250-587 BCE* (Peabody, Mass.: Hendrickson, 1993).

[9] 1 Pet 2:5, 9; Ex 19:6; Is 61:6; Rev 1:6; 5:10.

[10] 1 Cor 7:12-16; 1 Pet 3:1-4. See Lee Strobel and Leslie Strobel, *Surviving a Spiritual Mismatch* (Grand Rapids: Zondervan, 2002).

can to free the will of the addicted spouse. Any intoxicant or mind-
altering drug such as alcohol, marijuana or other narcotic can physically
and mentally and emotionally master someone. We cannot make our
spouse or child or other family member become a Christian, but we can
place that person in a drug absent, Holy Spirit present environment so
the will can become more free to choose good over evil. As Rev. Joseph
Kellermann concludes: "*It is not true that an alcoholic cannot be helped
until he wants help.* It *is* true that there is almost no chance that the alcoholic will stop drinking as long as other people remove all the painful
consequences for him."[11]

As well, if one spouse is ill, in other words, the "natural" physical or
emotional abilities are temporarily impaired, that affects the roles that
one can do in the marriage. Again, this impairment in no way affects
one's masculinity or femininity. However, temporarily the other spouse
will have to take a heavier load (or, if they can afford it, hire help). In
the middle years of their life, Aída's parents were relatively traditional
when it came to household duties. Her mother cooked and cleaned the
house and shopped; her father worked outside the home and gardened
on the weekend. But during the senior years of their life, when Aída's
mother developed a heart condition, her father shopped and took on
vacuuming the house. In other words, as long as the couple keeps in
dialogue, roles can be adjusted. Similarly, how much a spouse earns has
nothing to do with masculinity or femininity. What counts is whether
a person works responsibly as that one is able (2 Thess 3:7-13; 1 Tim
5:13-14). Doing a certain role does not make one masculine or feminine, just as being in a garage does not make one a car.[12]

MARRIAGE AND DECISION MAKING

How are decisions made in a home of shared leadership, a democracy?

---

[11]Joseph Kellermann, *Alcoholism: A Merry-Go-Round Named Denial* (Virginia Beach, Va.: Al-
Anon Family Group, 1969), p. 12. See also Janice Keller Phelps and Alan E. Nourse, *The
Hidden Addiction and How to Get Free* (Boston: Little, Brown, and Company, 1986); Buddy
Scott, *Relief for Hurting Parents: How to Fight for the Lives of Teenagers* (Lake Jackson, Tex.:
Allon Publishing, 1994).
[12]See also Aída Besançon Spencer, "What Are the Biblical Roles of Female and Male Followers
of Christ," *Priscilla Papers* 18, no. 2 (Spring 2004): 11-16.

As of this writing, the summer of 2007, we have been married thirty-five years (after having been friends for six previous years). So, we grew up together in the faith and in our marriage. We never remember any undue difficulty in coming to a joint, major, family-affecting decision. For example, we have not regretted one major move that we have made. Given the information and leading we had at the time, we can see how God used each choice to lead us to our present ministry. The difficulty in getting a handle on a decision has arisen when the question is new to us (so there is no precedent or experience) or we do not have enough information, because all the options look like they would serve God's kingdom. Over the years we have developed strategies for the process of decision making, the criteria for decision making, and the conflict that may accompany decision making.

Five aspects of the process of decision making. Our process for all major decisions has five aspects, beginning in prayer. Proverbs beautifully exhorts, "Commit your work to the LORD, and your plans will be established" (Prov 16:3) and "The human mind plans the way, but the LORD directs the steps" (Prov 16:9). The first proverb emphasizes the importance of directing one's actions toward God's wisdom and sovereignty. The second proverb discusses the interrelationship between human will and God's sovereignty. We direct our steps. We then need to be sensitive to God's leading as we walk (see also Jas 4:13-15; Prov 19:21). Second, we get all the information and helpful advice we can find. Many a proverb reminds us of the importance of advice: "Fools think their own way is right, but the wise listen to advice" (Prov 12:15); "The ear that heeds wholesome admonition will lodge among the wise" (Prov 15:31), and "Listen to advice and accept instruction, that you may gain wisdom for the future" (Prov 19:20). Third, we will write the positives and negatives to every choice down two columns. In this way, we gather up the input of everyone involved. Fourth, we may get additional information if needed. Fifth, we will pray again and assess the columns together, as Proverbs teaches, "Iron sharpens iron, and one person sharpens the wits of another" (Prov 27:17).

Six criteria for the basis of decision making. On the basis of what criteria do we decide? First, we ask, what would more advance God's kingdom? As Paul exhorts, "And whatever you do, in word or deed, do everything in the name of the Lord Jesus" (Col 3:17). He then asks the Colossians to pray that "God will open to us a door for the word, that we may declare the mystery of Christ, for which I am in prison" (Col 4:3). God's will is not always the easy, comfortable route. As in Colossians, Paul does not ask to leave behind his chains, but the "open door" is an opportunity to advance God's kingdom, even there in prison. Second, we assess, how does this new possibility fit with each of our ministry models and our particular spiritual gifts? After much observation and study, Bill has concluded his ministry model or style is a community model. He builds community, using his gift of encouragement. Aída's is a kingdom model, using her gift of organization to help move people to action to advance God's reign. Third, we question, can someone else do this better? Or, is it a ministry only we can do? Fourth, we consider, how would each choice affect each member of our family? What will this cost our family? Is it a higher price than the benefit we can give? Fifth, as we talk this over, we seek consensus and the peace of Christ (Col 3:15; Phil 4:7). True consensus fulfills the needs of all parties. Without consensus, we will not make any major decisions. Sixth, if we receive an offer of another job or call, we ask, are we losing more leaving here than we could achieve going there? Is our ministry complete here and ready to close? Or, do we have more to do? For important decisions we always make a joint decision. One person never makes a final decision on important matters that affect the others. It may disrupt the ministries they are doing.

Before we were married, Bill had a call as a college chaplain at Rider University. Aída then searched for another call in the area, in the interim teaching English as a Second Language at a maximum security prison, where, as a volunteer, she organized several Bible studies and worship services. It took a year for her to find a call as a chaplain at a nearby college. Then, we found a joint call teaching with New York Theological Seminary that fulfilled both our callings. Bill's next sense of call as a writer was such that he could pursue it anywhere. Thus, he was able to move to Kentucky while Aída pursued her doctoral education and then move to Massachusetts when she obtained her teaching position at Gordon-Conwell Theological Seminary. (In Kentucky, Aída took a semester off to have our son. Since Aída's doctoral studies had classes that only met three times a week and Bill took an evening position teaching adult literacy and GED high school equivalency, between both of us we had the time to rear our young son.) Thus, originally we were going to rotate whose career has priority. Bill had the first call; Aída had the second. Then, we found that a new calling, writing, had more flexibility than the other calling, teaching. Eventually, Bill decided to return to teaching, and has been doing that half time at Gordon-Conwell Theological Seminary, writing the other half of the year. Now, as we grow older, we have decided that any new calls will have to fulfill both our career goals simultaneously.

Recently, we had an opportunity to consider a change in ministry. After spending several weeks going through our six criteria for decision making, we decided not to accept this opportunity. We concluded that we could advance God's kingdom in the new placing and still use our ministry models and spiritual gifts, and we could do the ministry well. However, having just lost Aída's father and mother, we would be too adrift leaving our only adult son. We did not have Christ's peace. We also thought we would lose more than we gained. We did not sense we would have as much support from our new employers as we had from our past employers. We still had some important ministry goals toward which we'd been working that were not finalized in our present call. Thus, after prayer and research, we said no to this new joint career opportunity.[13]

On less important but daily decisions, one of us may have expertise and make the final decision, keeping the other informed. Or, one of us may research an area and present the findings with a recommendation

---

[13]We also think Christian institutions should become more family friendly: developing half-time positions with full benefits (e.g., see success of Kellogg six-hour shifts, Van Leeuwen, *My Brother's Keeper*, pp. 230-35, 244-45), offering day care for parents who choose to use it, offering paid maternity and paternity benefits, offering free classes for spouses and children, allowing committees to meet at times flexible for parents, helping the second spouse find a position when the other spouse is hired. Evangelical Christians should be at the forefront of organizing institutions that enhance family life and ministry, but unfortunately, this is not always the case.

for a joint decision. For example, when we needed to have our driveway resurfaced, Aída called and arranged the estimates. Together, we discussed the pros and cons of each. Then she arranged the work at a time convenient for both of us. When we need to plan timing, Bill, who has a good sense of time, proposes a time schedule for trips, meetings and tasks. After feedback from Aída, we schedule accordingly. In other words, we find we do not both have to do every task for joint decisions. We can rely on one another to do a good job in our area of specialty, as long as we keep in good communication.

Every once in a while we deadlock on a small decision. For instance, one of us wants to drive while the other thinks the first person is too tired. What do we do then? If even after discussion, we cannot agree, after prayer, we can also abide by Proverbs 18:18 ("Casting the lot puts an end to disputes and decides between powerful contenders"). We choose it out and let the Lord decide (Prov 16:33)! One interesting observation we have noted is that these instances were more frequent in our early years and extremely rare now.

Four steps for handling the conflict that may accompany decision making. Bill's mother warned us when we were first married that we would take a while to adjust to each other because we were two different people reared in two different homes with different customs.[14] A good marriage will have conflicts or disagreements as it moves toward unity. Conflict is natural; resolution of it is Christlike. Conflict can be helpful, causing growth, if the goal is eventual reconciliation. As John Chrysostom explains: "For there is nothing which so tempers our life together as the love of man and wife. For this many will lay aside even their arms, for this they will give up life itself" *(Homily 20 on Ephesians 5.24)*. Mediator Mischelle Causey-Drake suggests that "conflict is ba-

---

[14]For example, Jack Balswick and Judith Balswick write that if a couple claims never to have conflicts: "they haven't been married very long; they don't talk to each other very much; one spouse has all the power and the other has none; or they are in denial." *A Model for Marriage: Covenant, Grace, Empowerment and Intimacy* (Downers Grove, Ill.: InterVarsity Press, 2006), p. 118. See also chap. 9 of Patty Lane, *A Beginner's Guide to Crossing Cultures: Making Friends in a Multicultural World* (Downers Grove, Ill.: InterVarsity Press, 2002). Elizabeth Achtemeier adds that "the more intimate the marriage is, the more conflicting desires and views are likely to come to the surface." *The Committed Marriage*, Biblical Perspectives on Current Issues (Philadelphia: Westminster Press, 1976), p. 172.

sically caused by the frustration of a need. The question is, How do you respond to it?"[15] She suggests that the first step in dealing with conflict is to ask whether to overlook it or pursue it. Is it a minor offense? Is it one's own fault (e.g., Mt 7:5)? Proverbs warns "The beginning of strife is like letting out water; so stop before the quarrel breaks out" (17:14). Sometimes we are simply tired and grumpy, and a restful sleep is all we need or a good laugh at a frustrating situation. The second step is to look at the root problem to try to understand the conflict. We need to listen and observe before disagreeing. Many proverbs recommend we observe and listen: "If one gives answer before hearing, it is folly and shame" (18:13) or "The purposes in the human mind are like deep water, but the intelligent will draw them out" (20:5), and "The one who first states a case seems right, until the other comes and cross-examines" (18:17). Gary Chapman warns us to watch out for four "fowls," unhealthy, nonlistening, patterns of communication: the Dove ("I Want Peace at Any Price"), the Hawk ("It's Your Fault"), the Owl ("You're Not Being Logical") or the Ostrich ("Ignore It and It Will Go Away").[16] The third step is to deal with the conflict as soon as possible in the best possible way. A "word in season" is good and can bring healing, but rash words are "like sword thrusts" (Prov 15:23; 12:18). Paul wants us to try to resolve anger within the day (Eph 4:26-27). Jesus

---

[15]Mischelle Causey-Drake, "The Bible and Conflict Management," *Discernment: A Newsletter of the Center for Applied Christian Ethics* 6, no. 2 (Spring 1999): 7.

[16]Gary Chapman, *Covenant Marriage: Building Communication and Intimacy* (Nashville: Broadman & Holman, 2003), pp. 44-49. The Balswicks identify five styles of conflict: the withdrawer, the yielder, the winner, the compromiser, the resolver. *Model for Marriage*, pp. 126-131. Otto Kroeger and Janet M. Thuesen discuss how personality types might cause conflict and they provide tips for resolving conflict. For example, *Type Talk: The 16 Personality Types that Determine How We Live, Love, and Work* (New York: Bantam Doubleday, 1988), p. 112. Herbert Anderson and Robert Cotton Fite, *Becoming Married,* Family Living in Pastoral Perspective (Louisville: Westminster/John Knox, 1993), pp. 130-33 write that good communication is direct, begins with "I," incorporates both rationality and feeling, is timely, and well-intended. They add that marriages that endure and flourish have achieved a mutual recognition that "honors the spouse as a separate and unique subject." See also Matthew McKay, Martha Davis and Patrick Fanning, *Messages: The Communication Skills Book*, 2nd ed. (Oakland, Calif.: New Harbinger Publications, 1995), chaps. 10-12; Matthew McKay, Patrick Fanning and Kim Paleg, *Couple Skills: Making Your Relationship Work* (Oakland, Calif.: New Harbinger Publications, 1994); Gilbert Bilezikian, *Beyond Sex Roles* (Grand Rapids: Baker, 1985), pp. 212-14; Patricia Gundry, *Heirs Together: Applying the Biblical Principle of Mutual Submission in Your Marriage* (Grand Rapids: Suitcase Books, 1980), pp. 138-47.

recommends we see a person privately (Mt 18:15). Electronic mail is one of the worse means of resolving conflict,[17] face-to-face conversation in a restful setting is the best. Disagreements also need to be separated from power struggles. We remind ourselves that the truth is in Jesus, not ultimately in either spouse. Finally, above all, persevere. Do not give up quickly when things are hard. Love "endures" (1 Cor 13:7). "A friend loves at all times, and kinsfolk are born to share adversity" (Prov 17:17). "Two are better than one . . . for if they fall, one will lift up the other" (Eccles 4:9-10).

Sometimes conflict may be caused by traditional differences of approach by a man and a woman. However, we agree with noted Christian psychologist Mary Stewart Van Leeuwen, who concludes that "the complexity of human functioning eludes simple stereotypes about what men and women 'are' or 'should be' like."[18] As a result, psychological and sociological studies should be treated as descriptive, not prescriptive. The Bible's teachings, in contrast, are prescriptive. Yet, it does not present any clear sex-based giftings. As we saw in the last chapter, husbands are told to love their wives (Eph 5:25), but so are wives told to love their husbands (Tit 2:4). Wives are told to manage their house-

---

[17]Patrick Vaughn points out that electronic mail often "stifles and garbles communication. The absence of facial expressions and voice inflections can produce painful results." Since e-mail "creates the illusion of distance and anonymity," people "often tend to inject unwarranted criticism in an e-mail that they would not express verbally in face-to-face or telephone conversation. E-mail inadvertently promotes distortion of data and indiscriminate venting." Email is good for short and specific dissemination of information. "E-mail: Uses and Misuses in Congregations," *The Parish Paper* January 2007 (HrbMiller@aol.com).

[18]Van Leeuwen, *Gender and Grace*, p. 105. The reason Van Leeuwen is accurate is because God created first of all "Adam" or "the Human." "Male and female" have one name (Gen 1:26-27; 5:2). Then we are told that "the Human" is a "them," "male and female," a "them" (Gen 1:26-27, repeated after the fall in Gen 5:1-2). All of us are "Adam" or "the Human." Before we are gender specific, we are "human." Our humanity precedes our maleness or femaleness. Why? Because as humans we were created to reflect or mirror *one* God. God has only *one* name (Mt 28:19). But that one name has three Persons, Father and Son and Holy Spirit, who are one but also distinct from each other. We are human before we are male and female, like God who is revealed as one before God is explained as three. In other words, we do not worship three Gods who have something in common but one God in three Persons. That is why all of us, males and females, can worship one God who can meet all our needs. Unlike ancient religions, we do not need one god (or set of gods) for the men and another god (or set of gods) for the women (Mithras vs. Isis!). That does not mean we believe in unisex, rather we hold to priority. God did create two sexes, male and female, but their unity as the human species precedes their diversity. Aída Besançon Spencer and others, *The Goddess Revival* (Grand Rapids: Baker, 1995), pp. 88-91.

holds (Tit 2:5; 1 Tim 5:14), and elders as well are told to manage their households (1 Tim 3:4). Thus, leadership in the home should not be based on gender. If any studies of male-female differences enlighten your understanding of yourself or your spouse, go ahead and consult them. If you discover true individual differences between a male and a female (and eventually the children) in each marriage, they should be understood and appreciated, not considered weaknesses. But, do not let any study imprison you or your spouse into thinking it is infallible and you must fit within its patterns.[19]

Counselors Herbert Anderson and Robert Cotton Fite wisely remind us that the struggle to share power "pervades almost every aspect of marital life together." Making decisions about "who does the housework, who cares for the children, whose family tradition predominates, how leisure time is organized, how decisions are made, or who writes the Christmas letter" are opportunities to share power. "When everyone is empowered, love flows more freely and conflicts are settled more quickly."[20] Remembering that Christ is our only Ruler and High Priest can help us (1) share leadership in the home by performing the priesthood of all believers and (2) make decisions that lessen conflict. Solomon around three thousand years ago realized the importance of coparenting when he began his Book of Proverbs: "Hear, my child, your father's instruction, and do not reject your mother's teaching; for they are a fair garland for your head, and pen-

---

[19]Naomi L. Quenk agrees that in regard to the Myers-Briggs Type Indicator a "frequent error is the assumption that all women 'should' be Feeling types and all men 'should' be Thinking types" since in the United States 57% of males prefer Thinking decisions, whereas 75% of females prefer Feeling decisions. She adds that the Thinking-Feeling "dichotomy is the only one of the four [Extraversion-Introversion, Sensing-Intuition, Judging-Perceiving] that has consistently shown a gender difference in prevalence." *Essentials of Myers-Briggs Type Indicator Assessment* (New York: John Wiley, 2000), p. 76. Van Leeuwen warns us of the limitations of social science testing on gender differences in "Opposite Sexes or Neighboring Sexes? What Do the Social Sciences Really Tell Us?" *Women, Ministry and the Gospel: Exploring New Paradigms*, ed. Mark Husbands and Timothy Larsen (Downers Grove, Ill.: InterVarsity Press, 2007), pp. 171-99. See also Sharon Jayson, "Men, Women Are Equal-talkers," *USA Today*, 6-8 July 2007, 1A.

[20]Anderson and Fite, *Becoming Married*, pp. 127, 129. In a study of men and women in eleven large conservative United States churches, "only 20 percent of the participants defined their *beliefs* as unequivocally egalitarian, but 60 percent of them defined their *practice* as unequivocally egalitarian." Alice P. Mathews and M. Gay Hubbard, *Marriage Made in Eden: A Pre-Modern Perspective for a Post-Christian World* (Grand Rapids: Baker, 2004), pp. 139-40.

dants for your neck" (Prov 1:8). Coparenting is still a jeweled treasure today, as is fully shared home leadership of husband and wife, that imparts to children a healthy model for their future life of shared harmony with their own spouses and children.

STEVE AND CELESTIA TRACY'S
VIEWPOINT

Until recently, gender-differentiated marital roles have been widely, overwhelmingly accepted in the Western world. But that dramatically changed with the advent of the modern feminist movement in the early 1960s when Betty Friedan wrote her monumentally influential book, *The Feminine Mystique*, in which she discussed the "problem that has no name."[1] She argued, based on her study of women in her same life circumstances, that even middle-class, college-educated women with a comfortable life do not find life purpose and satisfaction simply living out the traditional domestic gender role given to wives. Hence, for the past four decades fierce debates have raged over whether women can find fulfillment in being wives and mothers, and whether any gender-based roles are morally and biblically appropriate. So, it now seems strange, even heretical, in many circles to suggest gender-differentiated marital roles. As with the previous chapter, we tread gingerly on this sensitive subject, one that does need to be addressed both practically and carefully.

We would like to share an e-mail (used with permission) to introduce the topic of marital roles and some of the questions it raises. The following came from a single professional woman who had asked to read our manuscript chapters as we completed them. After reading the headship and submission section, she wrote:

---

[1]There were certainly earlier feminists in the late eighteenth through the early twentieth centuries, but they tended to focus on suffrage (the right of women to vote). Once the nineteenth amendment was passed in 1919 giving women the right to vote, American feminism lost most of its momentum. The modern feminist movement is generally understood to have begun with the publication of Betty Friedan's book, *The Feminine Mystique* (New York: Dell Publishing, 1963). This is often referred to as the second stage of feminism, and focused on gaining full social and economic equality for women. On the history of feminism, see Estelle Freedman, *The History of Feminism and the Future of Women* (New York: Ballantine, 2002); on modern evangelical feminism, see Pamela D. H. Cochram, *Evangelical Feminism: A History* (New York: New York University Press, 2005).

When I first saw the title my stomach ended up in my mouth! And I thought—*I must read this but how on earth am I going to get through all this headship/submission language!* So it was a bit of a hard read but as I read and saw what you both were developing in this chapter I got a meaning for headship and submission that to me felt more biblically appropriate and correct. I ended up going to bed straight after I read it. What happened then surprised me but I was lying in bed and I just burst into tears—I tried to process what I was feeling/needing and I thought that if a man loved me, honored me and protected me and respected me in the way you described in this chapter then I would gladly submit to him for the rest of my life. And it would not feel like he was exerting power over me or dominating me. Rather, in loving me that way what I would want to do in return is love him with all I have.

What would cause a highly educated and accomplished professional woman to react to a discussion of headship in such an unexpected and emotional manner? Could it be that in spite of her painful experiences with gender traditionalism, and in spite of lifelong cultural conditioning that seeks to obliterate gender differences and gender roles, that the deepest longings of our heart tacitly point to innate, purposeful gender differences?[2] Could it be that in throwing out the dirty bathwater of patriarchy we have also thrown out the beautiful baby of gender differentiation?

INNATE GENDER DIFFERENCES IN CREATION

One of the most significant pillars of much modern feminism is the notion that basic differences between men and women are absolutely minimal. Gender differences while all too often real, are not essential; they

---

[2]Some secular researchers have strongly affirmed that denying innate gender differences is ultimately counterproductive and painful, for it is a futile denial of the essence of our gender. For instance, Shelley E. Taylor, a groundbreaking scientific researcher on stress argues, "Probably the saddest fallout of our efforts to squeeze men and women into the same psychological mold was our intense embarrassment over anything inconveniently female in nature." *The Tending Instinct: Women, Men, and the Biology of Our Relationships* (New York: Henry Holt, 2002), p. 4. Similarly, secular journalist Danielle Crittenden notes, "Pretending that we are the same as men—with the similar needs and desires—has only led many of us to find out, brutally, how different we really are. *What Our Mothers Didn't Tell Us: Why Happiness Eludes the Modern Woman* (New York: Simon & Schuster, 1999), p. 25. Crittendon's focus is on women's innate social/relational differences from men. See also Louann Brizendine who says that in denying our gender-differentiated brains we "begin fighting our own nature." *The Female Brain* (New York: Morgan Road Books, 2006), p. 6.

are the result of social conditioning.[3] The biblical creation account, however, clearly indicates otherwise. First of all, we see that God's explanation for making the woman is positively predicated on sexual differences. We read, "It is not good that the man should be alone; I will make him a helper as his partner" (Gen 2:18). While many if not most gender traditionalists understand "helper" to teach that women's role is to serve her husband (essentially a secondary role), this does not fit the text. The Hebrew phrase used here literally means "helper corresponding to" *(ʿēzer kĕnegdô)* and conveys the idea of one who complements as an equal by filling or completing that which is lacking.[4] This strongly suggests that men and women, while equal, are different and that those very differences create a bilateral need for the other gender. So, while gender differences have historically been emphasized, even exaggerated at the woman's expense, the biblical text clearly teaches that men need women and women need men for relational complementation. Thus, women exist not to serve men but to serve God with men, filling in the gaps that are lacking in men's natural composition. The other creation text that gives more specific aspects of male/female differentiation is Genesis 1:26. This is the condensed account of human creation as "male and female." The Hebrew terms for gender inescapably, even shockingly, emphasize gender differences and complementation. And these differences are placed in the context not of male superiority but of joint and equal creation in the image of God and rulership over all of creation. The root meaning of the Hebrew word for "female" *(nĕqēbâ)* is "to pierce" or "perforate" and hence "female" pictures the "one pierced." The

---

[3]This assertion is particularly true of the so called "second wave" feminist works, from 1963 to the early 1990s. There are countless feminist authors that insist that gender differences are a social construct. For a recent work that minimizes biological factors and champions nurture over nature in creating gender differences (while acknowledging that differences in hormones and brain structure do exist), see Leslie Brody, *Gender, Emotion and the Family* (Cambridge, Mass.: Harvard University Press, 1999).

[4]Thus, Gordon Wenham notes that this phrase conveys complementation and literally means "helper like opposite him." So he translates it "helper matching him." *Genesis 1-15* (Waco, Tex.: Word, 1987), p. 68. Victor P. Hamilton also notes the significance of this phrase, "Thus the new creation [the woman] will neither be a superior nor an inferior, but an equal." *The Book of Genesis Chapters 1-17* (Grand Rapids: Eerdmans, 1990), p. 175. It should also be noted that ʿēzer is almost always used in the Old Testament of God himself and does not indicate an inferior.

Hebrew word for "male" *(zākār)* seems to denote the male organ (and was often used in the context of circumcision).[5] This graphically erotic language pictures gender differentiation at its most basic level—human genitalia and the act of sexual intercourse. More specifically, the man is pictured as the one whose gender gives him an external sexual organ, while the woman is pictured as the responder who literally receives the man into her body in the most sacred act of intimacy. While such literal Hebrew terms may appear crude to modern ears, we must remember that this is God's language for gender and is in the context of his "very good" creation (Gen 1:31). Furthermore, we must not remove these terms from the original context. While they describe sexual intercourse with anatomical precision and may sound almost coldly pornographic, this act is placed in the context of loving intimacy that produces life. Thus, even the most foundational gender differences are beautiful and divinely purposeful. Let us delight in these differences!

THE INTERSECTION OF GENDER DIFFERENCES AND GENDER ROLES

I (Celestia) studied architecture and design in college. One of the architectural concepts I learned at that time which has continued to shape my thinking over the years is this: *form follows function*. That is, design reflects the intended purpose or function. If this is true in human design, how much more precisely it must be true of God's creation. God is not random but is wonderfully and strategically creative. The differences he built into men and women (their design) have a logical and beneficial purpose, allowing them to best carry out his purposes for their lives as males and females (their function).[6] In the next section we

---

[5]Francis Brown, S. R. Driver and Charles A. Briggs, eds., *The Brown-Driver-Briggs Hebrew and English Lexicon: with an Appendix Containing the Biblical Aramaic* (Peabody, Mass.: Hendrickson, 1996), s.v. נְקֵבָה and זָכָר.

[6]To this extent we agree with the many secular Darwinian scientists who argue that innate gender differences are (at least historically) necessary and purposeful. The decisive difference is that we assert that a personal, transcendent Creator wisely introduced these differences to allow us to carry out his purposes in our lives. Secular scientists, however, argue that these purposeful gender differences are the result of blind chance that furthered the survival and evolution of the species; they do not necessarily have positive significance in the modern world. On the secular assertion that it is absurd to assert that function flows out of (blind chance produced) biological design, see Taylor, *The Tending Instinct*, p. 15.

will elaborate on gender differences, but first we need to clarify gender marital roles. Before we can explain marital gender roles, however, we must carefully clarify what we mean by *role*. By *role* one might mean "ultimate purpose" as expressed in a declaration I have heard several times: "My role in life is to glorify God." By this broadest definition of role, men and women have identical roles. They are to glorify God by using their gifts and other resources to advance his kingdom. *Merriam-Webster* gives two other common definitions of *role*.[7] The first is "a socially expected behavior pattern usually determined by an individual's status in a particular society." This definition of role when applied to marriage limits and demeans women because it views a woman's *role* based on status and societal expectations. And the woman inevitably has the lower status, and thus an inferior role. Furthermore, this definition leads to a narrow and restrictive understanding of a woman's role based on stereotypical behavior, regardless of a woman's unique divine gifting. With this approach to *role*, the wife's divine mission and sphere of work is typically understood to be "domestic activity."[8] This definition is also very problematic for single Christian women, leaving them without a clear way to fulfill their life *role*. This first definition is expressly not what we mean by *role*. The second definition given by *Merriam-Webster* is, "a function or part performed especially in a particular operation or process." This is much closer to what we mean by role. By marital role we mean the unique part that a man or woman plays in

---

[7]*Merriam-Webster's Online Dictionary*, s.v. "role," available at <http://www.m-w.com/dictionary/role> (accessed 4/11/2007).

[8]This understanding of role is reflected in the famous German dictum often attributed to Martin Luther regarding the role of women, "*Kinder, Küche, Kirche,*" (children, kitchen, church). Many gender traditional evangelicals subscribe to this restricted role for women, and assert that women's God ordained role is foundationally (and, for some, exclusively) domestic. For instance, Douglas Wilson argues that a woman's "assigned orientation is toward the home"; pregnancy is the beginning of a woman's divine calling; feminism has led women into positions for which they are not "naturally suited" such as positions of civic responsibility. *Federal Husband* (Moscow, Idaho: Canon Press, 1999), pp. 38, 85, 81. See also Martha Peace who argues that apart from very unique circumstances, a wife should not work outside the home but should focus on serving her family. She gives specific examples of what this should look like: keeping up with the ironing, making sure your husband has clean underwear in his drawer, keeping a running list of needed food and cleaning supplies, and (except for starting a load of laundry), completing one task before starting another. *Becoming a Titus 2 Woman* (Bemidji, Minn.: Focus Publishing, 1997), pp. 111, 117-19.

carrying out the joint tasks of marriage (crafting the relationship, building vocations/ministries and raising children). *This definition places gender uniqueness in the context of a couple's corporate responsibilities and mutual mission.* Thus, both the husband and the wife as a *one-flesh* entity are to build a strong, godly marriage, nurture children, and build their ministries and vocations. They do this together but each plays a unique part in this task based on their gender as well as their individual gifting. Clearly, there can be considerable individual variance and overlap here—this understanding of marital roles, while gender distinctive, is not narrow.[9] Remember that in the last chapter we saw much overlap and mutuality in the work of the Father and the Son. But just as the Father and the Son, in their great mutuality of work, do have some unique roles, so husbands and wives play some unique roles in the joint marital task. This is why they are given some different marital commands (headship/submission). So how can we describe husbands' and wives' unique roles?

Since we depart from the traditional model that tends to view marriage roles strictly and narrowly (her domain is the home and her role is to submit; his domain is the outside world and his role is to be the authoritative head), we find it best to begin with an image of our role model rather than a sterile definition. Picture a small medieval fort on the edge of a lawless and dangerous wilderness. While this technically is the King's land (or so the ancient writings say), no one has ever seen him here. For as long as anyone can remember, the local inhabitants have raped, pillaged and murdered each other. Anarchy and suffering reign. It's all they have ever known. Many have never even heard who their reputed King is; they don't know and they don't care. But the King knows them. One day he sends a peasant couple he has surprisingly adopted to inhabit the fort, transform it into a castle, and extend his rule. He gives them matching thrones and delegates to them his authority to have dominion over this unruly place in his name. He places them as king and queen in this wild outpost. They know they

---

[9]For a similar approach to marital gender roles, see Gary Thomas, *Sacred Influence: What a Man Needs from His Wife to Be the Husband She Wants* (Grand Rapids: Zondervan, 2006), pp. 77-89, esp. p. 82.

could never do this alone, aren't sure they can even do it together, but obey their orders. They reign together work together and play together, often in parallel or similar tasks. But their work isn't identical. The king's unique focus is clear—he is the knight who initiates protection and provides for those in the fort. The queen's task and focus is also clear—she is the queen of hearts. Her expertise is in the sophisticated realm of relationships. She often sees, hears and feels the needs of her citizens long before the king does. He respects and values her intuitive wisdom and wouldn't think of leading without her. Her voice has become embedded in his own. He marvels at the interdependence of their kingdom rule. How dependent on her he has become! She is his closest confidant, lover and friend. Her eyes can be fire when she must confront the destroyer of love. She protects hearts—first her own, then his. Feminine wisdom tells her, if the kingdom is destroyed, it will not be from outside marauders but from within. Her role is very active. He trusts her implicitly and knows he has been changed by her soulful wisdom and active love. He is a wiser and kinder king because of her. Together they skillfully build the castle, extend the kingdom and train future heirs of their throne. This is their joint and sacred work that ensures the taming of the wilderness long after they are gone.[10]

To summarize and clarify:

1. We believe marital gender roles focus on mutuality and equality. Husbands and wives rule together as equals. Their mission is a joint mission. Even the more specific tasks they are given in Scripture as wives and husbands show great mutuality and overlap. Thus, we want to be very clear that in noting gender differences, this is a matter of emphasis not a rigid separation of the sexes. We do not reduce "true femininity" to passivity, softness or emotionality. Nor do we reduce "true masculinity" to strength or assertiveness.[11] We can particularly

---

[10]We love Dan E. Allender and Tremper Longman's summary thesis statement: "God's intention is for our spouses to be our allies—intimate friends, lovers, warriors in the spiritual war against the forces of the evil one." *Intimate Allies: Rediscovering God's Design for Marriage and Becoming Soul Mates for Life* (Wheaton, Ill.: Tyndale House, 1995), p. xvi.

[11]Thus, we take great issue with those such as Mark Chanski who ignore the plain statement of Gen 1:26 giving dominion to the husband and the wife, and assert that men need to rise up, resist the influence of feminism that is destroying our culture, and be truly masculine by exercising godly dominion and not being feminine (passive). In other words, the essence of

see overlapping male female duties/authority with respect to parenting. Both parents are to instruct their children and are to be equally obeyed (Prov 1:8; Col 3:20) and equally honored (Ex 20:12; Lev 19:3). The penalty for not honoring or obeying fathers or mothers is identical (Ex 21:15; Prov 30:11, 17). Fathers *and* mothers are to take a rebellious son to the elders (Deut 21:19-20). If a woman is accused of not being a virgin when she married, her father *and* her mother are to bring evidence of her virginity to the elders (Deut 22:15). Fathers *and* mothers are to comfort and have tender compassion for their children (Ps 103:13; Jer 31:9; 1 Thess 2:7). Fathers *and* mother are described as together bearing children (Zech 13:3).[12]

2. We affirm that husbands and wives do have some gender-differentiated tasks and strengths/abilities, all of which contribute to the joint marital mission. In general terms (not rigidly) we would describe the wife's role in the joint task of marriage as responsive and nurturing. The husband is characterized by initiating, protecting and having overarching responsibility for the well-being of the family. Where do we find these concepts in Scripture? We saw these respective roles in the biblical commands regarding male headship (protecting, empowering, initiating) and female submission (responding). We see them fleshed out in numerous Scripture passages. The following are just a few. Throughout Scripture, men are responsible to care for and sacrificially protect their families, the vulnerable, and even their communities.[13]

---

masculinity is domination and power; the essence of femininity is seemingly softness, responsiveness and emotionality. Mark Chanski, *Manly Dominion in a Passive Four-Ball World* (Merrick, N.Y.: Calvary Press, 2004), pp. 12-15, 167-73. With slight variations, see also Leon J. Podles, *The Church Impotent: The Feminization of Christianity* (Dallas: Spence, 1999), pp. 43-44, 58-59; 84-85. The dangerous roots of a rigid reduction of masculinity to strength and unemotional rationality and the reduction of femininity to softness, passivity, and emotionality is brilliantly demonstrated by Prudence Allen, *The Concept of Woman: The Aristotelian Revolution, 750 B.C.–A.D. 1250*, rev. ed. (Grand Rapids: Eerdmans, 1997). In this landmark work, Allen traces philosophical understandings of women over the centuries and shows the dominant influence of Aristotle who argued for the ontological (in one's very essence or being as a person) supremacy of males based on the essence of maleness (even in the fertilization process itself) consisting of activity, and the essence of femaleness being passivity and emotional irrationality.

[12]This mutuality in parenting does not, however, eliminate all unique responsibility or leadership for fathers, but it softens it, see Gen 24:23; Ex 22:17; Num 30:3-5; Deut 22:16; Lk 15:12; Gal 4:2.

[13]For instance, in Neh 4:13-14 when surrounded by the enemy, Nehemiah placed men with

Women also protect (cf. Ex 1:17-20), but this is primarily a responsibility carried out by men. The more dangerous, aggressive protection such as through military conflict, is almost exclusively a male activity in Scripture.[14] Note for instance, that when their lives were threatened by Herod, God came to Joseph and told him to lead his family to safety in Egypt (Mt 2:13-14). Closely related is the task of material provision, which is a particular responsibility for husbands.[15] Let us note that Proverbs 31:10-31 makes it patently clear that godly wives, even those with children, are not restricted to the domestic sphere; they can work outside the home. But even in this passage the emphasis on the ideal wife's attunement, and responsiveness to her husband and children is clear.[16]

In the New Testament women are directed to care for their household, including caring for their children (1 Tim 5:14; Tit 2:4-5). In fact, nurturing children, serving believers, and caring for the needy are given as some of the best evidences of a woman's godliness (1 Tim 5:10). Women are very often described and characterized by their relational sensitivity and nurturing. This is not a patronizing gender stereotype, for Scripture forcefully and positively uses women as the personification of gentle, nurturing love.[17] Of course husbands are also to love their families (Ps 103:13; Eph 5:25) but tender responsive nurturing is viewed in Scripture as a characteristically female trait and virtue.[18] While many secular feminists repudiate the personification of women

---

weapons at the vulnerable places in the city and instructed them to courageously fight for their children, wives and homes. See also Gen 14:1-16; Jer 22:1-3, 15-17; 41:7-16; cf. 1 Macc 3:2.

[14]See for instance Ex 17:9; Judg 1:1-9; 6:1-6, 7:1-25; 1 Sam 17:9-58. One of the only exceptions to this is when Deborah the prophetess went with Barak into battle against the Canaanites because Barak would not go himself. Thus, due to his abdication of his responsibilities, God said he would give victory but Barak would not get the honor, a woman (Jael) would (Judg 4:9).

[15]This helps us make sense of the curse in Gen 3:17-19, where the curse to Adam was that thorns and thistles would grow, making his task of provision much more difficult. Conversely, the woman's curse is that she will have pain in childbirth (v. 16), her sphere of (somewhat) particular responsibility.

[16]See esp. vv. 12, 15, 21, 27.

[17]Num 11:12; Ps 131:2; Is 49:13-15; 66:13; Mt 23:37; 1Thess 2:7.

[18]For this reason it is natural that children in time of crisis tend innately to go to their mothers for comfort and care. Thus, during the horrible foreign invasion, which created great famine, children cried out to their mothers asking for bread, and passed out in their mothers' arms (Lam 2:11-12; cf. 2 Kings 4:19).

as gentle and nurturing, this need not and should not be a patronizing description.[19] The beauty of the woman's particular task of tender, responsive nurturing is perhaps best pictured in the frequent, universally positive descriptions of women nursing their infants, something that only women can do.[20] In fact, this very metaphor is used of God himself (Is 49:14-15; cf. Is 66:10-13).

Finally, Scripture places particular responsibilities on husbands for their families. *They do have an authority of love* (Eph 5:22-31). One of our favorite passages affirming this is Deuteronomy 24:5 where a new groom is given the responsibility of not taking on any military or agricultural responsibilities for the first year of his marriage so he could focus on devoting himself to bringing happiness to his wife. The particular responsibility of a husband toward his family helps us understand why even though both Adam and Eve ate the fruit (Eve actually ate first, Gen 3:1-6) God imputes that first sin to Adam (Rom 5:12-19; 1 Cor 15:21-22).

Since men and women are both made in God's image, why would they have somewhat different roles? Actually, it is because we are made in God's image, and that image is given its fullest expression in humans male *and* female (Gen 1:26), that God ordained these differences. Because of our different gender qualities as men and women, we respectively highlight somewhat different aspects of God's character. For instance, husbands in some unique ways highlight God's strength and justice, whereas wives in some unique ways highlight God's grace, mercy, and tender care.[21] It is instructive that God is described using both masculine and feminine imagery.[22] Together, a

---

[19]For instance, see the fascinating comparison of men and women based on traditional gender traits found in 1 Esd 4:1-35. The speaker concludes that women are actually stronger, and in a sense, superior to men.

[20]Num 11:12; Ps 22:9; Song 8:1; Is 49:15; Joel 2:16; Lk 11:27; cf. 2 Macc 7:27.

[21]For a similar assertion that while there is much overlap in the characteristics of men and women, both as individuals and as two collective genders, that men and women's gender differences allow them to highlight somewhat different aspects of God, see Allender and Longman, *Intimate Allies*, pp. 148-55.

[22]For instance, in Deut 32:3-43, Moses alternates between male and female allusions in praising God. He is described in masculine imagery/qualities as a rock (v. 4), a Father and a creator (vv. 6, 18), and an avenging warrior (vv. 41-43). He is also described using female imagery or qualities such as a mother eagle who cares for her young (v. 11), and a mother who birthed Israel (v. 18).

man and a woman bring their own respective gender-shaped qualities to the marriage to carry out the divine mission. Together they give a fuller picture of God. The qualities each brings are equally valuable and essential.

ADDITIONAL EVIDENCE FOR INNATE GENDER DIFFERENCES THAT FACILITATE GENDER ROLES

The most obvious male/female gender differences certainly support this understanding of marital gender roles. God made the female body such that it receives the man. Furthermore, the woman is the one who carries the developing child for nine months, gives birth, and nurses her baby with her own breasts. God has designed the female body to nurture and respond. The man is the one who enters the woman—in this sense he leads and initiates in a life giving way. God designed the man to carry out his role of initiating, providing, leading, and protecting. Are there other innate gender differences beyond mere genitalia that harmonize with our assertion of gender roles (male initiation, protection, responsibility and female responding and nurturing)? While this is certainly a complex and contentious subject, there is rapidly mounting scientific evidence of innate gender differences, particularly in terms of brain structure and chemistry (particularly hormones such as testosterone, estrogen and oxytocin).[23] As neuroscientist Cynthia Darlington notes, "the evidence for clear and important differences in brain function between males and females is overwhelming."[24] Modern

---

[23]We have surveyed dozens out of hundreds of peer reviewed scientific journal articles that give strong evidence of innate biological gender differences, and intend to present this data in a future journal article. For an overview of recent scientific evidence of biological gender differences, see in particular the following books written by secular scientists: Simon Baron-Cohen, *The Essential Difference: The Truth About the Male & Female Brain* (New York: Basic Books, 2003); Louann Brizendine, *The Female Brain*; Anne Campbell, *A Mind of Her Own: The Evolutionary Psychology of Women* (Oxford: Oxford University Press, 2002); Cynthia Darlington, *The Female Brain* (New York: Taylor & Francis, 2002); David C. Geary, *Male, Female: The Evolution of Human Sex Differences* (Washington, D.C.: American Psychological Association, 1998); Shelley Taylor, *The Tending Instinct*. For a practical explanation of male/female brain differences, see the works of educational psychologist Michael Gurian, especially *The Wonder of Girls: Understanding the Hidden Nature of Our Daughters* (New York: Pocket Books, 2002), and *The Minds of Boys: Saving Our Sons From Falling Behind in School and Life* (San Francisco: Jossey-Bass, 2005).

[24]Darlington, *The Female Brain*, p. 201.

scientific research has shown that men and women have far more bio-logical similarities than differences.[25] At the same time, there are some key differences between the respective genders (individual men and women are unique creations of God and will reflect these differences to greater and lesser degrees).[26] While many differences have been suggested,[27] we will summarize and briefly explain some of the most well-documented differences, all of which facilitate men and women in carrying out their respective gender roles and bringing their respective unique strengths to the marital tasks.

Male assertiveness/aggression: *Focus on power and status over rela-tionships.* As a gender, men are markedly stronger and more aggres-sive than women. One of the definitive studies of aggression analyzed homicide rates across various cultures for over seven hundred years, and discovered that there is no known culture in which female fatal violence comes close to male violence. Male-on-male violence occurs thirty to forty times more frequently than female-on-female, and often in the context of saving face (retaining one's social status).[28] More recent studies of violence validate this gender difference in aggression finding, and specifically refute the notion that this is the result of social conditioning.[29] Similarly, studies (including a meta-analytic study of 150 risk experiments) reveal that males are significantly more risk taking and women are considerably more risk aversive.[30] Males, beginning in early childhood and continuing into adulthood are more

---

[25]Campbell thus speaks of a "single fundamental human design in *A Mind of Her Own*, p. 269.

[26]In noting differences, we are speaking of statistical differences between the genders.

[27]See, for instance, Janet Shibley Hyde, *Half the Human Experience: The Psychology of Women*, 6th ed. (New York: Houghton Mifflin, 2004). Hyde notes the following commonly proposed gen-der differences: emotions, self-esteem, use of language, aggression, nurturing ability, empathy, anxiety, activity, spatial ability, verbal ability mathematics ability and brain lateralization, pp. 94-104, 215-21, 280-82.

[28]M. Daly and M. Wilson, *Homicide* (New York: Aldine de Gruyter, 1988).

[29]Terrie E. Moffitt, Avshalom Caspi, Michael Rutter and Phil A. Silva, *Sex Differences in An-tisocial Behavior* (Cambridge: Cambridge University Press, 2001). This book was based on a study of 1,000 males and females ages 3 to 21 years and won the Maccoby Book Award from the American Psychological Association. The researchers found that females are less anti-social (less frequently and less seriously so). Furthermore, this study specifically refuted the common belief that social context (parental gender differentiated treatment) explains the sex differences in antisocial behavior, pp. 235, 240.

[30]J. P. Byrnes, D. C. Miller and W. D. Schafer, "Gender Differences in Risk Taking: A Meta-analysis," *Psychological Bulletin* 125 (1999): 367-83; Campbell, *A Mind of Her Own*, pp. 69-100.

physical, assertive, and dominant in their play and in their social interactions than females.[31] Their relational interactions also tend to be much more focused on power and status and less on relationships than is characteristic of females.[32] In terms of the reasons for greater male aggression, dominance and task orientation, there is considerable evidence that these differences are, at least in large measure, the result of differences in male brain structure and hormones, particularly the presence of the hormone testosterone and possibly lower male levels of the brain neurotransmitter serotonin (which appears related to impulse control). Testosterone in particular accounts for most of the unique male gender traits, including differences in brain structure (and from puberty on males have roughly ten to twenty times more testosterone than females).[33]

Female intimacy/relationship orientation and heightened emotional/relational sensitivity. Shelley Taylor, a world-renowned expert on stress and health, argues that, based on our differing brains and hormones, men respond to stress in assertive, aggressive ways ("flight or fight") whereas women's biology leads them to connect with others, especially other women. She calls this the female "tending instinct."[34] She mar-

---

[31]Raymond H. Baillargeon, Mark Zoccolillo, and Kate Keenan, "Gender Differences in Physical Aggression: A Prospective Population-Based Survey of Children Before and After 2 Years of Age," *Developmental Psychology* 43 (2007): 13-26; Campbell, *A Mind of Her Own*, pp. 104-9; Eleanore E. Maccoby, *The Two Sexes: Growing Up Apart, Coming Together* (Cambridge, Mass.: Belknap Press, 1998); R. C. Savin-Williams, *Adolescence: An Ethnological Perspective* (New York: Springer Verlag, 1980).

[32]R. F. Baumeister and M. R. Leary, "The Need to Belong: Desire for Interpersonal Attachments as a Fundamental Human Motivation," *Psychological Bulletin* 117 (1995): 497-529; Savin-Williams, *Adolescence*; Sally Helgesen, *The Female Advantage: Womens Ways of Leadership*, rev. ed. (New York: Doubleday, 1995).

[33]On the relevance of male brain structure to aggression and dominance, see Brizendine, *The Female Brain*, pp. 5-6. For research studies on the relevance of lower serotonin to heightened aggression and lower impulse control in males, see Campbell, *A Mind of Her Own*, pp. 82-90. On the role of testosterone to lower empathy, greater aggression, and increased physical play, see Baron-Cohen, *The Essential Difference*, pp. 95-109; Rebecca Knickmeyer, Simon Baron-Cohen, Peter Raggatt and Kevin Taylor, "Foetal Testosterone, Social Relationships, and Restricted Interests in Children," *Journal of Child Psychology and Psychiatry* 46 (2005): 198–210; R. C. Knickmeyer et al., "Gender-typed Play and Amniotic Testosterone," *Developmental Psychology* 41 (2005): 517; V. L. Pasterski et al., "Prenatal Hormones and Postnatal Socialization by Parents as Determinants of Male-typical Toy Play in Girls with Congenital Adrenal Hyperplasia," *Child Development* 76 (2005): 264-78.

[34]Shelley Taylor, "Evolution, but No Revolution: The 'Tend and Befriend' Theory of Stress and Coping," *Psychology of Women Quarterly* 27 (2003): 194–95. Gurion similarly summarizes the

shals much evidence to demonstrate that both genders have the capacity to nurture, but biology has given females a significantly enhanced capacity. Simon-Baron Cohen, one of the world's leading experts on autism, similarly and succinctly states the female gender distinction: "The female brain is hard-wired for empathy."[35] Abundant research demonstrates that women are more focused on social and family relationships and place greater value on them than men.[36] For instance, one research study found that boys were fifty times more competitive than girls, whereas girls were twenty times more likely to share and take turns.[37] Furthermore, females do seem to have superior nurturing abilities, as evidenced by studies in the developing world that found the greatest factor in infant mortality was mother mortality.[38] Females also score higher on tests measuring empathy quotient, and studies from widely varying cultures reveal they also score higher on tests that measure the ability to accurately read emotion in facial gestures.[39] Females' greater relational orientation, nurturing and emotional sensitivity are biologically based, and are particularly the result of greater levels of estrogen and oxytocin.[40] They are probably also the result of brain

biologically-based female difference, calling it "the intimacy imperative," *The Wonder of Girls*, pp. 52-63.

[35]Baron-Cohen, *The Essential Difference*, p. 1.

[36]For two fascinating secular developments of the value of the unique female psyche and values, particularly the manner in which women tend to be relationship oriented (as opposed to the male task, power, hierarchy orientation), see Carol Gilligan, *In a Different Voice: Psychological Theory and Women's Development* (Cambridge, Mass.: Harvard University Press, 1993) and Helgesen, *The Female Advantage*.

[37]Baron-Cohen, *The Essential Difference*, p. 30.

[38]Campbell, *A Mind of Her Own*, p. 53.

[39]Baron-Cohen, *The Essential Difference*, p. 32; Darlington, *The Female Brain*, pp. 107-26. We cannot simply attribute these differences to social conditioning. Tests conducted with newborns as well as infants reveals that girls are more relational and emotionally astute. Newborn infant girls fixate on human faces, whereas newborn boys tend to fixate on inanimate objects. One-year-old girls looked at their mother's faces ten to twenty times more than boys the same age, and much more accurately read their mothers' nonverbal signs of approval or disapproval: J. Connellan et al., "Sex Differences in Human Neonatal Social Perception," *Infant Behavior and Development* 23 (2001): 113-18; Svetlana Lutchmaya and Simon Baron-Cohen, "Human Sex Differences in Social and Non-Social Looking Preferences at 12 Months of Age," *Infant Behavior & Development* 25 (2002): 319-25.

[40]Brizendine, *The Female Brain*, pp. 18-26, 36-37; Gurion, *The Wonder of Girls*, pp. 26-96; Kerstin Uvnäs-Moberg, *The Oxytocin Factor: Tapping the Hormone of Calm, Love, and Healing* (Cambridge, Mass.: Da Capo Press, 2003), pp. xvi, 7, 67-68; Shelley Taylor, "Tend and Befriend: Biobehavioral Bases of Affiliation Under Stress," *Current Directions in Psychological*

structure differences, particularly the greater use of the right hemisphere of the brain in women.[41]

These gender differences should make it patently clear that God has made women and men beautifully different. Husbands and wives equally and critically need each others' unique gender traits and strengths to fulfill God's calling for marriage. We would now like briefly to flesh out the marital tasks in three areas by illustrating from our own marriage. In describing the three overarching tasks of marriage in terms of designer love, designer work and designer parenting, we intend to communicate that husband and wife jointly and mutually enter into this adventure. Husband and wife together must customize (personally apply) biblical principles to their own situation, strengths and weaknesses in order to build their marriage, family and ministry.

DESIGNER LOVE: CRAFTING THE RELATIONSHIP

In terms of the marriage relationship itself, our mission is to deepen our *one-flesh* bond and stimulate each other to deeper levels of Christlikeness, so that we will glorify God by demonstrating more and more of his character, individually and collectively (cf. Eph 5:25-32). Allender and Longman put this well, "Marriages grow as each spouse invites the other to be more like Jesus Christ."[42] The irony of marital intimacy is that we must look to Christ, not to each other, to meet our deepest needs and to fill our soul. Thus, I (Steve) am not the priest of our home, Christ is! God is our creator, redeemer and sanctifier. Paradoxically, as we individually grow in intimacy with Christ, we grow in our intimacy with each other. We also grow in our ability to sharpen each other.

So where do gender differences come to play in this joint mission? As a husband, I feel my love for Celestia is largely expressed through my initiation of support and taking active responsibility for our relationship and Celestia's physical well-being. Throughout our marriage, starting with the first night of our honeymoon, God impressed on me that as a loving husband I should initiate times of devotion and prayer.

Science 15 (2006): 273–77.
[41]Darlington, *The Female Brain*, pp. 107-26; Gurion, *The Wonder of Girls*, pp. 26-96.
[42]Allender and Longman, *Intimate Allies*, p. 143.

When other challenges emerged, such as finding a new church or dealing with health or financial emergencies, I initiated and took unique responsibility, all the while acting in partnership with Celestia. I presented my plans to her and we discussed them, prayed over them and often modified them together. What if with a given plan or decision we haven't been able to agree, even after lengthy discussion and reflection? On those rare moments (something is very wrong if this happens frequently) I have taken responsibility for making a final decision. This has occurred two times in thirty years. As we reflected on these incidents Celestia told me that both times I demonstrated a love for her and the Lord that prompted her to trust in God's direction through me. Yet this does not render Celestia's role a passive one. I greatly need her feminine wisdom, coaching and even her bold rebuke.[43]

I (Celestia) have sought to craft our relationship in many ways. I seek to "receive well" Steve's initiation and care. I have a strong personality and lead naturally, often feeling more decisive and confident than Steve. I have learned to respect and value his loving leadership. I have learned that my verbal affirmation and support is critical for him. He sees himself reflected through my eyes. I must consistently use "magic eyes" that see him as the man God created him to be. "Receiving well" was reflected two years ago when we both felt led to move out of the suburbs into inner Phoenix. We spent countless hours talking, praying and surveying neighborhoods. After a year's search, Steve believed we should buy a particular house. I tried to get excited but couldn't and remained ambivalent. However, I supported his desire to buy the home. Upon

---

[43]I'll clarify this in Celestia's own words: "I love Steve well and help us glorify God together by coaching him emotionally and relationally. He loves as deeply and passionately as I do, but my female brain most often perceives people's needs and vulnerabilities in ways that Steve's does not." Thus, I am thankful that Celestia loves God and me enough to coach me boldly and persistently. She did this on a return flight after an exhausting and nerve racking trip to the Mayo Clinic. I quickly became frustrated that the overhead bins were overflowing, and I had no where to put my briefcase. Having paid a premium for the flights to begin with, I was beginning to fume. In my frustration, I didn't even notice the flight attendant trying to help me as I tossed my briefcase aside. Within minutes Celestia respectfully confronted me with my loss of perspective and insensitivity. She had made several observations that I had missed. She then gently but boldly explained how inappropriate and discouraging my behavior had been, and gently made a few wise suggestions for dealing with my frustrations in the future. Though her comments stung deeply, I knew that she had hit the bull's eye of truth. She loved me (and God) too much to let such behavior go unchallenged.

moving in I immediately shifted gears, making plans to remodel and create the warm environment that would enhance our witness and ministry in this community. I chose to love what Steve loved in this new home and God has blessed me with joy in this space. Finally, I craft our intimacy by providing the physical and domestic support that Steve loves—balancing my time in order to create a "prepared place" in which he feels respected and loved. Every time he walks in the door I want him to experience my care.

DESIGNER WORK: BUILDING VOCATIONS/MINISTRIES

Our mission in building vocations is to develop and steward our God-given strengths so that we can serve others and meet our family's needs. This aspect of marriage often raises questions regarding whose career should take precedence and who should make the most money. We believe such questions don't get at the heart of the issue because they presuppose that one spouse's career must take precedent. They also do injustice to the *one-flesh* nature of marriage in which everything is defined corporately. Moses' description of leaving, cleaving and becoming *one flesh* in Genesis 2:24 pictures a death to the single-life experience/identity and the conception of a new inviolable family and identity. This new *one-flesh* creation should be the reality that shapes and guides all life choices, including hobbies, friendships, family budget and careers.

One of secular feminism's fatal (and most destructive) errors is its unmitigated emphasis on the wife's own individual fulfillment, particularly with respect to her career. To some extent traditional patriarchy, for different reasons, can have a similar effect, using career to weaken marital oneness.[44] Therefore, the most helpful guiding career question is, *what career choices will allow us as a couple to best serve our family and allow us together to best steward the gifts God has given us?* And the answer to this two-part question and the issues surrounding it are rarely static but will change over the stages of life. While both hus-

---

[44]This can happen through the doctrine of "separate spheres" in which the husband alone works outside the home, making his vocational world his alone, separated from his wife and her exclusively domestic world.

band and wife have separate strengths and skills, they should prayerfully strive to develop and use their respective gifts together, each supporting and empowering the other. All career choices are for the collective benefit of family to the glory of Christ.

What has this philosophy looked like for us? Shortly before we got
married, I (Celestia) changed my major from architecture to home
economics/education in light of our joint calling to pastoral ministry. I
then worked full time as a teacher to put Steve through seminary. Upon
graduation, I was grateful to be able to stay home and focus on our
young children. During this stage of family life, Steve provided financially for us. Once all our children were in school I felt God's call to
professional counseling. Steve emotionally and financially supported my
graduate education by continuing to work full time until we left for his
doctoral studies in England. Upon our return to the United States a few
years later, I maintained a part-time private practice until our children
graduated from high school. During these years, Steve had been transi-
tioning his research focus to gender, sexuality and abuse, so we could
more closely work and minister together. Now that we are empty nest-
ers, we both work full time in separate careers in separate offices, but
our lives and work are quite interwoven. I am a counselor with a mind of
a theologian, and Steve is a professor with a heart of a clinician.

In keeping with our understanding of servant headship, even when
we have both had full-time paychecks Steve has sought to cover most of
our fixed family expenses from his income. This takes much of the
weight off of Celestia's shoulders. Ironically, Celestia's counseling income is considerably more than my (Steve's) teaching income. Does
that impugn my masculinity? Not in the least! It is delightful for me to
help her passionately live out God's call upon her life and watch her
succeed. Today, it is particularly fulfilling for us to use our respective
gifts and training to write, speak and lead together!

DESIGNER PARENTING: RAISING CHILDREN

In succinct terms, our joint parenting mission is to create, nurture and
develop life in all its fullness (Gen 1:28; Ps 127). From start to finish
this is a joint enterprise. Celestia and I have often described our parent-

ing as "tag-team wrestling." We have spent countless hours over the years praying, reflecting and strategizing on how we can meet our children's needs and nurture them in the Lord. At the same time our individual effectiveness with a given parental task varies from child to child and event to event. Our unique gender directs these tasks in differing ways. Celestia was obviously the one who nursed our children. Her female brain and chemistry has given her unique nurturing skills, which was the primary reason we purposed for her to be a stay-at-home mom while our children were young. Her attunement to their physical and emotional needs continues to bless them even as they have grown into adulthood. A significant aspect of Celestia's nurturing expression is seen in the way she has created a warm, loving environment through her care of the home, through her engaged presence when the children arrived home from school, to the notes of encouragement she still leaves for us. A young woman who lived with us for several years after experiencing the trauma of a father who abandoned her family describes it well: "Celestia has an incredible ability, in large and small ways, to create a home that gives the message 'somebody cares about you here.'" None of these activities are exclusively maternal, but Celestia is able to carry them out in a manner that reflects her unique female attunement and nurturing.

In our home we live by the motto "we work and play together." Steve certainly assists with the physical care of the home even cooking at times. We both discipline and instruct our children in spiritual matters. When I think of Steve's protective role in parenting, I think specifically of the adolescent years. Beginning with puberty, our girls needed even more of his undivided attention. The time that he spent protecting and providing for them communicated to them a sense of worth and value that was a stabilizing corrective to the erratic attention of adolescent boys and our culture! Additionally, the relationship he established with their subsequent boyfriends was another form of protection. He would meet with them on the front end of relationship and clarify our guidelines for dating our daughter. These young men were then asked to articulate a plan for sexual purity in the relationship. Both of our daughters reported that while their boyfriends liked Steve they were afraid of him. Steve would often smile and say, "That must mean I'm doing a good job!" Steve's ongoing interest in and support of our daughters' relationships served as another circle of protection for them. Similarly, in fathering our son, Steve's initiation of support, guidance and correction in Luke's adolescence have been critically significant. Luke and I are the most similar in temperament (minus the testosterone, of course) and had consistently enjoyed a close relationship. When he grew into midadolescence, I became acutely aware of needing Steve's involvement and backup. My relationship with Luke began to change, and suddenly he required his father's voice and strength. Several times I would declare to Steve, "I'm just not strong enough for him. He won't take me seriously enough. He needs a dad's strength and he needs it right now!" I was dependent upon Steve to be there. By God's grace he was.

We would like to conclude and summarize this chapter on marital roles by sharing Celestia's "Millennium Mission" that she wrote in 1999, just days before the new millennium. I am incredibly proud of her wise, godly articulation of the unique ways she as a Christian woman purposed to live out the various spheres of her life in partnership with me, to honor our Lord.

My mission is to live with love and integrity.
To profoundly impact the lives of others for God's kingdom.
I will do this as I make careful and calculated choices,
consistent with my deepest values.
I value my relationship with Jesus Christ and will seek
to balance my time in such a way as to prioritize that relationship.
This requires a quiet, focused time each day to
journal and reflect on God's words to me.
I will maintain a mentor in my life to guide,
support and offer truth.
I will live each principle that I teach so I do not develop
a dissonance between who I think I am and who I really am.
I will remember every day, the ease at which a heart can self-deceive.

I value my relationship with my husband.
I will make choices about my time that consider him first.

I will schedule daily time at the beginning and
end of each day to reflect with him.
I will endeavor to share every feeling, thought and
dream as I become aware of its significance.
I will work to make his needs and dreams as
important to me as they are to him.
I will seek to know him and to accept the man I find him to be.
I will offer the best of me.

I value my relationship with my children.
I will prioritize their emotional needs at the
same level as their physical needs.
I will remain faithful to prioritize my time in order
to be predictably available to them.
I will pray for them and with them on a daily basis
for God to be unleashed in their lives.
I will, with God's help, harness my fears about their safety
so I can say "Yes!" to God's call on their lives.
I will encourage risk-taking and passionate choices
in their service of God.
I will remember that they are ultimately His.

I value my relationship with others.
I will be respectful and kind when I do not feel
like being respectful and kind.
I will hold onto truth, but not at the expense of grace.
I will endeavor to set boundaries that protect my relationships
with people God has ordained to be in my life.
I will seek God's balance of mercy.

CONCLUDING DIALOGUE

In many respects this chapter confirmed for us the need and value of this book project. At first blush, it seemed that we would be able to predict accurately the other couple's response on marriage roles. After all, differing marital role distinctions lie at the heart of the egalitarian/complementarian divide, so our chapters seemed rather predictable. In fact, we often agreed, in both theory and daily practice, on many aspects of roles that we could not have anticipated. On the other hand, many of our disagreements were also unexpected and enlightening. This reminds us of the danger of labels and the value of honest dialogue.

Areas of agreement. We identified over a dozen major points of agreement in the Spencers' and the Tracys' respective chapters. In terms of foundational principles that effect marital roles and decision making, both couples affirmed that men and women are equally gifted by God; marriage creates a wholly new existence in which both husband and wife experience a "death" to their former single life; husbands and wives share a joint "marital mission"; Christ, not the husband, is the priest of the home; and the husband and wife rule together as equals. (The latter two principles set the Tracys apart from many hierarchical nonegalitarians.) While there were obviously significant areas of disagreement regarding specific marital roles, both couples agreed that when roles are defined most broadly, they are identical for men and women. As the Tracys stated, men and women are both "to glorify God by using their gifts and other resources to advance the kingdom." Both couples desire to avoid making marital roles overly rigid, and emphasized the need for ongoing dialogue and adjustment. For instance, the Tracys appreciated the Spencers' assertion that "as long as the couple keeps in dialogue, roles can be adjusted." And the Spencers appreciated the Tracys' statement, "Husband and wife together must customize (personally apply) biblical principles to their own situation, strengths and weaknesses."

Furthermore, both couples are against the "separate spheres" concept and agree that the wife's sphere is not restricted to the home. Both are also opposed to Aristotle's view of women that has wrongly dominated Christianity (women are by essence soft, passive and intellectually inferior, and thus have a rigidly distinct and inferior role).

While some unexpected differences emerged in terms of parenting, both couples emphasized the importance of joint or coparenting and gave personal examples of how they had done this within their own families. Though the Tracys and the Spencers had noticeably different models of decision making in the presence of irreconcilable differences of opinion, the Tracys strongly affirmed the Spencers' first criteria for decision making: "What would most advance God's kingdom." We all agree that this is *the* foundational decision-making question. The Tracys also found the Spencers' criteria for decision making to be both biblical and helpful, and have employed all five principles in their own marriage. The Tracys also resonated with the Spencers' steps for dealing with marital conflict, and felt it was perhaps the most helpful section of their chapter (ask whether to overlook or pursue a conflict, look at the root issue to understand the conflict, deal with conflict as quickly as possible, persevere). Perhaps the greatest number of agreements came in the area of careers. Both couples agree that neither spouse's career goals should take precedence over the other's; whose career gets priority might change over life; the amount of financial income does not define masculinity or femininity and based on gender one sex should not automatically earn more than the other.

Areas of disagreement. Though we had not entirely anticipated this, our strongest disagreements revolved around the nature of gender itself, particularly the existence of innate male/female differences and, if they exist, their relevance to marital roles. As we saw in the previous chapter, differing hermeneutical approaches were foundational to these disagreements. The value and place of social science research also emerged as a significant methodological difference. The Tracys build their model of gender differentiation by, first of all, appealing to the creation account to demonstrate that with the creation of the first man and woman, God purposefully built innate differences into the two genders so they could more fully and distinctly image him. They surveyed specific biblical data on fathers, mothers, husbands, and wives, to demonstrate that these innate gender differences were designed by God to allow husbands and wives to make some differing contributions to the "mutual marriage mission." Their hypothesis is that "form follows function." Thus, the Tracys devoted considerable attention to science/social science research that they argue strongly documents innate biological gender differences, particularly male assertiveness/aggression and focus on power and status over relationship, and female intimacy/relationship orientation and heightened emotional/relational sensitivity. Furthermore, the Tracys argue that the scientific data regarding innate gender differences harmonizes beautifully with their understanding of the biblical data that assigns some unique gender tasks to men and to women. They define *role* as "the unique part that a man or woman plays in carrying out the joint tasks of marriage—unlike the Spencers who define *role* simply as a "task or function." Thus, the Tracys place gender uniqueness in the context of a couple's "corporate responsibilities and mutual mission." So, they believe that their model creates greater marital unity and beneficial complementation, for each partner brings unique strengths to the common marital tasks. They would see the Spencers' model as failing to account for and benefit from gender complementation, such as seen in the Spencers' example of parenting based on taking distinct shifts, with the parent off shift not interfering with the other.

The Spencers, on the other hand, recognize biological differences between men and women but see these as incidental. That is, they are wholly material and unable to define the spiritual dimension or dictate who will lead and who will follow, defining neither tasks nor leadership. Instead, they see gender differences as God creating two "others" so that each learns to love an "other" as preparation to love the entirely "Other." They see the Bible as promoting complete equality of role and function, tracing these back to pre-Fall Genesis, arguing that Genesis does not contain gender differences in its commands to rule. They believe, since the Fall all traditions are fallen and, therefore suspect, couples should therefore not settle for society's roles or even the Christian culture's roles for themselves. They believe the right and the left have politically dictated and directed definitions of roles, and Christians should not be "conformed to this world." The Spencers see roles correctly and primarily dictated by each spouse's gifting. They believe that God intends "shared leadership, husband and wife lead[ing] from the basis of their spiritual gifts, their strengths, where Christ is the only ruling high priest." In fact, they see Celestia's "strong personality" and ability to "lead naturally," matched by Steve's selfless willingness to bike thirty miles to provide transportation for her as mutual leadership, as they themselves try to practice it, each trying to defer to the other, each leading the other (e.g., Celestia confronting Steve on the plane flight seems the kind of mutual care and encouragement in the full sense that includes correction). Thus, both in the church and in the home, the Spencers maintain that leadership should be chosen by "spiritual gifts and natural gifting and education and godly characteristics," different gifts kicking in to lead or protect or caretake the family at different times. Therefore, they see psychological and sociological studies as useful only when helpful. The Spencers identify five resources for decision making: (1) spiritual gifts, (2) natural and learned abilities, (3) equal division of labor, (4) accepted responsibility, (5) time factors. They will not move forward without consensus, since they believe God intended joint rule for both spouses. The Spencers see both spouses as responsible for providing the family sustenance and see traditional definitions as unworkable if the man is not physically capable of protecting/providing and woman not gifted in intuitive sensibility. They also recognize that, along with the similarities listed above, some of these values may transcend both models and be characteristic of Christian marriage itself. The Tracys assert that normally, by God's design, women play the more nurturing role but note that there are occasional exceptions to this principle based on individual circumstances. The Spencers, however, believe that males and females can be equally nurturing but it may be expressed in different ways.

Chapter Four

MARRIAGE
AND INTIMACY

STEVE AND CELESTIA TRACY'S
VIEWPOINT

SPIRITUAL FOUNDATION

> God's relationship with humans is one of intimate bonding . . . all hu-
> man intimacies are "rehearsals" for the ultimate reunion of humans with
> their Creator. Stated inversely, we might say that all humans are bond-
> ing beings, such that their yearning for intimacy is an internal magnet
> which draws them, often unwittingly, toward God, for whose intimate
> relationship they are created.[1]

Donald Joy beautifully articulates the ultimate basis for all human
intimacy, including marital sexual intimacy. We long for intimacy because God made us relational beings just as he is a relational being. Our
creation therefore, ultimately drives us to God himself. In a culture
obsessed with sex and fixated on personal sexual pleasure as the ultimate purpose for relationships, it is essential that we step back and get
the bigger picture. Contemporary notions to the contrary, neither Hugh
Hefner nor Hollywood created sex, God did! And he had a wonderful
purpose for doing so. The nature and foundation of human intimacy is
seen most clearly and succinctly in the creation account. From Genesis
1:26-28 we can draw three truths about intimacy: (1) God is relational,
and exists in intimate relationship within his own divine being;[2] (2) our
specific gender as male or female flows out of our creation in God's

---

[1]Donald M. Joy, *Bonding: Relationships in the Image of God*, rev. ed. (Nappanee, Ind.: Evangel
Publishing House, 1997), p. ix.

[2]Gen 1:26 reads, "Then God said, "Let *us* make humankind in *our* image, according to *our* likeness" (italics added). For an exegetical defense of the view that the plural pronouns "us" and
"our" refer in some manner to relationality (some call it "fullness") within the Divine being,
see D. J. A. Clines, "The Image of God in Man," *Tyndale Bulletin* 19 (1968): 62-69; Victor P.
Hamilton, *The Book of Genesis Chapters 1-17* (Grand Rapids: Eerdmans, 1990), pp. 132-34;
Gerhard Hasel, "The Meaning of 'Let Us' in Gn 1:26," *Andrews University Seminary Studies*
13 (1975): 58-66.

image.[3] Our gender as male or female gives us the capacity and longing for intimate relationships;[4] (3) Marriage gives us a unique (but not the only) matrix in which to express godlike intimacy, for it provides one of the most intimate types of human interaction (sexual intercourse), which in turn results in one of the most godlike activities—the creation of life in the very image of God.[5] In short, humans are relational beings created by a relational God and thus made for intimacy. Sexual intercourse is God's design and creation. This is why sexual intercourse must always be appreciated and enjoyed in the context of the marital bond, a lifelong covenant relationship. Biblically, marriage is created by a covenant, forming a new *one-flesh* entity in which all of life (finances, dreams, souls, bodies) are shared (Gen 2:24-25). Thus, while sex does not create marriage, it should never be divorced from it, for "sexual union expresses, reinforces, and reenacts the marital covenant itself."[6]

We would like to share with you the "love template" God has taught us. In our model, sexual oneness flows out of relational bondedness. Thus, dynamic sex in marriage is a designer sex that does not come from technique or an emphasis on the body, but is instead the spontaneous and natural result and expression of oneness. In marriage God intends for couples increasingly to know and be known by each other in order to build a deep spiritual, emotional, relational and sexual intimacy. This helps us understand the beautiful biblical expression for marital sexual intercourse found in Genesis 4:1—"Adam *knew* Eve his wife; and she conceived" (KJV, italics added). This metaphorical expression for sex comes from the Hebrew verb *yāda*ʿ, which has a literal meaning of "to

---

[3]Gen 1:27 reads, "God created humankind in his image, in the image . . . male and female." In other words, human creation in the image of God is described or explained as the creation of two different genders.

[4]On the way sexuality is beautifully designed by God to drive humans to intimate relationship, see Lewis B. Smedes, *Sex for Christians* (Grand Rapids: Eerdmans, 1976), pp. 32-33; see also Stanley J. Grenz, "The Purpose of Sex: Toward a Theological Understanding of Human Sexuality," *Crux* 26 (1990): 27-34.

[5]Gen 1:28 reads, "God blessed them, and God said to them, 'Be fruitful and multiply, and fill the earth.'" This verse gives divine sanction of sexual intercourse in marriage in two clear ways. (1) God sanctions sex by blessing the couple in the context of the command to be fruitful. (2) God sanctions sexual intercourse by commanding Adam and Eve to be fruitful and multiply (essentially a command to engage in sex since that was the one and only way they could obey the command).

[6]Steven Tracy, "The Marriage Mystery," *Christianity Today*, January 7, 2002, p. 63.

know." This suggests that the physical sexual union should flow from and express a deeper nonphysical union. We can picture our intimacy model as follows:

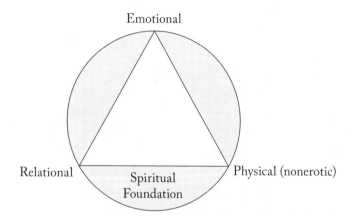

Our model emphasizes spiritual intimacy as the foundation of the entire marital relationship. This means each partner is committed to his or her individual spiritual growth and oneness with Christ, which then gives each the supernatural desire and ability to love the other. I can only unselfishly love and honor Steve, respecting his often very different needs, if I am filled with the Holy Spirit, living and breathing a kingdom culture, and not the narcissistic "it's all about me" culture of the world. Germinating out of this spiritual foundation are the three dimensions of bonding: emotional, physical and relational. Therefore, as these three dimensions are strengthened, sexual expression becomes more natural, healthy and dynamic. We would like to invite you to take our challenge—instead of focusing on new sex techniques or the size and shape of your body or body parts,[7] attend instead to the quality of the following three dimensions of intimacy in your marriage. Enhance and deepen these and see what happens to your sex life!

---

[7]For candid personal accounts of the extreme and destructive emphasis in our culture on physical perfection attained through cosmetic surgery, see Virginia L. Blum, *Flesh Wounds: The Culture of Cosmetic Surgery* (Los Angeles: University of California Press, 2003) and Alex Kuczynski, *Beauty Junkies: Inside Our $15 Billion Obsession with Cosmetic Surgery* (New York: Doubleday, 2006).

BONDING: THREE DIMENSIONS

Emotional

You do not just live in a world but a world lives in you.
You are a world.
Each carries his world on his back the way a
Snail carries his shell.[8]

Emotional intimacy is the ability to know and express (communicate) your feelings to your spouse and have them understood and validated.[9] Clearly, this necessitates both partners' commitment to emotional health and cannot be established individually. Romans 12:15 tells us to "Rejoice with those who rejoice, weep with those who weep." This involves working hard to make a deep emotional connection with each other. It involves a willingness to share and an ability to trust and be vulnerable (see Jas 5:16). It also involves a commitment to active listening. "The purposes of a man's heart are deep waters, but a man of understanding draws them out" (Prov 20:5 NIV).

Steve and I are writing this chapter in the mountains of Colorado. We have just returned from an exhilarating but demanding ministry trip in East Africa. Our recent drive here was the first time we have been privately alone with each other in nearly a month. We were more physically exhausted than we realized. The law of survival dictates that the energy around emotional connecting is the first to go. We have now been together for five days, and have had to work deliberately to reestablish our emotional and spiritual connection (with God and then each other). We could not effectively begin this chapter without our emotional and spiritual bond back in place. Emotion is the conduit

---

[8]Frederick Buechner, *Telling the Truth: The Gospel as Tragedy, Comedy & Fairy Tale* (New York: HarperCollins, 1977), p. 3.

[9]Social science research shows that healthy communication—the accurate expression of one's own feelings and needs as well as an understanding and validation of those feelings and needs by one's partner, is strongly correlated with marital and sexual satisfaction. Daniel M. Purnine, and Michael P. Carey, "Interpersonal Communication and Sexual Adjustment: The Roles of Understanding and Agreement," *Journal of Consulting and Clinical Psychology* 65 (1997): 1017-25; Howard J. Markman, Frank J. Floyd and Scott M. Stanley, "Prevention of Marital Distress: A Longitudinal Investigation," *Journal of Consulting and Clinical Psychology* 56 (1988): 210-17.

through which we experience, not only each other, but God himself. Frederick Buechner in his reflections on Isaiah 53 states:

> To see a man weep is not a comely sight,
> Especially this man whom we want to be stronger and
> Braver than a man,
> And the impulse is to turn from him as we
> Turn from anybody who weeps
> Because the sight of real tears,
> Painful and disfiguring,
> Forces us to look to their source where we
> Do not choose to look because
> Where his tears come from,
> Our tears also come from.[10]

Nonverbal communication. Research shows that just 7 percent of our communication comes from mere words.[11] Nonverbal expression such as gestures, posture, voice pitch, speed and intensity make up the remaining 93 percent! That is a startling statistic to read in an era of instant messaging and e-mail. This speaks of our sophisticated design by a triune God for knowing and being known. We are designed and equipped for deep connection and our personal well-being depends on it. Unlike the rest of creation, this is uniquely true for us as men and women. For instance, our cat Kimia is most content at night to sit beside me on her soft throw. She declares her complete satisfaction with our relationship with a rumbling purr. She doesn't care to really know me. She doesn't stir with a quiet discontent at the emotional separation between us. She doesn't feel lonely or displaced at the end of her day when she cannot recount her exploits and victories—the birds she caught or the neighbors she visited. She doesn't feel agitated and worthless when I, or other loved family members, do not prioritize time with her. She is just a cat.

However, in stark contrast, we are driven to connect as people. Our postmodern cultural obsession with the body and sex is an example of

---

[10]Buechner, *Telling the Truth*, p. 37.
[11]Albert Mehrabian and Susan R. Ferris, "Inference of Attitudes from Nonverbal Communication in Two Channels," *Journal of Consulting Psychology* 31 (1967): 248-52.

our misdirected, but *desperate* need for intimacy. This connection will either be a healthy and real intimacy, or it will be a false intimacy. It will be either an unstoppable sexual compulsion or a satisfying and meaningful connection that, in marriage, is designed to be imaged and expressed through sexual oneness.[12]

Verbal communication. Emotional verbal communication is the ability and desire to put our inner world into words. It involves a commitment to live in marriage like Christ lived on this earth, "full of grace and truth" (Jn 1:14). We are often instructed in Scripture to speak the truth and to speak it in love.[13] This cannot be done apart from emotional maturity and godliness. It is important to note what honest and respectful emotional communication is and is not. It is not venting. Venting is a rash and reckless spewing of negative and angry emotion that disregards the spouse.[14] Venting is for the benefit of the "spewer" and not for the edification of the hearer. In other words, venting is for my own emotional relief, not Steve's. Venting can be destructive and must be rooted out of our marriages. However, emotional dishonesty is also sin because it is a lie that impedes oneness. Intimacy is predicated on truly knowing and being known. Hence, it is our responsibility to communicate honestly but respectfully what is in our heart to our spouse: joy, guilt, regrets, pleasure, love, commitments and fears. All that is inside of us needs to be shared so we can understand and respond to each other at the deepest level—who we truly are, not what we pretend to be or what we wish we were.[15] Otherwise, a creeping separateness will slowly erode

---

[12]For an excellent discussion of sexual compulsion as false intimacy, a sinful and misguided pseudo intimacy, which avoids the cost of real intimacy, see Harry W. Schaumburg, *False Intimacy: Understanding the Struggle of Sexual Addiction*, rev. ed. (Colorado Springs: NavPress, 1997).

[13]Prov 12:18-22; 28:23; 31:26; Eccles 12:10-11; 2 Cor 5:11-13; 6:6-7; Eph 4:15, 25, 29.

[14]Scripture warns against the danger (to others and to oneself) of verbal venting, that is, of speaking rashly. Inevitably, this is done with little or no concern for others. For instance, see Prov 12:16-18; 15:28; 18:4-7; Eccles 5:2; cf. Prov 21:23. When we speak of rash and angry venting, we are not addressing the meaningful sharing of deeper frustrations and pain. Emotional communication involves the sharing of all primary emotion with the purpose of knowing and being known. However, reckless anger is a secondary emotion that is often a psychological defense that protects us from our truer pain. Therefore, the spewing of this anger is not a part of true intimacy but instead will in time diminish the safety and closeness within the relationship.

[15]While the distinction between unhealthy sharing of one's negative emotions and healthy emo-

our relationship. Again, verbal emotional communication is to be done for the edification of the other and the good of the relationship. Does this take work and time? Absolutely, but the rewards are great.[16]

Physical (nonerotic touch)

A kiss can be a comma, a question mark,
Or an exclamation point.
That's basic spelling that every lover ought to know
—Mistinguett

Physical intimacy is nonerotic affectionate touch that spouses give to each other. Tender touch is a powerful and essential way to communicate love and deepen the relational bond. Nonerotic affectionate touch says, "I value you," versus, "I want something from you"; "I enjoy and love you," versus, "I need you." Our modern American culture is very uncomfortable with nonerotic, affectionate touch. By our cultural standards, the frequent biblical accounts of adult friends and family members, especially men with men, embracing and kissing each other seems strange and makes us uncomfortable.[17] But nonerotic affectionate touch is a powerful and critical means of communicating love and deepening relational connection. It is also an indirect yet critical factor in marital sexual union.[18] For instance, for most women, there is a direct correla-

---

tional honesty may seem to be rather subjective, the key is one's motivation. The former is selfishly motivated merely for one's own emotional relief while the latter is motivated by a desire to deepen the relationship, even at the risk of saying things that are painful to say and painful to hear. In Scripture we see this kind of healthy emotional sharing with respect to building intimacy with God. For instance, many of the Psalms are painful laments to God about the psalmists' fears, frustrations, disappointments and unmet longings. It was because the psalmists refused to be satisfied with a shallow (nonintimate) relationship with God that they poured out their hearts to him. See, for instance, Ps 10:1; 13:1-5; 22:1-3, 19-22; 35:17-22; 38:1-22; 42:1-11; 55:1-5; 60:1-12; 74:1-2, 10-12; 79:1-13; 88:1-13.

[16]For example, research has shown that even short-term education/training in marital communication improved couples' self-reports of marital and sexual satisfaction compared to a control group of couples who did not receive the education/training. Alvin Cooper and Cal D. Stoltenberg, "Comparison of a Sexual Enhancement and a Communication Training Program on Sexual Satisfaction," *Journal of Counseling Psychology* 34 (1987): 309-14.

[17]Gen 29:13; 33:4; 45:15; 48:10; Ex 4:27; Ruth 1:9, 14; 1 Sam 20:41; Lk 7:38; Acts 20:37; Rom 16:16.

[18]Physical affection from the husband is also critically important for creating a healthy sexual relationship because research has shown that one of the greatest factors that affects a woman's sexual desire is how she feels about her body, and roughly 2/3 of Christian women surveyed re-

tion between a husband's tender affection initiated toward his wife and her sense of self-worth and beauty. This is particularly true in our pornography-saturated culture. This physical (nonsexual) energy by a man toward a woman redeems her sense of worth. In our marriage, Steve offers me the same high levels of affectionate touch independent of my physical condition. I have many memories of his tender care during our "sensate" time together that followed weeks and at times months of postsurgical recuperation.

Recent scientific research shows God's intricate design of our bodies in this bonding process. In particular, research on the hormone oxytocin shows that one of the primary means by which oxytocin production is stimulated is through physical touch.[19] Hence it has been dubbed "the cuddle hormone." Oxytocin has also been shown to stimulate social bonding as well as trust.[20] Oxytocin is also critically related to sexual intercourse, for oxytocin increases libido and prepares the body for sexual intercourse. Sexual arousal and intercourse also increase levels of oxytocin, creating a healthy self-reinforcing "love cycle" (see diagram).[21]

Unfortunately, in our culture we often move straight to the erotic and bypass or even demean nonerotic, nurturing physical touch. Consider for instance our cultural schizophrenia regarding the female breast. When it comes to erotic images of breasts, there are seemingly no limits on their exposure. Female breasts are exposed on national television for the largest single viewing audience of the year (the Super Bowl), yet even discreet breast feeding of infants has resulted in women being arrested or removed from public areas. Nonerotic touch is often

---

ported they are negatively affected sexually by one or more aspects related to their body image. Archibald D. Hart, Catherine Hart Weber and Debra Taylor, *The Secrets of Eve: Understanding the Mystery of Female Sexuality* (Nashville: Word, 1998), pp. 71, 76-77.

[19]One of the best nontechnical treatments of oxytocin by one of the world's leading experts is Kerstin Uvnäs-Moberg, *The Oxytocin Factor: Tapping the Hormone of Calm, Love, and Healing* (Cambridge, Mass.: Da Capo Press, 2003).

[20]C. Sue Carter, "Developmental Consequences of Oxytocin," *Physiology & Behavior* 79 (2003): 383-97; Michael Kosfeld et al., "Oxytocin Increases Trust in Humans," *Nature* 435 (2005): 673-76; Kerstin Uvnäs-Moberg, "Oxytocin May Mediate the Benefits of Positive Social Interaction and Emotions," *Psychoneuroendocrinology* 23 (1998): 818-35.

[21]On the complex relationship between oxytocin and sexual behavior, see C. Sue Carter, "Oxytocin and Sexual Behavior," *Neuroscience and Biobehavioral Reviews* 16 (1992): 131-44; Janice Hiller, "Speculations on the Links Between Feelings, Emotions, and Sexual Behaviours: Are Vasopressin and Oxytocin Involved?" *Sexual and Relationship Therapy* 19 (2004): 393-412.

Diagram. Self-reinforcing "Love Cycle."

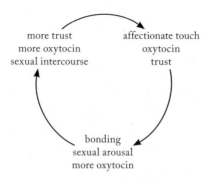

not a part of our cultural experience. Oh that we would learn to value and offer affectionate, nurturing touch to our spouses!

Recent technology, particularly ubiquitous Internet pornography, is making marital bonding through affectionate touch a greater challenge. Thus, we strongly suggest that couples familiarize themselves with the cultural and relational effects of pornography.[22] In particular, pornography programs individuals (especially men) to focus entirely on the sex act and the sex organs. It can literally extinguish the drive toward nurturing, loving touch, even erotic affectionate touch.[23] In this way, Satan is "crouching at the door" of our marriages and is constantly seeking to devour all that is good and life giving. Today pornography is not only consumed through the Internet but has been mainstreamed into the culture around us. Satan no longer needs a door—his destructive influence is in the air!

---

[22]On the relational, personal, and cultural affect of pornography, see Azy Barak and William A. Fisher, "The Future of Internet Sexuality," in *Sex and the Internet: A Guide for Clinicians*, ed. Al Cooper (New York: Brunner-Routledge, 2002), pp. 263-80; Al Cooper, ed., *Cybersex: The Dark Side of the Force: A Special Issue of the Journal of Sexual Addiction and Compulsivity* (Philadelphia: Taylor & Francis, 2000); Pamela Paul, *Pornified: How Pornography Is Transforming Our Lives, Our Relationships, and Our Families* (New York: Times Books, 2005).

[23]Much research demonstrates that pornography usage has a strong and rapid affect on men's attitudes and responses to women, causing them to objectify, demean and become callous toward women, fixate on sexual intercourse, and become dissatisfied with their partner's physical appearance. Jack Glascock, "Degrading Content and Character Sex: Accounting for Men and Women's Different Reactions to Pornography," *Communication Reports* 18 (2005): 43-53; Doug McKenzie-Mohr and Mark P. Zanna, "Treating Women as Sexual Objects: Look to the (Gender Schematic) Male Who Has Viewed Pornography," *Personality and Social Psychology Bulletin* 16 (1990): 296-30; Dolf Zillmann, "Effects of Prolonged Consumption of Pornography," in *Pornography Research Advances and Policy Considerations*, ed. Dolf Zillmann and Jennings Bryant (Hillsdale, N.J.: Lawrence Erlbaum Associates, 1989), pp. 127-57.

For example, kissing has become a lost art. I (Celestia) have discovered through marital therapy as well as church marriage ministry that it is not unusual today for couples to have sex (notice I did not say "make love") without kissing or even looking into each other's eyes. What a loss! Song of Solomon 1:2 is instructive for married couples: "Let him kiss me with the kisses of his mouth! For your love is better than wine." Remember, practice makes perfect! Over the years Steve and I have developed what we call "ritualized touch." This is affection that is turned into habit— holding hands during prayer and kissing afterward, greetings and good-byes that always involve kisses and hugs, holding each other at night after going to bed, and touching each other in passing, just to name a few. Have fun with this dimension and customize your relationship.

Relational dimension

My love has two lives, in order to love you.
That's why I love you when I do not love you.
And also why I love you when I do.
—Pablo Neruda[24]

Relational intimacy is the bond created by valuing, prioritizing, and treating as sacred my marriage relationship and my spouse. It is broader than emotional and nonerotic physical intimacy and is reflected in countless actions that flow from our commitment to treat each other and our relationship as absolutely unique. Since Celestia is the only person on the planet I have a *one-flesh* sacred covenant relationship with, all day long my actions and attitudes should reflect a unique valuing and prioritization of her and our relationship over literally every other human relationship. We do this in large and small ways, from not allowing other people, even our children, to come between us, to the way our budget and our schedule give each other a supreme place of priority, to the pet names and intimate secrets we share, known only to each other. As a couple learns to value and prioritize each other in this way, they also communicate the deepest levels of love to each other,

---

[24]Pablo Neruda, "Tonight I Can Write," from *Twenty Love Poems and a Song of Despair*, trans. W. S. Merwin (London: Cape, 1969).

ultimately giving each other the love, respect and value already imbued to them by their Creator. Relational intimacy continually forces me to transcend what I (Celestia) *feel* like doing in the moment. This dimension requires time and a good deal of unselfishness! For instance, Steve has an academic's specialized brain and is quite focused when he is researching and writing. He needs to think deeply and quietly about things before he is comfortable talking about them. He is rational, deliberate and linear. I, on the other hand, am very extroverted and external in my processing. I need to talk things through to make sense of them. I am full of emotion and that is typically expressed relationally. Clearly we have a dilemma! Our commitment to the relationship is to address both sets of needs mutually and as sensitively as possible.

I prioritize and "fine tune" my relationship with Steve in a way I do not with any other person. This can, and often does, take a good deal of time and energy but it significantly strengthens our relational bond and closeness. For instance, I feel most loved by Steve when he will walk and talk with me at night, and Steve feels most respected by me when I allow for the differences in our temperaments and am patient with his less emotional and more methodical style of relating. Through the years of our marriage I have grown beyond patience to gratefulness for these very different traits within him. Individual and gender differences are part of God's good design for complementation in marriage. I have seen God use my husband to be an extension of God's own arm of protection and care in my life. In summary, deepening this bond requires shifting focus from ourselves to our spouse, for relational intimacy is based on a commitment to bless the other person and honor our unique relationship. It is a commitment I make to his well-being—to respect and value his feelings and needs. Hence, building a strong relational bond must be important enough to be prioritized.[25] When we invest the time and energy needed to build marital relational intimacy, God is glorified, since he made us for this. We are also blessed because relational intimacy leads naturally to sexual intimacy.

---

[25]For instance, marriage therapist Willard F. Harley suggests that a couple needs fifteen hours per week of focused interaction time to maintain their relational/emotional closeness. *His Needs, Her Needs: Building an Affair-Proof Marriage* (Old Tappan, N.J.: Revell, 1986), p. 58.

SENSATE HOUR

Do you love me because I'm beautiful?
Or am I beautiful because you love me?
—Cinderella

Like most couples, over the years we have juggled the demanding responsibilities of raising children, dual careers, graduate school and ministry, all the while trying to maintain an intimate and dynamic marriage. While this has been a challenge, we have found that one of the best tools to help us keep our marriage healthy and passionate is what we call "the sensate hour."[26] It has become part of our relational "glue," and we recommend this discipline to other couples. The purpose of this time is not sex in and of itself, but the enhancement of a couple's bondedness/intimacy in every dimension. This includes their sensory enjoyment of each other, which in turn, will powerfully energize sexual intimacy. The "sensate hour" involves focusing on each other the last hour of the evening before going to bed. This takes place without television or any other form of visual entertainment.[27] More specifically, we direct our energy to each other by sharing our hearts, connecting verbally, emotionally, and physically with affectionate touch. We focus on the sensual enjoyment of each other. We play our favorite music, burn specifically fragranced candles,[28] and end the day talking while

---

[26]"Sensate" comes from the Latin word for "senses" and refers to a focus or preoccupation with things that can be experienced through the five senses. In our sensate hour we try to use all five senses to experience, enjoy, affirm and bond with each other. We try to focus not only on our own sensual experience but also on our partner's. Our broad usage of "sensate" encompasses but is not limited to the more technical meaning of "sensate focus" found frequently in the marital sexuality and sex therapy literature. This latter meaning refers to a focus on giving and receiving sensual pleasure primarily through touch, with an emphasis on a trajectory leading to sexual intimacy, see Douglas Rosenau, *A Celebration of Sex: A Guide to Enjoying God's Gift of Sexual Intimacy*, rev. ed. (Nashville: Thomas Nelson, 2002), pp. 22-34, 99-100; John P. Wincze and Michael P. Carey, *Sexual Dysfunction: A Guide for Assessment and Treatment*, 2nd ed. (New York: Guilford Press, 2001), pp. 123-29.

[27]Steve and I laughed when we read about a recent study of over five hundred Italian couples that found that couples who had a television in their bed room had sex half as often as the couples who did not. This should come as no surprise, for marital sexual intimacy can be easily sabotaged. The study was conducted by Serenella Salomoni, and the results were reported in *National Review of Medicine* (January 30, 2006): 1, available at <www.nationalreviewofmedicine.com/news_in_brief/2006/nb3_issue02_jan30_pg2.html>.

[28]The importance of selecting certain specific fragrances that are only used in the bedroom is that those scents become paired with the experiences of relational safety, comfort, attention,

we cuddle and give each other back rubs. While the sensate hour does not lead to sex every night, it certainly creates the bond, the atmosphere, and the occasion for regular and healthy sexual intimacy. Lest some readers object with "That's a great idea for couples who don't have our busy schedule," let me add that we developed our sensate hour while we were both in graduate school, working and parenting small children. We created an orderly routine in which we attended to the children's needs, prayed with them and sang while tucking them into bed. Knowing we had addressed their needs, we were free to close and lock our door. When our children became nocturnal adolescents we would sign off for the night, complete with Ray Charles and again, a shut bedroom door! Our kids knew they were to respect our privacy and not come knocking unless their room was in flames, the dog was foaming at the mouth or one of them was hemorrhaging on the floor. Furthermore, there have been many nights when I have given to Celestia at the end of her day our sensate hour then, once we have prayed and she has gone to sleep, I returned to my study to work for several more hours. Since marital intimacy is a top priority for us, the sensate hour is an essential part of our daily routine.

SEX AS AN EXPRESSION OF BONDEDNESS

While there are significant gender differences regarding sexual intimacy,[29] we will close this chapter by briefly mentioning three broad principles for healthy marital sex.[30] Since sex in marriage is a wonderful and honorable blessing from God, *couples should embrace, protect and cele-*

---

and love. In time this becomes a powerful and comforting neurological association that helps to mitigate previous destructive sexual experiences.

[29]One of the best summaries of gender sexual differences is found in *The Secrets of Eve*, 249-60. Based on fascinating research, the authors demonstrate that men and women differ: in how they think about sex, in what they want from and enjoy about sex, in their energy resources for sex, in their concerns about body image, in how often they want sex, and in how they connect sexually. These conclusions are based on research, not on their gender-role convictions.

[30]Due to our limits on chapter length, all we can do here is give a few brief principles. While there are many Christian books now on the specifics of sexual intimacy, we consider the following to be among the best: Rosenau, *A Celebration of Sex*; Douglas Rosenau, James and Carolyn Childerston, *A Celebration of Sex after Fifty* (Nashville: Thomas Nelson, 2004); Christopher and Rachel McCluskey, *When Two Become One: Enhancing Sexual Intimacy in Marriage* (Grand Rapids: Revell, 2004).

brate the gift of sex. First Corinthians 7:1-5 is the most detailed New Testament treatment of marital sex. In this text Paul speaks to Corinthian couples who were struggling with their sex lives. In verse one Paul quotes the Corinthians when he says, "It is well for a man not to touch [sexually] a woman." Apparently, some of the Corinthians had become convinced that they should not have sex with their spouse. Paul emphatically refutes this, asserting that married couples absolutely should be having sex ("each man should have [sexually] his own wife and each woman her own husband"). In other words, they should *embrace* sex as a gift. We know that Corinth was a very immoral city (cf. 1 Cor 5:1-2; 6:15) and these believers had pagan pasts. So, undoubtedly, some of these Christian couples just couldn't accept sex in marriage as pure and holy. Many couples today have the same struggle and need to learn, based on the truth of Scripture, to embrace sex in marriage. This is done by viewing sex with our spouse as an act of worship to the God who gave us this gift, by prioritizing our sexual relationship, and by healing from past promiscuity or sexual abuse that prevents us from enjoying sex—the giving and receiving of pleasure.

In verse two Paul says married couples should be having sexual relations because of "cases [various kinds] of sexual immorality." While Paul viewed marital sex as holy, he was plainly concerned that the gift of sexuality would be marred and corrupted by Satan who delights in enticing us with illegitimate sources of sexual fulfillment when our sexual needs are not met in marriage. Like all of God's gifts, sex must be *protected*. This is particularly true in our current sex-obsessed, hedonistic culture. Perhaps more than at any time in American history, couples face unprecedented sexual temptations around them and must be very diligent to protect their sexual purity. Research shows that roughly 20 to 25 percent of married people will be sexually unfaithful to their spouse, and Christians are no exception to this trend. In fact, one research study found that religious commitment only makes a significant difference in lowering sexual infidelity if someone was in a very happy marriage.[31]

---

[31]David C. Atkins, Donald H. Baucom and Neil S. Jacobson, "Understanding Infidelity: Correlations in a National Random Sample," *Journal of Family Psychology* 15 (2001): 746. The researchers suggest this data may indicate "when the primary relationship [marriage] is less

Those who reported they were "pretty happy" or "not too happy" in their marriage were two to four times more likely (respectively) to report having been sexually unfaithful than those in "very happy" marriages. In other words, couples cannot afford to coast; even those in fairly happy marriages are in real danger of sexual infidelity.

Over several decades of collective professional and pastoral counseling, Celestia and I have ministered to several hundred individuals who have had sexual affairs, including many Christian leaders. Very few of these individuals were looking for an adulterous relationship. From their perspective, it just happened. Or did it? While there are different kinds of affairs with different characteristics,[32] what we see most often is couples who gradually drift away from each other, growing more lonely and emotionally starved, one day deciding they are in love with someone else who makes them again feel alive and loved. This is why an ongoing, daily commitment to attend to the three dimensions of bonding, including the sensate hour, is so important.

In addition to this, here are a few practical steps Celestia and I have taken to protect our marriage sexually: (1) As a part of our devotional life, we both practice the discipline of journaling. We prayerfully reflect on our inner life and record our: struggles and pain, questions, victories, and in the context of all of this, what we receive from God's word. We seek to identify inner patterns of fear, insecurities or frustration.[33] Otherwise, we are less able to love each other well and can be more emotionally and sexually vulnerable. (2) We have committed to absolute honesty in our relationship. We keep no secrets from each other and give each other access to all of our lives (professional confidences would be the only exception). We have each others' e-mail pass-

---

than ideal, the dissatisfaction with the relationship may override religious values," 746.

[32]Dave Carter distinguishes three types of affairs with different causes and characteristics: one night stands (single experience, lustful, no emotional attachment), entangled affairs (develops gradually, strong emotional attachment), and sexual addiction affairs (repeated affairs, impersonal, less related to state of the marriage). *Torn Asunder: Recovering from Extramarital Affairs* (Chicago: Moody Press, 1992), pp. 50-57.

[33]Roy Bell and Stanley Grenz give a helpful explanation of the importance of identifying and dealing with our deep-seated insecurities, since they lie at the heart of most affairs, *A Betrayal of Trust: Sexual Misconduct in the Pastorate* (Downers Grove, Ill.: InterVarsity Press, 1995), pp. 133-34.

words and share our daily schedule with each other. We also commit to complete honesty about our relationship. We regularly ask each other the hard questions: How could I better meet your emotional needs? Is our sexual relationship satisfying to you? How could it be better? What could I change to encourage you or make you feel more loved or respected? We share honestly with each other whenever we feel a strong sexual or emotional attraction toward or from someone else. While this can be difficult, it has allowed us to fine tune our marriage. It also greatly reduces the power of secret sexual attraction, for it is no longer a secret. (3) As Celestia mentioned in chapter two, I subscribe to Covenant Eyes, an Internet tracking service that monitors my activity for potentially sexually inappropriate usage and sends a report weekly to my accountability partner who is my supervisor at Phoenix Seminary. (4) I have written out an extensive list itemizing the cost of an affair—what might well happen physically, sexually, spiritually, vocationally, emotionally, financially, and so forth, if I were unfaithful to Celestia. (5) We make love regularly, which leads us to our final Pauline principle for healthy marital sex.

God wants us to *celebrate* the gift. Paul told the Corinthians in 1 Corinthians 7:3, 5, to have very regular sexual relations. In verse three the command "let him keep on fulfilling his duty" (author's translation) is in the present tense, indicating continual action. The language used here is language of obligation—"depriving" in verse 5 is a verb which means "to defraud" and indicates taking away what rightfully belongs to another (as in the man who is financially defrauded in 1 Cor 6:7-8). The only exception to this rule of regular sex is for a limited, mutually agreed upon time of abstinence for the purpose of prayer. God is telling us that meeting each other's sexual needs in marriage is so important that it is absolutely nonnegotiable. It is to be a top priority. It saddens Celestia and me how often we meet Christian couples who go months or even years without making love. And this is not because they are on a long-term prayer program! It is sobering that in a large national survey of married couples married five years or less, the second most problematic marital issue reported was "frequency of sex."[34] In a survey of the general population, roughly a quarter of couples responded that they were dissatisfied with their sex lives, men more so than women, particularly with the frequency of intercourse.[35] Each couple must carefully work out what "regular" and mutually satisfying sexual relations mean for them. This will vary somewhat over the stages of life. The key is that we refuse to accept a mediocre sex life. Establishing a long-term healthy marital sex life requires a commitment and sacrifice—continuing to educate ourselves through solid Christian sexuality books, having sometimes embarrassing conversations with our spouse, learning, adapting to and valuing differing sexual needs, and even seeking outside medical or therapeutic assistance if necessary. A couple's regular celebration of sex honors our heavenly Father, provides moral protection, and brings great joy and fulfillment!

---

[34]Gail S. Risch, Lisa A. Riley, and Michael G. Lawler, "Problematic Issues in the Early Years of Marriage: Content for Premarital Education," *Journal of Psychology and Theology* 31 (2003): 253-69.

[35]Kate M. Dunn, Peter R. Croft and Geoffrey I. Hackett, "Satisfaction in the Sex Life of a General Population Sample," *Journal of Sex & Marital Therapy* 26 (2000): 141-51. The good news is that overall, married men and women report relatively high levels of emotional and sexual satisfaction, in fact significantly more than do sexually active singles. Linda J. Waite and Kara Joyner, "Emotional and Physical Satisfaction with Sex in Married, Cohabiting, and Dating Sexual Unions: Do Men and Women Differ?" in *Sex, Love, and Health in America: Private Choices and Public Policies*, ed. Edward O. Laumann and Robert T. Michael (Chicago: University of Chicago Press, 2001), p. 266.

BILL AND AÍDA SPENCER'S
VIEWPOINT

When Genesis describes the first act of sexual intimacy, the Scripture explains it metaphorically in 4:1: "And Adam knew Eve his wife" (KJV). The Hebrew word used is *yādaʿ*. This is the same word the tempter used to beguile Eve to disobey God and consume the forbidden fruit in Genesis 3:5: "Because God *knows*," the evil one lures her, that humans will alter by "*knowing* good and evil" (Bill's trans.), if she and her husband ingest the forbidden item, making its contents now a part of themselves. Their foolish compliance makes them like the sexual victims of the HIV virus, taking the infection into themselves and having their lives inexorably altered by this one event.

The parallel use of the term *yādaʿ* applied positively to sexual intimacy reveals that the physical act achieves a deep knowledge that produces unity at a level so profound that it alters the very nature of those involved. The status of humanity changed forever when our primal parents "knew" good and evil. The ramifications were profound: aging and death. In contrast, but also in parallel, when Adam and Eve "knew" each other through sexual intercourse, that act of gaining "knowledge" was so profound that it altered their lives and the course of humanity forever: a new human was the result—their son, Cain. Genesis 2:24, as we saw in chapter one, describes the ramifications of such life-changing intimacy between man and woman becoming husband and wife, as cemented by the sign of sexual union: parents are left; spouses unite; they become one being in God's sight *(one flesh),* a new creation is "born," and this union, we now discover in Genesis 4:1, produces more creatures, our children.

When two individuals become *one flesh,* they comprise a new dynamic living creature—a third entity in God's sight. "Dynamic" suggests dynamo, a center to their relationship radiating out life to every area of their being just as a dynamo sends out impulses of electricity that change and enliven machinery. In parallel, marriage itself is a living unity that pumps out energy into every area of our being, our relationship with our spouse, our entire perspective of and approach to the world and those in it to whom we relate. Everything we do and think becomes charged with this new life.

Such a life-changing act of covenant, or permanent agreement, is exactly what's missing in a relationship without the *one-flesh* commitment. There is no new living creation, no center. Nothing holds it together. No divine bonding exists. So, once the physical attraction begins to wane, or interests change, casual partners begin to grow apart, splitting up again into two individual parts and moving out and away from each other. Changing to another liaison is somewhat similar to changing to another job. Such relationships begin with no vows, no ceremony, no permanent agreement, and then disconnect, often leaving at least one of the partners grieving and feeling disconnected.

But the *one-flesh* creation is a center that keeps deepening every aspect of the new being that has been created, joining wife and husband inseparably, so nothing short of death breaks the bond. While the younger widowed are free to remarry and even counseled to do so in Scripture (see 1 Tim 5:14), and therefore many such Christians do, the older widowed sometimes find remarrying difficult. A common reality among seniors is that, when one spouse dies, the other is often not long in following. This was the case with Bill's grandparents. His grandfather mourned the death of his grandmother for a year and could not be consoled. "I see her everywhere," he said over and over. He had himself been fairly healthy when his wife died during an operation, but he languished and succumbed a year later. Aída's mother lasted a year and a half after her husband, but there was no joy left in her. Nothing anyone of us could do could keep her from following. Bill's mother took an immediate radical increase in the stages of Alzheimer's when his father died. Something had already died besides each of their spouses—the *one-flesh* relationship of their marriage until death parted them was now itself dead. Something very holy and very profound happens in marriage—something that alters our very beings. All of this background explains why we believe the *one-flesh* union, born of the ultimate knowledge of another that is marriage, is at the center of the greatest gift marriage gives us: authentic intimacy.

Drawing from the information in Genesis, we have compiled the following definition of intimacy: Intimacy in marriage we see as the gift of knowing one's spouse in a relationship of trust where both partners are determined to be one in accord at the deepest levels: the spiritual, personal, relational, emotional (psychological), and physical. It is complete bonding. Let's take a look at each of these aspects.

SPIRITUAL INTIMACY

Nurturing the *one-flesh* bond with spiritual intimacy comes as we build our marriages consciously on a three-way relationship with God. Practically worked out, such bonding begins with personal preparation in daily individual prayer and devotional reading in the Bible that informs family times of worship and prayer together with our spouse. As husband and wife, both of us try to stay mindful of God's presence in our marriage, attempting to act toward each other in ways that please God, remembering God is watching how we treat each other, and recognizing God should be the boss of every marriage, including ours, so neither of us needs to struggle for ultimate power, since God has that. When we are drawing close to God in obedience in these matters, we notice God spiritually prompts us to act toward each other in the way Jesus acted toward the church: with tender care for its well-being.

This concern of God for each of our marriages was the source of a wonderful rabbinic legend that recounts how a Roman woman once asked a rabbi what God had been doing since the world was created. "Arranging marriages," replied the rabbi. "Is that His occupation?" asked the aristocrat. "I, too, could do it. I possess many male and female slaves, and in a very short while I can pair them together." The rabbi responded: "If it is a simple thing in your eyes, it is as difficult to the Holy One, blessed be He, as dividing the Red Sea." To prove him wrong, she lined up all her male and female slaves and announced they were married to each other, but the next morning "they appeared before her, one with a cracked forehead, another with an eye knocked out, and another with a broken leg." She was shocked. "What is the matter with you?" she asked. One of the female slaves moaned, "I don't want him." A male slave retorted, "I don't want her."[1] The lesson was demonstrated poignantly to her and to us all: Each of us needs God's guidance to seek a spouse and stay together when we are married. Clearly, when we draw near to God, James 4:8 promises, God will draw near to us. God will also draw us closer to one another in our marriages. But, before doing that, God begins work on each of us individually.

PERSONAL INTIMACY

God begins our sense of intimacy within ourselves at birth, as we define ourselves and then ultimately redefine ourselves in marriage. When one is an infant, one's self is defined by one's own needs. The world, as one perceives it, appears to exist to serve these needs. But, this is not to say that infants have no sense of relationship. When our son was eleven years old, we were walking in San Juan one beautiful sunny day as the conversation lounged around to the topic of memory: what was the earliest memory any of us could recall? Steve said, "I remember when I was looking up at some lights and somebody took me out of dad's hands and I started yelling because I wanted to be back with him." We puzzled over that memory, reliving every doctor's visit when Steve was a baby—where dad, who worked at night and spent every day with his boy, held him tightly for shots and examinations. But none of these would do. Then as Steve described the soft voice Bill used, the lights above, the figures with covered faces who took him away, his crying as they washed him and his quieting down only when he was back in Bill's arms, we suddenly realized thunderstruck that he was accurately describing the delivery room from his perspective. It was a scene we had never described to him and indeed had all but forgotten. He had had a natural childbirth with Lamaze and modified Leboyer techniques, dimmed lights, soft voices, no spanking and introducing ourselves gently as he opened his eyes and looked at our faces. Even before language,

---

[1] A. Cohen, *Everyman's Talmud* (New York: Dutton, 1949), p. 163, citing *Gen.R.68.4*.

he remembered interacting in the events of that day. And so relationship was already stamped upon him at birth.

As we mature, all of us define ourselves within the context of our
familial relationships. We begin to expand our sense of self outside the
family with our early friends. We bond with them, defend them to our
parents, and, when they are our best friends, sometimes fight with
them against all comers—or run away with them! When we marry,
that tendency concretizes profoundly as our sense of self within the
one-flesh relationship now includes our spouse. Two independent people
have become interdependent and have been made one—two selves who
have become a united self. When children are born, we see them as an
extension of ourselves—our sense of self expands once again. At some
profound moment in our maturing, we may even begin to understand
that every child in the world is in a sense our child. The great souls of
the human race, and the Christians most blessed and blessing to others,
are those whose sense of self has so expanded as now to include the
neighbor, the widow, the orphan, the sufferer. "I have great sorrow and
unceasing anguish in my heart," wrote Paul to the Romans in 9:2-3.
"For I could wish that I myself were accursed and cut off from Christ
for the sake of my own people, my kindred according to the flesh." So
far had Paul's sense of self-definition expanded that he would even give
up the hope of glory for the salvation of Israel.

In her fascinating study *The Search for Intimacy*, we notice Elaine Storkey also begins her definition of intimacy in this very personal way:

> At its most basic *intimacy is knowing that I am not alone in the universe*.
> But that *knowing* is not simply a cerebral process. It is something I ex-
> perience, and live within; something that shapes my understanding and
> acceptance of reality . . . Intimacy is the sharing of closeness, of bond-
> ing, of reciprocation. It is the engulfing of warmth and care. It is the
> experiencing of *Another*.[2]

Here we see the biblical image of knowing, in this case a profound
realization that God is present and in relationship with us. This security of knowledge undergirds our ability to expand our sense of self to

---

[2]Elaine Storkey, *The Search for Intimacy* (Grand Rapids: Eerdmans, 1995), p. 4.

allow that intense level of intimacy with which we regard and care for ourselves to include others, as Jesus' Golden Rule describes (Mt. 7:12), and ultimately to encompass our spouse and our children.

Can we still have an area in our beings where we don't share our deepest feelings with our spouse—or even with our God? Yes, but the price we pay is that we will forfeit complete intimacy. Holding out a part of our past, hiding some of our deepest aspirations, masking our real fears, keeping back either negative or positive aspects of ourselves from those who love us may keep us from truly experiencing the full *one-flesh* intimacy of marriage. This is not to say we have to parade every evil act we have ever done in our lives for review before our suffering spouse. If we have confessed a sin to God and been forgiven, we should forget it as thoroughly as God has already done. Further, caring Christians, especially those in formal ministry, are sometimes told secrets by parishioners who beg us not to share the information with anyone, even our spouses, so that every minister becomes a repository of many secret confessions that are taken to the grave. But, beyond the obvious exceptions, we are saying that our self now includes another self and true intimacy involves real disclosure of our hopes and dreams and fears and failures and successes. Important things not shared can become time bombs that may detonate later in our relationship and cause great damage to our trust level. Godly, caring honesty about ourselves is the miracle plant food for trust. And, in parallel, true personal intimacy within the *one-flesh* redefining of our personal understanding of self also means that we now receive hopes and dreams and fears and failures and successes from the new self that has been joined with ours. Reflecting the God who is three persons in one, our marriage has made us two persons in one unity—a unified self in relationship.

RELATIONAL INTIMACY

Adam knew Eve before he "knew" Eve.[3] Since Christ's death for us has

---

[3]Although the Bible in its marvelous economy of presentation takes only two chapters to describe their relationship, we are not certain if Adam's age in Gen 5:5 is reckoned from his creation or his expulsion from the garden. If the latter, then, we really have no idea how many eons they lived together in obedience to God and in harmony together. However, as we noted at the outset in the case of Ananias and Sapphira, Adam and Eve's relational bond was also

freed us from the curse, then we too should try to recapture an edenic kind of relating, as John Chrysostom wisely counseled husbands to nurture their relationship with their wives with lavish expressions of love:

> Never call her simply by her name, but with terms of endearment, with honour, with exceeding affection. Honour her, and she will not need honour from others; she will not want the glory that comes from others, if she enjoys that which comes from thee. Prefer her before all, on every account, both for her beauty, and her discernment, and extol her. Thus wilt thou persuade her to give heed to none that are without, but to scorn all the world except thyself. Teach her the fear of God, and all things will flow in smoothly to thee as from a fountain, and the house will be full of ten thousand blessings. *(Commentary on Eph 5:33)*

There was no apostle more vulnerable to error than Peter, so God inspired him to write, "Above all, maintain constant love for one another, for love covers a multitude of sins" (1 Pet 4:8). Let's face it, all of us humans are fallen, and we need as much mercy as possible. So, this is how God treats us all, with mercy. Jesus, God-Among-Us, came to earth enjoying our company at banquets and weddings and other festivities, counseling, healing and saving us. Above all, Jesus showed constant love and mercy, along with helpful correction.

Like God, we need to be slow to anger, slow to judge, quick to forgive, tender and caring in our interactions. Those of us who want mercy so much ourselves should be showing much mercy to others. Particularly, we should show daily tenderness and mercy to our spouse in all our dealings, large and small. One way we can do it is through polite discourse. From early on we treated our son respectfully and taught him to treat us that way. It was all "please and thank you," even when he was a toddler. Today he is a man and his discourse with us remains "please and thank you." It is part of a whole attitude of tenderness. Caring is an attitude that starts with respect.

---

their undoing. Each of us has a responsibility to steward our relationship with the same care we are to steward our own bodies to help each other remain in holy living. This, of course, is not a mandate for controlling the other's will, privately nagging until they do what we consider to be right, or publicly shaming them to correct their behavior. Rather, we should use a positive approach, making it our practice to be respectful and loving to each other in public and in private.

One great tragedy we wanted to avoid is that of a fundamentalist family whose daughter went with a friend of ours when we were all dating. Every time we went to pick her up we could hear shouting in the house, then she would slam the door, get in the car, and snap, "Drive!" between clenched teeth. Our buddy married her and they are both wonderful Christian people, but it was all hammer and tongs. The marriage broke up and today they have new spouses, trying again. We believe the attitude in the original family doomed the children's relationship from the start. We each have to set a tone for our family—it can either be adversarial or cooperative. Politeness, tenderness, supportiveness are each a part of the ways that Christ builds the church. They should be the way we build our homes. They nourish the soil in which intimacy grows, because no one under attack feels they can show something vulnerable. Instead, they construct walls. Families that are broken into armed camps don't have communal moments, they have detentes and peace talks. Self-protection is the rule of the field of battle—that and preemptive action. It is all about losing and gaining ground, not about planting the seeds of love. But intimacy thrives on love.

Therefore, we should be proactive and seek ways to make our beloved feel supported and respected. If our spouse needs more education, we should invest our best efforts there. We did that ourselves when we were just turning 30. Aída felt called to teach as our work in Newark, New Jersey completed, so we packed up and moved to Louisville, Kentucky, so she could study. What we avoided by doing this was what one family we know, full of wonderful and capable Christian people, underwent. Father and both children were professionals. Mom's attempts to start an Internet business were the standing joke of the family. Four decades into the marriage, mom suddenly left to the shock of all. Fires that smolder sometimes burst into flame and fire can either warm us or burn us. We need to kindle the gifts of each member of the family. No one is there to support everybody else but receive no support. A victory for each member of the family is what we should be seeking.

For instance, board games are fun, but in daily life we should make certain we never compete with each other. First Corinthians 12:26 teaches us: "If one member suffers, all suffer together with it; if one member is being honored, all rejoice together with it." We can't do that if we are at odds with one another. One author we knew used to carry on a "healthy" competition with her husband. She published far more than he did. She assured us this competition spurred them both on. One day it spurred him out of the house for good. A victory for one should be a victory for both, a failure by one should not be a source of secret rejoicing for the other but a catastrophe for both. We should be working to comfort each other and help each other succeed. In this way we will grow more godly together, closer to God, and be drawn closer by God to each other.

Don't let the world set your thinking about marriage. The world is all about familiarity with no commitment. We are all about commitment that produces greater and greater familiarity. Christians and non-Christians are going in different directions. Christians build intimacy on faithfulness to our vows, complete trustworthiness to honor our partner with tender care and not abuse, life-long commitment to stay together. Our values are completely different from the casual ones of many in the world. We don't marry with a prenuptial agreement in the back pockets of our tuxes or down the cleavage of our wedding gowns. So, since the laws of our new country are different from those outside our border, why should we look to those outside to interpret how our marriages should be going? If they have anything helpful to say, of course, we listen, just as countries should listen to wisdom that comes from other nations. But Christian marriages are not in the United Nations. The world does not vote on how we work out God's values in our lives together. Guiding that is the responsibility of the church, not the task of the world.

We're not writing here about a right to abuse each other. God never allows domestic abuse in any Christian home and will not bless an abuser. Malachi 2:16 warns us that God hates a husband who "covers his garment with violence" in his interactions with his wife, and 1 Peter 3:7 reminds husbands to keep in mind their wives' lesser physical strength (a weaker vessel = body) and show them consideration. What we are saying is that worldly relationships often set their standards within a post-Fall climate of estrangement, and we're trying to live out lives redeemed by Christ. We use a different currency than they do. The coin of the fallen world that is forged with the motto "Me first and foremost" should not purchase the viewpoint of the Christian home. In essence, every happily married couple has to learn to replace "me" with "we." A deep part of intimacy is becoming familiar with what is unique about our spouse, what our spouse really values, so that a "we," a joint set of values and a united perspective, can be forged together. Such cooperation turns familiarity into intimacy and it helps secure the marriage bond.

Each loving act of tenderness should represent a protecting brick in the wall of commitment that surrounds our marriages. Jack and Judith Balswick cite researcher F. Dickson's study of "couples who have been happily married for fifty years or more" and summarize what is common within the findings: "(1) They treat each other with mutual respect and dignity. (2) They have established a comfortable level of closeness. (3) They have a shared vision and course of action."[4] As we look at this list, we can discern a progression. Tender respect draws marriage partners closely together, and they blend thought and action. In our case, we have tried (not always successfully, but we are steadily improving) to treat each other tenderly and respectfully in public and private (even when we disagree). We try to do as many activities as we can together. Since we ended up as teachers, we try to have each other present when a student visits, and, when Steve was a child, we tried to include him in on our ministry calls. The point is we realize that our marriage commitment has bonded us together, therefore we reason that when people want us, they want us both—otherwise, why has God enriched the church with singles?

Within our own relationship, such closeness has made us more tolerant of each other. We try to choose our disagreements wisely and stick to the point, not drag in a lot of old quibbles. We have also put a moratorium on sarcasm and even put-down humor. These do nothing to nurture loving feelings—in fact, they thwart love. Humor can be a wonderful way to defuse tension. Bill, who uses it often, thinks that

---

[4]Jack O. Balswick and Judith K. Balswick, *A Model for Marriage: Covenant, Grace, Empowerment and Intimacy* (Downers Grove, Ill.: IVP Academic, 2006), p. 151.

truth is what is amusing. Humor is about bringing out painful truths in situations where an artificial construction has been disguising it. When the truth is spoken, the relief makes one laugh and feel better. A humorless relationship is one in jeopardy. At the same time, however, humor can simply be a mask for cowardice, to deflect a couple from sitting down and sharing what we really care about. With our spouse we should be able to listen and share about our deepest concerns and aspirations—and sometimes listen to these over and over again. Others may scoff or be impatient, but a spouse is in for the long haul, takes every revelation seriously and invests a lifetime to help the beloved work through it: "Love never gives up" (1 Cor 13:4 *The Message*).

That is why it is so important at the outset to marry the right person, or make sure *you* are marriageable before you enter into the covenant. When a person shows trustworthiness, consistently looking out for the spouse's best interest, a normal spouse, who is not so damaged that response is no longer possible, should feel enough trust to draw closer in more and more intimate ways. Putting Paul's advice into action in a marriage is effective therapy for the diagnosis of post-Fall estrangement. We need to be, and to marry, a person who can be invested in relationally.

The end of all this investment in our marriage relationship should be joy. The rabbis understood this, when they wrote in the *Babylonian Talmud*:

> Blessed art Thou, O Lord our King, God of the universe, who has created joy and gladness, bridegroom and bride, rejoicing, song, mirth, and delight, love, and brotherhood, and peace, and friendship. Speedily, O Lord our God, may be heard in the cities of Judah, and in the streets of Jerusalem, the voice of joy and the voice of gladness, the voice of the bridegroom and the voice of the bride, the voice of the singing of bridegrooms from their canopies and of youths from their feasts of song. Blessed art Thou, O Lord, who maketh the bridegroom to rejoice with the bride (*Ketub.* 8a).

Men and women love each other; God ordained it so. And the monogamy of the *one-flesh* relationship is the foundation of that love, as we focus ourselves on each other and embark on a life of joy. But, now, a note of caution about that process of embarking is in order.

Falling in love and living in love seem to be two different things. We remember once hearing a famous movie actor, infamous for his divorces, explain that he liked getting married, it was being married that he found dull. A marked difference does appear between people who have just fallen in love and those of us married for many years, though we still call our two conditions love. To gauge this difference, Rutgers and Stony Brook Universities researchers Helen Fisher, Arthur Aron and Lucy Brown used an MRI machine to distinguish physical changes in an examinee's "ventral tegmental area and the caudate nucleus" of the brain, as it fuels with dopamine when presented a photograph of someone with whom that person has fallen in love within the previous 7 months.

University of Pisa (Italy) psychiatrist Donatella Marazziti has chronicled blood serotonin levels of people in love under 6 months and noticed a parallel between these and patients suffering from obsessive-compulsive disorder. National Geographic author Lauren Slater summarizes the result: "Love and mental illness may be difficult to tell apart." She notes that researchers confirm that couples eventually do move "from the dopamine-drenched state of romantic love to the relative quiet of an oxytocin-induced attachment. Oxytocin is a hormone that promotes a feeling of connection, bonding."[5]

If these observations are true, then God has hard-wired each of us who are married to focus first on our beloved in a manner intense enough to mimic madness, but has then moved our responses to another part of our brain to maintain our marriages. Therefore, falling in love and staying in love are two phases designed into us by the divine Designer and, as we stay in touch with God and each other together, deep bonds develop.

Roberts and Wright, in their marriage preparation manual *Before You Say "I Do,"* counsel couples to expect "three stages" in their mar-

---

[5]Lauren Slater, "True Love," *National Geographic* 209, no. 2 (2006): 35, 38, 45. Interesting to note is that as far back as Plato's *Phaedrus*, Socrates had noticed "four divisions of the divine madness," describing them as "prophecy," "mystic madness," "the poetic," and "the madness of love," which he terms "the best" (p. 48).

riage, the first of *enchantment*, which they describe as "On Cloud 9, Perfect . . . Ecstasy." The second they call *disenchantment*, where couples are "Upset . . . Irritated . . . Bitter." And the final stage they term *maturity*, characterized by "Feet on the ground . . . Let's work it out . . . Together, we can make it."[6] We think this sounds like every formulaic movie we ever saw, usually described in the reviews as "boy meets girl; boy loses girl, boy gets girl." But, if the MRI machine and these counselors are correct, such movies are indeed based on an observable fact: relationships must mature to achieve true emotional intimacy.

EMOTIONAL INTIMACY

One of the most precious gifts of a truly solid commitment to another based on a foundation of trust is the healing that comes to each partner of the aspects we are able to confess about ourselves that seem to us most shameful. These are the shortcomings we can share freely with only two persons: God and our spouse. They may be the only ones, even beyond our parents, who know about our tendencies to sin and the bad habits that have plagued us in the past. We may have addictions that may threaten our marriage and with which we must finally deal in the environment of support, if we have not been wise and courageous enough to deal with them earlier. In fact, the addicted have already made themselves *one flesh* with the addiction, that having been their real spouse. Thus, nothing renovates a marriage like ending an addiction to drugs or pornography or whatever it is. Another form of healing is the letting go in this supportive environment of past liaisons with others that hinder the new bonding. Several times in our ministry we have worked with "the other woman" in an adulterous relationship, helping these let go and seek a spouse of their own. Since a healthy marriage is a healer of emotions, whatever else hinders emotional intimacy, be it anger, or the inability to handle stress healthily, or the effects of past emotional wounds, has the opportunity to be addressed. For example, to avoid some of the pain we saw in others' lives, Aída suggested a rule at the outset of our marriage that we never let anger

---

[6]H. Norman Wright and Wes Roberts, *Before You Say "I Do": A Marriage Preparation Manual for Couples* (Eugene, Ore.: Harvest House, 1978), p. 25.

invade our bedroom and always resolve quarrels that day (cf. Eph 4:26; Mt 5:21-24). Kari Malcolm, in her wonderfully wise book *Building Your Family to Last*, explains the power of resolving conflict with those we love:

> I am grateful for family members who have ministered to me in this way as I have confessed my sins, my doubts, and my hang-ups. I have confessed at times to my parents, brothers, sister-in-law, husband and children. For example, before we prayed together at night, I used to sit at the bedside of my children and give them time to review the day's events. Sins were often confessed. I confessed and they confessed. Those were very holy moments of the day when the slate was wiped clean between us and our God and between each other.[7]

Such are healing moments, as James 5:16 reveals. But such communion must be going both ways, benefiting both partners. Over and over, we have seen self-centeredness and fear of change balk at and block a progress toward intimacy. This is why we have invested so much of our thinking in God's redefinition of our sense of self through means of the *one-flesh* bonding.[8] We are, after all, the children of fallen primal parents, and the history of alienation is the context of every female and male relationship since the first humans fell from perfection. When the effects of the Fall are felt in our marriages, they destroy our sacred intimacy and reintroduce the age-old warfare that comes with two strong combatants vying for power. We have to take our commitment to be emotionally bonded very seriously. Pastoral counselors Herbert Anderson and Robert Fite especially offer this warning:

> Men often mistake physical intimacy for emotional intimacy and are confused when their wives complain of the distance between them even though they make love frequently. . . . Physical intimacy is the delightful companion of emotional intimacy; but sex becomes distorted and ultimately disappointing when it is cut off from emotional closeness. While sexual attraction may be what draws people together, it is rarely

---

[7]Kari Malcolm, *Building Your Family to Last* (Eugene, Ore.: Wipf & Stock, 2006), p. 65.
[8]Gary Chapman, in *Toward a Growing Marriage* (Chicago: Moody Press, 1979), p. 114, observes that "selfishness is the greatest barrier to oneness, and we are all afflicted with the disease. We are our own greatest enemy in attaining marital unity."

what keeps them together. . . . Without such respect and open communication between husbands and wives, fears and resentments are likely
to build up that will eventually restrict the sexual pleasure that may have
characterized the early stages of the relationship.[9]

PHYSICAL INTIMACY

When wholeness is being achieved on the spiritual, personal, relational,
emotional level, we have discovered that physical expression of love is at
its gentlest, most tender and most satisfying. Further, we have discovered that sexual love is a skill, an art that is achieved more and more
fully as the years go by. We might view this as using the *one-flesh* relationship as a passport into our own brand new world. If we see our
marriage vows as allegiance we swear to a new country, named "married," and our borders the love of our spouse and our loyalty to that
love, we realize a spouse contains much unexplored territory. "To know
someone" takes a lifetime of exploration into another person's world
that has now become our world too. It is indeed an expression of the
greater and greater bonding within all the areas of intimacy this chapter describes. One way to underscore this truth is by examining the
alternative.

As we write, the most high-profile book on sexuality, the one that
has all the buzz here in Massachusetts, has been written not by a doctor
or psychologist, but by a young Tufts University graduate who majored
in human sexuality, community health and American studies, and, as
an undergraduate, wrote a weekly column on sexual issues in the student newspaper. Her *Hooking Up: A Girl's All-Out Guide to Sex and*

---

[9]Herbert Anderson and Robert Cotton Fite, *Becoming Married* (Louisville: Westminster/John
Knox , 1993), pp. 125, 127. One popular book we reviewed on marriage reduced males simply
to sexual beings and counseled, "Consider what drives a man. Well, sex, of course and if not
that, then how about sex? Or maybe some sexual sublimation—food or beer or making money
or racecar driving or beating his best friend at squash. But basically, here's what he wants: to
have sex with you" (Jamie Callan, *Hooking Up or Holding Out: The Smart Girl's Guide to Driving
Men Crazy and/or Finding True Love* [Naperville, Ill.: Sourcebooks Casablanca, 2007], p. 10).
As a result, the book recommends ways women can keep men interested by holding them off as
long as possible, gratifying them sexually if they begin to lose interest, then holding off again
to keep the game going. The entire thesis of the book is that dishonesty and head games are the
basis of a lasting relationship. It is the exact opposite of what all of the writers of the present
book have discovered, and what counselors Anderson and Fite have expressed so well.

Sexuality is a frank, well-researched and popularly written manual for every young woman who contemplates participating in sexual activity outside of marriage. Rather than merely the salacious romp of the Hollywood persuasion that it sounds, the resulting book is actually quite harrowing and sad. After a sobering chapter, detailing all the sexually transmitted diseases that one risks, author Amber Madison concludes:

> In a nutshell, there are many STDs out there, and many people have them. Because vaginas have more fragile skin than penises, it's twice as easy for you to get an STD from a guy than vice versa. The only truly safe sex act is masturbation (or abstinence, but that's not sex at all). So, when you have sex, you have to be very careful. If you're sexually active, there is no absolute guarantee that you will be able to avoid STDs completely.[10]

Of her own experience, she writes:

> In the days before I was supposed to get my period, I would go into full-blown stalker mode, searching for any sign of it . . . And I would always be positive that "this month it just wasn't coming". . . Until one month— it actually didn't come at all. It was a nightmare come true. I made my boyfriend buy the test because I didn't want to pay ten dollars and confess to a cashier that I might be pregnant. I was so freaked out that, not only did I insist on taking it at my boyfriend's place, but I also actually made him come into the bathroom with me. The toilet in his college apartment was clogged, so in order to take the test, I had to hold on to the grimy shower wall and pee in the bathtub. I squatted down over the drain and peed over both the test and my feet. And all I could say while I waited was, "I'm so scared."[11]

---

[10]Amber Madison, *Hooking Up: A Girl's All-Out Guide to Sex and Sexuality* (Amherst, N.Y.: Prometheus, 2006), p. 102.

[11]Ibid., pp.127-28. Despite the often touted peace of mind contraception is supposed to ensure to the unmarried, Amber Madison confesses, "After I started having sex, I would spend the week before my period agonizing over whether or not it would actually come, and whether or not I was pregnant. It didn't matter how many kinds of contraception I used. I was always nervous" (p. 127). And, despite the multi-partner premise of the book, she herself recommends monogamy, "If you are going to have sex, it is safest to do it within a long-term monogamous relationship (where both you and your partner are having sex only with each other). If you are having sex with only one person, and that person is having sex with only you, it greatly limits your exposure to STDs. The more people you have sex with, the more likely it is that you will get an STD. Although there is always a risk of contracting an STD when you're having

What should be a nonissue for sexually monogamous couples—sexually transmitted diseases—and a source of joy for married couples—the advent of a child—become calamities for those who seek intimacy outside of the safe house of monogamous marriage.

But so common is this misunderstanding that *Webster's Dictionary* settles for "familiarity" for its primary definition of "intimacy." Interestingly, its second definition parallels Amber Madison's topic, "an intimate act; especially illicit sexual intercourse: a euphemism."[12] How is it that such a beautiful term became associated with risk-taking actions outside the intention of the One who created sex? Clearly, the answer is that humanity has chronically misunderstood God's directions. We live in a biblically illiterate age. Few people have a clue that God has such a healthy view of God's own gift of sex. "Rejoice in the wife of your youth," reads the book of Proverbs 5:18-19, "a lovely deer, a graceful doe. May her breasts satisfy you at all times; may you be intoxicated always by her love" (cf. Eccles 9:9). And in the New Testament the apostle Paul writes:

> The husband should give to his wife her conjugal rights, and likewise the wife to her husband. For the wife does not have authority over her own body, but the husband does; likewise the husband does not have authority over his own body, but the wife does. Do not deprive one another except perhaps by agreement for a set time, to devote yourselves to prayer, and then come together again. (1 Cor 7:3-5)

Which sounds more healthy and upbuilding? A clandestine, risk-filled, casual encounter among strangers that may make the body familiar to each other but leaves the soul a stranger; or this healthy, lusty union of two halves of humanity, liberated in the security of a marriage bond to become *one flesh* again and again by divine blessing?

We ourselves schedule set times together weekly and refuse to take outside commitments on scheduled nights. We also resist long absences that would keep us apart from one another. The parody of the old adage

---

sex, your risk is much lower if you have one partner for an extended period of time—and that partner is remaining faithful to you" (p. 89).

[12]Noah Webster, *Webster's New Universal Unabridged Dictionary*, 2nd ed. (New York: Dorset & Baber, 1972), p. 962.

"absence makes the heart grow fonder," "absence makes the heart go wander," echoes the warning in 1 Corinthians 7:5. We should be exploring all the gifts God gave us together with our spouse. Enjoying sex, sharing aspirations, building a life together, these are all things God intended for married couples. If either husband or wife finds himself or herself unable to function correctly, in other words, one is sexually fearful, competitive rather than cooperative, more interested in individual than shared pursuits, that one should immediately seek responsible Christian counseling to help identify and deal with the problem. One man we knew wooed his wife with lots of attention, but when she married him, he left her home alone every single weekday and weekend night to work on his several cars in his garage. After two years of living with a stranger, she left him. He tried to woo her back, but it was too late. He sadly discovered you can't take a reconstructed BMW to bed with you on cold nights.

We also consider protecting our marriage from outside invasion as a joint responsibility. Unlike the unmarried, who are never more than visitors, this is our home; we belong here. This is our turf. And we both need to defend that turf against interlopers. Our borders are sacred, as we remember God set them for us. And those who would invade them are strong. None of us should ever underestimate the power of temptation or overestimate our ability to withstand it, whether it is live and in person or on the Internet. In regard to live temptation, avoid all conversation with those with a crush on you. Your spouse can also intervene and chase alienators off. It is actually a very effective way to deal with them. On the Internet, men especially should keep in mind that, if pornography didn't work, it wouldn't be a multimillion dollar industry. Of course, it's going to work on you—take that as a given.[13] Therefore,

---

[13]Of the people who engage in "visual pornography," 90 percent are male, 10 percent are female, according to Mary Stewart Van Leeuwen, *My Brother's Keeper: What the Social Sciences Do (and Don't) Tell Us About Masculinity* (Downers Grove, Ill.: InterVarsity Press, 2002), p. 214. In *Pornified: How Pornography Is Transforming Our Lives, Our Relationships, and Our Families,* Pamela Paul points out that pornography is not matrimony-oriented. Because it is a type of adultery (as Jesus specifies in Mt 5:28), it is causing many divorces. She concludes, "Pornography has a corrosive effect on men's relationships with women and a negative impact on male sexual performance and satisfaction. It plays a rising role in intimacy disorders" (New York: Henry Holt, 2005), pp. 141, 163, 167, 267.

keep an updated spam policing system in place, don't subscribe to cable stations with sexually oriented programming (we ourselves don't subscribe to any cable and don't watch broadcast television as a rule). At work, never cover glass office windows; a fishbowl situation is a great protection. The list is endless for those who want to protect themselves and their fidelity. What we are trying to avoid is polluting our healthy view of sex with the world's unhealthy one.

The same apostle Paul counseled the new Roman followers of Jesus: "Do not be conformed to this world, but be transformed by the renewing of your minds, so that you may discern what is the will of God—what is good and acceptable and perfect" (Rom 12:2). Simply because we've made a confession of faith and asked Jesus to become the ruler of our lives doesn't mean we have all our thoughts immediately, miraculously straightened out. As Paul told the young Timothy, "Work hard to show yourself genuine to God, a worker with no need to be ashamed, interpreting correctly the word of truth" (2 Tim 2:15, Bill's translation). In no more crucial area is that advice needed than in each one of us learning "how to control [our] own body in holiness and honor" (1 Thess 4:4) and keeping the marriage bed "undefiled" (Heb 13:4).

Jesus interpreted the Trinity's intention for marriage in a definitive statement in Matthew 19:3-9: One man, one woman (v. 4) unite (v. 5) by God's decree becoming a new united person in God's eyes that no one should redivide by enticing one half away from the other or by either spouse leaving the union to unite with some third party outside of it (v. 6). Divorce is not what God ordained (v. 8). Sexual betrayal murders the *one flesh* that God brought together (v. 9). Intimacy dies with adultery, but thrives on fidelity. That is our Lord's teaching.

Instead, faithfulness in marriage is the bottom-line prerequisite for a foundational basis of trust into joy that stretches from Genesis 2:24 on throughout the Bible (e.g., Ex 20:14; Prov 7:5-27; Mt 5:31-32; 1 Cor 6:15-20). Breaking the marriage vow by having sexual relations with anyone besides one's *one-flesh* spouse destroys even physical intimacy by shattering its foundation of trust. If we can't be trusted to give ourselves entirely and solely to our spouse, we can't expect our spouse to give herself or himself totally to us. Intimacy needs complete trust to stand upon, for, without a sure footing, it topples down and smashes. Many bedrooms are littered with the shattered pieces. Small wonder, then, that the research done by the University of Chicago and the State University of New York discovered that "in real life, the unheralded, seldom discussed world of married sex is actually the one that satisfies people the most."[14] Further, a study of 130 couples by Steil and Turetsky found that "equality was positively related to sexual intimacy."[15] Why should such findings be the case? Because true equality is built on joint submission to Christ, shared leadership, joint determination of goals, equal distribution of power, division of tasks by gifts, mutual honor, respect, tenderness and kindness.

---

[14]Glenn Stanton, *Why Marriage Matters: Reasons to Believe in Marriage in Postmodern Society* (Colorado Springs: Piñon, 1997), p. 42. For suggestions on physical intimacy in marriage, see Douglas E. Rosenau, *A Celebration of Sex* (Nashville: Thomas Nelson, 1994).

[15]Judith K. Balswick and Jack O. Balswick, "Marriage as a Partnership of Equals," in *Discovering Biblical Equality: Complementarity Without Hierarchy*, ed. Ronald W. Pierce and Rebecca Merrill Groothuis (Downers Grove, Ill.: InterVarsity Press, 2005), p. 462. Dennis J. Preato has gathered up a number of helpful studies in his article, "A Fresh Perspective on Submission and Authority in Marriage," in *Priscilla Papers*, 19, no.1 (Winter 2005): 22-24. He notes Pennsylvania state demographers and sociologists Alan Booth and Paul Amato contacted 2000 men, women and some of their children six times per year from 1980-2000, then concluded with a random sample of 2,100 more married couples in 2000. Their conclusion? "Equality is good for a marriage. It's good for both husbands and wives. If the wife goes from a patriarchal marriage to an egalitarian one, she'll be much happier, much less likely to look for a way out. And in the long run, the husbands are happier too." University of Minnesota Professor Emeritus David Olson conducted a survey of 21,501 married couples, having them complete 30 background and 165 particular questions covering 20 marital issues. Eighty-one percent of the couples identified as egalitarian were reported as happily married and 98 percent of happy couples said they felt intimate with each other. "Couple inflexibility," inequality in sharing leadership, was identified as the primary cause of feelings of estrangement. In addition, University of Washington sociologists, Pepper Schwartz and Philip Blumstein surveyed 15,000 North American couples for a decade, publishing the results in 1983. They concluded "equality and shared power" led to long and happy marriages and "inequality experienced by women was a primary cause of unhappiness leading to the break up of marriages." Ashton Applewhite in *Cutting Loose: Why Women Who End Their Marriages Do So Well* discovered egalitarian marriages make women happy, basing her finding on a 1995 polling of 4,000 women. Baylor University Chair of the School of Social Work, Diana Garland, cites a 1980 study by Straus, Gelles and Steinmetz in her book *Family Ministry: A Comprehensive Guide* to relate happiness in egalitarian marriages to "300 percent" lower abuse rates. She further cites studies by "Bean, Curtis and Marcum 1977; Blood and Wolfe 1960; Centers, Raven and Rodrigues 1971; Locke and Karlsson 1952; Michel 1967" to conclude that egalitarian spouses "are more satisfied with their marriages than those in traditional relationships." Still, psychotherapist James P. Delphino, after 27 years in private practice, noted, "It's not common to meet couples with a shared view of power in their sexuality" ("Sex Makes the World Go 'Round'" in *Primetime A&E* [April, 2007]: 48), so there's still room for us all to improve.

Concluding Dialogue

A *reas of agreement.* The Tracys speak for both couples, when they observe, "If we didn't know better, we would say that surely we had read each others' chapters because they have such similar and overlapping content." In spite of our quite divergent backgrounds, training and gender-role convictions, as couples we independently built incredibly similar models of marital intimacy. There were more agreements in this chapter (terminology, use of Scripture, theses, illustrations, even practical personal illustrations) than in any previous chapter. We find this very affirming and encouraging, for it suggests that walking with God and loving your spouse for several decades reveals common truths about intimacy. It also suggests to us that Spirit-empowered love looks very similar in Christian marriage regardless of differing convictions regarding women's roles. (Of course, there are limits to this hypothesis. We aren't convinced that couples who hold a traditional, power-based male headship model would reflect the same convictions regarding intimacy. This would make for an intriguing future study.)

The Spencers too commented on the striking similarity of so many points of agreement that they felt that much of this chapter may have uncovered what was foundational to all Christian marriage, independent of perspective. They also appreciated the depth of bonding the Tracys had achieved and found the Tracys added dimension of bonding and "nonerotic affectionate touch which spouses give to each other" enlightening and helpful.

The Tracys too felt this will be one of the book's most helpful chapters for readers. The Spencers also believed it was the kind of information that they were searching for decades ago when they were contemplating marriage. The Tracys added, "Both couples' deep love for their spouses came through loudly and clearly." "Tender" is the word Celestia used to describe the Spencers' chapter. And the Spencers found the Tracys' chapter "very caring."

Steve also observed to the Spencers, "Though this may not have been a primary goal of the chapter, after I read yours it struck me that it is a strong polemic for biblical sexual morality by lifting up the beauty of marital love and the danger/damage involved in pre and extramarital sex." The Spencers observed the same agreement. Both couples agreed completely that sex and physical intimacy are sacred and to be reserved solely for the marriage bond. Both couples also saw the marriage bond as exclusive. It demands putting each spouse's priority on the relationship with the other spouse by emphasizing bondedness in every area of life. Consequently, both couples opposed pornography as detrimental to a good marriage, recognizing that contemporary culture was obsessed with sex. Each couple pointed out that sex belongs to God, who created it and therefore defines its proper use. The exclusive nature of sex to marriage, then, is God's determination and not subject to human whim or redefinition. Each couple emphasized the significance of sex in expressing the *one-flesh* relationship of marriage. Each cited the Hebrew word *yāda'* ("to know") as a foundational biblical motif that clarifies marital intimacy, expressing the increasing, deeper knowledge of the *one-flesh* union that is itself marriage. Both saw sexual union as a covenantal act that bonds and expresses intimate oneness. And each gave similar suggestions for protecting marital intimacy, including guarding against the danger of letting the world define or even influence one's view of sexuality. Both couples agreed that spouses had a mutual responsibility to protect each other and their home.

Both were struck by the similarities of the categories of intimacy independently selected (spiritual, relational, emotional, physical for the Tracys and spiritual, personal, relational, emotional/psychological, physical for the Spencers, both couples seeing the spiritual as foundational). Both agreed that intimacy begins with a relationship with God, since God, the Trinity, is relational and made humans, in God's image, as relational beings.

As a result of such an emphasis on intimacy, neither couple felt the need to go into great detail on the "how to" specifics of building a healthy marital sex life. This was because both couples are convinced that the key to building marital sexual intimacy is building intimacy in general. That is, deepen the love, emotional closeness, respect and relational intimacy, and a healthy, mutually satisfying sexual relationship will be the natural result.

To foster such a climate of intimacy, both couples emphasized the need for spouses to share completely and honestly with each other their feelings, fears, dreams and struggles. Both couples even gave the same single exception to this rule—professional confidences. In terms of sexual intimacy, both couples appealed to 1 Corinthians 7:1-5 and made very similar points. (The Spencers spoke of scheduling regular time together, whereas the Tracys spoke of "regular sexual relations" and of a "sensate hour.") Both appreciated Rosenau's *The Celebration of Sex* and emphasized the importance of premarital counseling.

Both couples also chose parallel scriptures dealing with suffering and joy as an essential component of a godly relationship (the Tracys picked Romanns 12:15, "Rejoice with those who rejoice, weep with those who weep" and the Spencers chose 1 Corinthians 12:26, "If one member suffers, all suffer together with it; if one member is being honored, all rejoice together with it").

Differences. The Tracys observed several differences in approach or emphasis, noting for example, "The Spencers fleshed out some of the implications of the *one-flesh* commitment in terms of how it changes not only the relationship but the two people. They gave excellent personal illustrations from their own families to show that in long-term bonded marriages, when one spouse dies, part of the other spouse also dies." The Spencers agreed and added that seeing "personal intimacy" as a separate category went along with their understanding of the need to expand one's self-identity to include the spouse with whom one was uniting into God's *one-flesh* redefinition, indicating that we need to define ourselves before we redefine ourselves in marriage. The Tracys blended their discussion of individual personhood into each section (e.g., "each partner is committed to his or her individual spiritual growth and oneness with Christ"). The Spencers wholeheartedly agreed with the Tracys' statement that "God is relational, and exists in intimate relationship within his own divine being." And, while they also agreed thoroughly that men and women are both made in God's image, they found themselves emphasizing personhood rather than specific gender, when the Tracys concluded "specific gender as male and female flows out of our creation in God's image." The Spencers felt instead that our personhood grows out of our creation in God's image, gender being assigned to each half of humanity for instruction in loving another to prepare us to love the Wholly Other and for procreation.

The Tracys added a dimension of bonding—(nonerotic) physical—which they define as "nonerotic affectionate touch that spouses give to each other." The Spencers appreciated this addition very much. The Spencers also observed the parallel between encouraging sex as spontaneous but also as a possible part of the routine of the sensate hour in the Tracys' presentation. The Spencers, who have a marital rule not to be separated from each other for more than one night, a rule they have observed strictly over thirty-five years of marriage except for emergencies, thought the "sensate hour" might also be part of the Tracys' solution to compensate for any long separations.

Each couple appreciated the other couple's wholesomeness, godliness and exemplary love for each other, and feel blessed to be sharing this discussion of marriage with them.

Chapter Five

Responses from Three Couples

Marriage for a
North American Hispanic Couple

Wanda R. and Robert (Bob) W. Pazmiño

From a Hispanic perspective in the United States and as we approach the sixty-year transition in our personal lives, marriage is experienced in the interlocking web of extended family with all of its joys and sorrows. When we married back in 1969, our extended families entered a relationship that has continued through these past forty years in regular interactions even when we personally have not been present at family gatherings and events. Though we live within four hours driving distance from both of our families of origin, on a daily basis our married life interfaces with the transitions of aging parents, young adult children and their children as they navigate their professional, family and spiritual lives.

In our particular case, we are privileged to live three miles from our son, daughter-in-law and six-year-old grandson. We are additionally blessed in together attending a local church where our son and daughter-in-law are assuming spiritual leadership as a deacon and member of the active outreach board respectively. Our spiritual life is nurtured in observing the wonder our grandson Oliver experiences in corporate worship and in assisting with his Christian education experiences both in the congregation and in our homes. Psalm 128:6 notes the following blessing: "May you see your children's children." This adds a dimension of joy to our married life while also serving in helping professions that address the various needs of hurting families and emerging church leaders who will care for those persons in their own ministries. Hispanic culture celebrates joy amid the suffering and challenges of daily or everyday life known as *lo cotidiano* in Spanish. Joy finds expression in daily life from the perspective of the fiesta often associated with Hispanic heritage. Fiesta celebrates the gifts of God for familial and communal life. These extended natural and faith family realities of our married life are not prominent in the descriptions of the Spencer or Tracy families and marriages, but often make up the warp and woof of marriages among Hispanic persons in the United States.

We would note that marriage is renegotiated in terms of role expectations at different stages of our lives with Christ as the center of the relationship. For example, when we were first married Bob worked full time in a psychiatric hospital with emotionally disturbed children for five years, and Wanda part time for a few years in a local public school after the arrival of our first child. This arrangement was possible with the generous support of extended family with whom we lived for three years. During masters and doctoral study for Bob, Wanda worked full time in law schools and Bob assumed the role of house husband for six years, interspersed with summer employment. This renegotiation renews the marriage covenant while inviting growth and making possible change in one's vocational calling.

Like the Spencer marriage, we affirm that spending time together is crucial with all these changes with the continuity of strong extended family ties that can serve to support a Christian marriage. Nevertheless, the biblical model of the husband leaving, cleaving and becoming one, as noted by both the Spencer and Tracy couples, can be a major challenge for Hispanic persons with their close extended family ties unless the process of becoming one includes sustained extended family ties that respect the boundaries of the new couple. The call to physically, emotionally and intellectually establish a marriage requires a new creation that renegotiates previous extended family ties. In addition, the conclusion that loyalty to Jesus supersedes all other loyalties, including familial loyalties, presents an important challenge for Hispanics where family itself, both extended and nuclear, is viewed as a gift from God to sustain personal, communal and social life. The call for humility and servanthood to sustain marriages is too often applied only to women in Hispanic marriages, but it must be noted that both patriarchal and matriarchal patterns persist in Hispanic families often dependent upon the faithful presence of married males in homes that is often related to equitable employment patterns.

We were married at age twenty-one, and we strive to maintain egalitarian convictions with decisions based upon the areas of one's giftedness in married life rather than set or dominant cultural role models that have been renegotiated. To this day Bob does the food shopping and majority of cooking while we both are employed outside of our home with Wanda as a liaison for Hispanic families in the local public schools and Bob as a seminary professor. In terms of the biblical discussion of headship, we tend to see headship as leadership and partnership in the areas of one's giftedness. In the discussion of marital roles and expectations, evangelical Christians can learn from progressive Christians regarding how the outworking of headship and submission historically has too often resulted in male privilege and power with passive female servility and deference practiced in evangelical subculture in the United States. An understanding of how a person's power is exercised under others to lift them up is essential rather than the common understandings of submission that fail to honor mutuality in relationships that is modeled for Christians in the life of the Trinity as the Tracys note. As the Spencers note, obedience to God without a regard to patriarchal conventions of authority are often required to survive in marriages especially for the Hispanic families Wanda encounters daily in her advocacy work in the public schools of Newton, Massachusetts. Too many Hispanic persons in the United States must daily struggle for their survival relying heavily upon the supports of extended family networks with relationship-building time for married couples sacrificed with work demands.

One issue we need to note is the place of personal, familial, and communal histories and cultural patterns as they influence any understanding of marriage in addition to the insights from medical, biological and social science research. For example, Bob's father often did cooking on weekends that Bob also practices. Our son David was a professional chef and culinary writer whose recipes are shared in *Cooks Illustrated*, and he is now a professor of the culinary arts. Family history influences marriage in practice. Married life in ethnic communities attends to historical and cultural patterns passed on across the generations with a necessary proviso noted by James Loder. In *The Logic of the Spirit: Human Development in Theological Perspective* Loder points out that "development is not destiny."[1] Historical and cultural patterns also noted in human development research are not set in stone. This insight applies to marriage with Christian faith affirming that Jesus as the head of marriage offers new life and renewal to all of life including married life for Hispanic persons and other ethnic persons.

We affirm the emphasis upon mutual submission to sustain a healthy marriage and see authority within marriage operating in terms of partnership. The five basic principles identified by the Spencers are helpful in caring enough to confront issues and conflicts. The emphasis upon intimacy is important as noted by the Tracys and insightfully diagrammed with application to Hispanic couples. With the strength of extended family ties, the diligent nurturing of marriage intimacy is crucial for Hispanic marriages over the long haul. First Peter 4:8 that notes "love covers a multitude of sins" is another key touchstone to sustain a strong and resilient marriage for Hispanic and all persons committed to their faith covenant. From our experience this covenant is supported through strong and sustained extended family ties. In many communities, these extended family ties are supported by local Christian churches where folk gather weekly for worship and instruction.

In reflecting back upon our life journey, Wanda notes that making Christ the center of our lives and home has been essential along with affirming and nurturing each other through various transitions along with close ties with our extended families. The shared activities of reading, music, travel, visiting art museums and galleries and now enjoying the "empty nest" has sustained our marriage through challenging times. With decision making, regular dialogue and joint prayer, asking God for wisdom, grace and patience in times of waiting are practices we would recommend for all marriages. Time to celebrate God's gifts of love, mutual respect and marital joys helps to put into perspective the struggles and losses that accompany our lives. The fiesta spirit of Hispanic culture honors these gifts for all Christian marriages.

---

[1]James E. Loder, *The Logic of the Spirit: Human Development in Theological Perspective* (San Francisco: Jossey-Bass, 1998), p. 142.

MARRIAGE FOR A
KOREAN AMERICAN COUPLE

Matthew D. and Sarah S. Kim

Our response to this book on Christian marriage will be communicated through the lens of a second-generation Korean American (SGKA) cultural perspective. That is, we (Sarah and I) are both Americans of Korean ethnic heritage who were born and raised in the United States. Being bicultural, we possess attributes and internalize values combining elements of both American and Korean cultures. Although we do not share the rich longevity of decades of marriage experience like the authors of this book, we have shared more than six happy years of married life together. The purpose of this response chapter will be to apply specific marriage principles that directly affect our bicultural Korean American context.

The purpose of marriage: Advancing God's kingdom. The first marriage principle in this book that we quickly noticed and embraced concerned God's purpose for marriage. Early on, both the Spencers and Tracys discussed the importance of married couples viewing "each other as colaborers in promoting Christ's reign in our world around us" and how "marriage should always advance the kingdom of God." Unfortunately, for many SGKAs, advancing God's kingdom is not their foremost intention or value in the pursuit of a marriage relationship. Rather, in ministering to Asian Americans, we have found that the central ambitions for marriage include: (1) to please parents through the act of marriage (by not remaining single and by finding a coethnic spouse); (2) to establish financial security through professional careers and the purchase of extravagant homes; and (3) to produce and raise offspring that will engender adulation from their local Korean American community.[1] These cultural values are a hybrid of Korean Confucian tenets which highly esteem the family unit, education and economic prosperity as well as the immigrant quest for the American dream. In various ways, these Korean Confucian cultural expectations become forms of idolatry for many married couples in Korean American circles.

As a couple, however, we have sought to challenge the pervasive spirit of materialism that consumes many in the SGKA church with biblical morals that sponsor prudence and stewardship. For example, even before considering marriage, Sarah developed several Christlike values through working with Christian organizations such as InterVarsity Christian Fellowship, which teach students that every aspect of their lives should glorify God and expand God's kingdom values. After several years of learning and growing in these constructive environments, Sarah translated directly this knowledge and experience to the marriage relationship where she understood that marriage is not self-seeking in nature, but for the purpose of reflecting and living out God's values of justice, mercy, reconciliation and incarnational living, among others. Ultimately, this book has reminded us of the importance of challenging SGKAs on their views of marriage and offering a safe haven to question more unconstructive ethnic and cultural values instilled in so many SGKAs, so that these spouses may spur one another on toward good deeds that advance God's kingdom.

Expectations in marriage: equality and one flesh. A second marriage principle that positively instructs our SGKA context involves biblical expectations in the marriage relationship. During our time in pastoral ministry, we have counseled several individuals and couples seeking to be married. One conspicuous expectation that many, if not all, of these individuals and couples share is that the future husband is anticipated to be the "spiritual leader" of the family. In many Korean American churches, young adults are instructed by pastors and other church leaders that, in all cases, men are to be the *head* of the household, which transpires into the role of "spiritual leader" of the family. For many SGKA young adults,

---

[1]See Matthew D. Kim, *Preaching to Second Generation Korean Americans: Towards a Possible Selves Contextual Homiletic* (New York: Peter Lang, 2007), pp. 103-21.

this concept of "spiritual leadership" in the home is rather amorphous. When asked what "spiritual leadership" means, men and women alike are unable to define what that looks like for their relationship. We believe that this ambiguity in gender roles is one ramification of observing first generation parents where many immigrant fathers had the final say when it came to domestic decisions, but failed to model spiritual maturity and direction in the home for their children.

Having grown up in a traditional Korean home, early on in our marriage, like Steve Tracy early in his marriage, I (Matt) believed that I was "the priest of the family" and that "God would speak to us through me." Consequently, I became easily frustrated and threatened when Sarah appeared to initiate forms of spiritual headship in our marriage. However, through both turbulent and peaceful waters in our married lives together, we (especially Matt) have come to the epiphany that God has brought us together to strengthen each other mutually in our personal relationships with Christ and in our respective roles in ecclesial ministry. For example, when Matt requires encouragement from an arduous week of pastoral responsibilities, Sarah is there to speak life-giving words of support from Scripture into his life. Similarly, when Sarah feels discouraged from the intrinsic burdens of being a pastor's wife, Matt sits beside her and reminds her to fix her eyes on the Lord Jesus Christ for whom she labors so diligently. Thus, we have realized that it is not two separate people seeking to have the final word or spiritual power, but rather two people under the headship of Christ who love and serve the other with a common aspiration of support and partnership. This is the model of biblical marriage that we hope to inculcate in our SGKA parishioners.

Another noticeable expectation in Christian marriage broached earlier in this book that is rather thorny for some SGKA couples is the concept of becoming *one flesh*. Yet, in the Korean American context, the struggles of being *one flesh* take a slightly different shape. That is, especially for Korean American males, it is cumbersome and at times unfeasible to disconnect themselves from the persuasion or even blatant control of their immigrant parents. However, as the authors of this book have stated so clearly, in Christian marriage, "the husband must leave home physically, emotionally and intellectually." Since Korean culture is heavily shaped by filial piety, the Confucian belief that children, in particular sons, should obey their parents at all costs, this complicates the marriage relationship on a number of different levels. We have witnessed how situations with in-laws can become so taxing that wives either live with constant frustration or in some cases leave the marriage relationship altogether.

Fortunately, for Sarah and me, our parents have, generally speaking, "let their children go." Two months after our wedding, we moved overseas to Edinburgh, Scotland, so that Matt could pursue his doctoral program. This physical absence from both sets of parents immediately facilitated the formation of our own family unit. During this time away from the States, we developed a system of communication where each called his or her parents once a week to share how we were doing. Sometimes Matt would call Sarah's parents and vice versa. This direct contact with in-laws established trust via open communication. Now that relationships have solidified, there are even moments when Matt's parents do not need to speak directly with Matt but are satisfied simply to handle any immediate situations and concerns with Sarah.

We recognize, however, that not all in-laws are so accommodating. For those couples struggling to detach themselves from unyielding parents, we encourage you to take a more "American" approach to in-law relations by explaining sensitively to parents how they may improve your marriage by maintaining boundaries. No parent wants their children to experience divorce or even marital strife especially on their account. Although not always viable, SGKA couples need to respect and build up the marriage relationship by pulling away from their parents so that they can create a healthy marriage with their spouse and become *one flesh*. This biblical principle is a crucial and often unspoken concern in many SGKA marriages that requires urgent attention.

Conclusion. Marriage in any ethnic and cultural context can be simultaneously frustrating and fulfilling. The authors of this work have presented valuable personal anecdotes and recommendations to further our understanding of healthy Christian marriages in practice. In this response chapter, we have only hinted at some of the challenges of ameliorating Christian marriages in the SGKA context. As noted, the contours of marriage for SGKAs are exacerbated by dual Korean and American cultural influences. Yet, what matters most is that biblical principles for marriage are practiced by all. As SGKA young adults and other Asian Americans read this book, we are hopeful that they will glean from the authors' joint experiences but most importantly place Jesus Christ at the forefront of their marriage partnership so that it will be lasting, vibrant, gratifying and ultimately bring greater glory to God.

Marriage for an African American Couple

Darin and Vicki Poullard

For the past five years I (Darin) have been privileged to serve as pastor of the Fort Washington Baptist Church located in Fort Washington, Maryland. Our membership is nearly 450, averaging close to 320 per Sunday. The congregation is predominantly African American. Many of the members are married with children, have earned degrees, own their homes, are successful in their careers of choice, are financially well off, are rearing their children in the Christian faith, and demonstrate a level of commitment to living the Christian life. They are highly intelligent, ambitious, and overall wonderful people of God. Serving this congregation has been one of my greatest joys.

As pastor, my time is consumed with ministering the word through teaching and preaching, visiting the sick, and overseeing the overall ministry. In addition to these things, considerable time is made available for church members who need premarital and postmarital counseling/spiritual guidance. Some people believe that with more success and fortune comes more happiness. However, soon after saying "I do," couples come to realize that neither their accomplishments nor their material possessions prevent marital strife. Thus, while serving a very prosperous body of believers, I've had to counsel more couples than I can recall.

For this book, I was able to identify thirty-two couples I've had in postmarital counseling. At times the issues being addressed were insurmountable and some couples ended unions that had begun with excitement and so much hope. There have been outbursts of anger, crying and even physical attacks in the middle of a session. On each occasion I've met with a couple, I've held on to the belief that through Christ and hearts of reconciliation saints could overcome their issues. To my disappointment and sorrow, many believing Christians have not been able to reconcile and resolve issues. In counseling sessions, we studied the Scriptures, clarified the issues, sought to communicate openly and honestly; I offered practical advice, gave assignments to be done at home, prayed with them and encouraged them to see things from a biblical perspective. In many cases, it was to no avail. What I so often needed during these sessions was a resource like the one prepared by the Spencers and the Tracys to help couples address and conquer issues that war against oneness.

In counseling sessions, I've tackled many, if not all of the issues raised in the book. Twenty-three out of thirty-two couples I've counseled complained of unfulfilled sexual desires and little to no intimacy. Neither husbands nor wives knew how to rekindle the flames of passion that once ignited so many memorable moments in their marriage. What factors cause couples to lose intimacy and passion? The Tracys contend that God is relational, and exists in intimate relationship within his own divine being. The male and female, as a result of being created in the image of God, have an intense longing for and capacity toward intimate relationships. Marriage provides one of the most intimate divinely sanctioned human relationships (*one-flesh* bond) and one of the most intimate types of human interaction (sexual intercourse). For couples who have lost sexual intimacy in their relationship, the Tracys argue that relational intimacy is a commitment to bless the other person and honor their unique relationship. They believe relational intimacy leads naturally to sexual intimacy. The Spencers believe that sexual attraction alone rarely keeps people together. Furthermore, physical intimacy is the delightful companion of emotional intimacy; but sex becomes distorted and ultimately disappointing when it is cut off from emotional closeness. Thus, intimacy includes sexual intercourse, but so much more than sexual intercourse is needed to maintain the intimacy.

For those couples destitute of intimacy, the insights of the Tracys (that intimacy must be a priority and commitment to the well-being, feelings and needs of one's spouse) and the Spencers (that Christians build intimacy on faithfulness to vows, on complete trustworthiness to honor one's partner with tender care and not abuse, and a lifelong commitment to stay together) would have helped. Sixteen of the couples who had a loss of intimacy had abandoned intimacy with a spouse for the exhilaration of a stranger (Prov 5:15-20). Adultery had conquered their intimacy. As the Spencers note, adultery is sexual betrayal! Sexual betrayal murders the *one flesh* that God brought together. Intimacy dies with adultery, but thrives on fidelity. When one is faithful to his/her spouse, that is, faithful to relational and emotional intimacy, sexual needs are satisfied. When sexual needs are left unfulfilled, Satan entices us with illegitimate sources of sexual fulfillment because of our vulnerability. If couples would follow the counsel of these authors and maintain, prioritize and commit to relational and emotional intimacy, and if they would jointly protect their marriage from outside invasions, rarely will the flames of passion be doused by adultery or extinguished because of neglect.

Unresolved conflict and anger consumed twenty-four out of thirty-two couples counseled. Twenty-five betrayed spouses could not dislodge themselves from feelings of distrust. Twenty-five spouses were convinced that his/her spouse had no respect for the relationship. Quoting Alice Mathews and Gay Hubbard, the Spencers wrote that marriage is for two fallen people who are reaching out to please Christ together:

> [Marriage involves] living out the intimate connection of two broken image-bearers who are in the process of being restored and who are committed to helping one another in the restoration process. It is about two broken image-bearers forming with one another a demonstration of God's transforming power.[1]

Some people have an unrealistic expectation of their spouse; entering the marriage union believing that he or she is beyond reproach, sin or selfish and uncaring acts that require forgiveness. I've tried to help couples resolve conflict and anger by embracing the truth that in marriage no one arrives as he or she ought to be, but through the grace of God, the transforming power of the Holy Spirit, having a heart filled with the Word of God, having a commitment to doing what is in the best interest

---

[1]Alice P. Mathews and M. Gay Hubbard, *Marriage Made in Eden: A Pre-Modern Perspective for a Post-Christian World* (Grand Rapids: Baker, 2004), p. 200.

of the spouse and the marriage, and maintaining a committed walk with Jesus Christ will enable one to grow to become more and more as he or she must be to protect the heart of his or her spouse.

Growing spouses wound loved ones less frequently because they govern their actions based on how their actions affect the hearts of those whom they love. I encourage couples to resolve anger by doing for their spouse what God so graciously does for us: he forgives us. I've challenged wives and husbands not to make one another plead for what God freely gives to one who sincerely repents of sin. Like the Spencers, I believe we will sin, but the hope is that we will seek to grow by forgiving and being forgiven. Encouraging couples to understand that forgiveness produces growth in Christlikeness, in many cases, has heightened anger, evoked feelings that one spouse had escaped a just punishment for their sin, and a perception that I, as the counselor, was ignorant of the depth of their pain by not having suffered the same trial with my bride. I've encouraged angry spouses to be assured that the punishment a spouse deserves has been sufficiently meted out on Christ. The repentant spouse did not get away; Christ bore the punishment. Thus, the offended spouse can forgive the spouse who committed the offense, as Christ has forgiven the offenses even of the indignant offended spouse. The Tracys are so right on the necessity of forgiveness:

> The reality of human sinfulness and the pain it can and will bring in marriage is what makes grace and forgiveness so essential. We have learned that forgiveness is as essential to marriage as love; for in fact these are really just two sides of the same coin. We are sinners who fail each other constantly, and only forgiveness, not score keeping will keep our marriage alive. . . . We resolve to expend as much time and energy as we must to resolve grievances against each other; we will keep talking until we have forgiven each other. Once we have forgiven our partner, we will never again bring up an old grievance.

Some spouses, completely consumed with anger, are now as guilty of sin as his or her spouse who committed the initial offense because they failed to realize that "an angry person stirs up strife and a hot tempered person abounds in transgressions" (Prov 29:22 NASB). Because of anger and the resulting transgressions, spouses who were initially offended, find themselves guilty of transgressions and needing forgiveness from the spouse who previously sought to be forgiven. Unresolved anger multiplies transgressions in a marriage (Eph 4:26; Jas 1:20), but love expressed through forgiveness covers all transgressions (Prov 10:12).

One area that couples really need training is in effective communication. Out of thirty-two couples, twenty-seven did not communicate effectively. During counseling some spouses demanded to be heard but had no interest in hearing their spouse. Some spouses became either defensive or angry while they listened to their spouse recount transgressions. At other times couples verbally assaulted each other, accused each other and demeaned each other as opposed to effectively communicate. Effective communication is vital and essential to relational/ emotional intimacy, to sexual intimacy, to conflict resolution, to becoming one flesh and to really addressing every area of the marital relationship.[2] It would have been helpful if the book had highlighted barriers to effective communication (i.e., anger, fear, bitterness, unresolved hurt, lack of trust in one's spouse to respond with empathy, inability to articulate one's feelings and concerns, etc.) and also included counsel on how couples could overcome the barriers. Without effective communication, it is difficult, if not impossible, for couples to experience all that God designed a marriage to become. Many people vent as opposed to communicate.[3] Communicating not venting is learned, is effectual in snuffing out anger before it ignites sin, is wholesome and edifying, and serves to liberate hearts from being held captive to bitterness, wrath, malice and revenge (Eph 4:25-32).[4] Even in our relationship with God

---

[2]Both the Spencers and the Tracys address communication to a degree; the Spencers, in regards to roles, decision making, conflict resolution and personal intimacy; the Tracys in regards to seeking forgiveness and honest communication as opposed to venting.

[3]The Tracys state, "Venting is a rash and reckless spewing of negative and angry emotion that disregards the spouse. Venting is for the benefit of the spewer and not for the edification of the hearer. . . . Venting is sin."

[4]The Spencers and the Tracys use as a focus verse Gen 1:26-28 to bring out facets of the marital covenant relationship. In marriage the single male and female become united and reflect humanity in its plurality even as the trinitarian God is plurality in unity. The Tracys, using the same biblical passage, focus on God's relationship within his own divine being and since we are made in his image, we have an intense longing for and capacity toward intimate relationships. In counseling sessions, drawing from these same passages I teach that within the

we must learn how to communicate effectively with God for the purpose of prayer (Lk 11:1; Jas 5:13-18), to ask forgiveness (1 Jn 1:9), and to confess Christ (Rom 10:9).

How might African Americans respond to this book? This book can create conflict between male and females in marriages where black males have understood that males are divinely appointed leaders of the family and wives are to submit to husbands (Eph 5:22-24). In this work, the authors believe that the Lord's will for marriage is mutual submission. Partners submit to Christ, to one another, and share leadership and authority based on giftedness not gender. The argument that male headship is for the purpose of lifting up and empowering one's wife so that they might work together as one versus headship meaning leadership and authority, may not be so readily embraced by black males, who have primarily maintained positional power in the home and the church rather than in society. Black males, who have been marginalized in America, may feel even further marginalized by these teachings on headship. Many black males may feel powerless in society and, based

---

Godhead there is communication (then God said). Even in his incarnation Jesus maintained communication with the Father (Mt 14:13, 23; 26:36) and as the ascended Son of God, he still communicates with the Father (Rom 8:27, 34; 1 Jn 2:1). Within the Godhead, there is collaboration (let us make humanity in our image). The trinitarian God collaborated for our salvation (Mt 3:16-17; Jn 14:16, 23, 26). There is cooperation within the trinitarian relationship (and God created humanity). Creation owes its existence to the cooperation between the Persons within the Trinity. What was determined within the Godhead was realized as the holy three functioned as the holy one. There is commitment within the Godhead (i.e., what the trinitarian God began together, the trinitarian God completed). Furthermore, there is commitment to their union. No member of the Trinity will ever abandon the holy others. Within the trinitarian relationship, there is no competition, no fighting for power, no lordship of one member over the other. There is loving submission by the Son to the Father for redemption's sake and there is loving submission by the Spirit to the will of the Son (Jn 14:16, 26; 16:13). Within the marital covenant, couples who reflect the image of God maintain communication, collaboration, cooperation, commitment and remove competition. There exists a loving and permanent companionship when the image of God is reflected in a marital union. Couples who reflect the image of God, while being two individually, functionally and theologically, are one (Mt 19:5). The husband and wife lovingly submit to one another for the sake of their union and to fulfill the goals of their union. According to the Spencers mutual submission is cooperation with others so that those others can exercise their roles with effectiveness. It is mutual deference and mutual understanding. Mutual submission means revolving leadership by gifting, ability, or responsibility. By communicating, by collaborating and not acting independent of one's spouse, by cooperating with one's spouse to fulfill plans and goals, by committing to one another to stay together and by not competing for power or lordship, couples model a mutually submitted love affair.

on the teachings of headship in the book, may feel they are losing power in the home.[5] The Spencers have written an absolutely superb study on authority, power, and headship. Both spouses are divinely empowered to rule and to exercise authority.[6] As the "head," husbands are given power to help save, deliver, give life, help mature, love, sacrifice for, sanctify, honor, care for, nourish and serve a person as Jesus did. This type of love is totally committed. When husbands and wives love this way there is no abandonment, no divorce, no loss of intimacy, anger is resolved, couples are selfless, the needs of both spouses are met, and the giftedness of each spouse is valued in the union. African American women, who for so long were considered to be on a lower plane than men, considered to be submissive by nature, and considered to be inca- pable of leadership, will joyously receive these new insights.[7] African American couples who embrace mutual submission learn that by doing so the male and female can exercise their marital roles with effective- ness. In a Christian marriage, the husband is not exalted above his wife, neither the wife above her husband. Christ is exalted above all.

---

[5]Quoting Nathan and Julia Hare, *The Endangered Black Family,* Theodore Walker writes, "The most talked about, but least understood, subject among black Americans today is black male- female conflict." Furthermore he writes, "They go on to speak of the problem of 'black male- female-schism' and of 'the displaced power struggle that presents itself between the black male and the black female' as an immediate threat to black family life in the U.S.A. . . . The Hares report that in addition to the black man's increasing inability to exercise the kinds of socio- economic power required to fulfill traditional family obligations, there is—in the wake of new morality, gay liberation, feminist and androgynous trends—increasing confusion and disagree- ment concerning the proper social behavior and roles of males and females. As socio-economic disadvantages increases, as it becomes less possible for black men to form viable, enduring, and mutually advantageous socio-economic relationships with black women, and as confusion about gender-specific roles increases, the opportunity for black male-female conflict is greatly increased." Theodore Walker Jr., *Empower the People: Social Ethics for the African-American Church* (Mary Knoll, N.Y.: Orbis Books, 1991), p. 79.

[6]In the beginning God blessed the male and female equally with shared responsibility (i.e., both were commanded to "Be fruitful and multiply and fill the earth" [Gen 1:28]); with shared authority (i.e., both were commanded to subdue the land and to rule over the natural creation (Gen 1:28); and with shared opportunities to enjoy all that God had given them (Gen 1:29- 30). As a result of sin, the woman was told that her husband would rule over her (Gen 3:16). As a result of redemption, the plans God had for shared leadership among humans have been reestablished. The male and the female are priests (1 Pet 2:9; Rev 1:5), the male and the female exercise gifts that edify (1 Cor 12:4-11), and the male and female are one in Christ (Gal 3:28). Oneness cannot exist where there are inequalities.

[7]Clarence Taylor, *The Black Churches of Brooklyn* (New York: Columbia University Press, 1994), p. 167.

Mature African American males will see that in Christ, there is no loss of power. In fact, one receives power to reject secular notions of masculinity that espouse lording oneself over another, to embrace Christ's model of power through submitted service to others (Mt 20:25-28). If the thirty-two couples I counseled could have received the truths in this book, seven would not have divorced, three would not have separated, and twelve would not be living together with issues still unresolved. Each couple would live as *one flesh* meeting each other's needs for relational, emotional and sexual intimacy.

CONCLUSION

I read for pleasure, mark you. In general I like wedding bells at the end of novels." So confessed A. Edward Norton in *A Victorian Gentleman*. Well, some pleasures transcend their age. A century later, we also love happy endings. In fact, everyone who ever looked for a happy marriage can resonate with Norton's words, " 'They married and lived happily ever after'—why not? It has been done."

Yes, it has. And our most ardent prayer as we conclude this dialogue is that our Lord who transformed mere water into the most refreshing wine at the wedding at Cana will transform these simple human words and enrich our readers or those they are helping to live happily married lives until he gathers us all up into the everlasting wedding feast of the Lamb that is his future destination for his beloved church.

What did we ourselves learn in our practice, reflection, and dialogue on marriage? Honestly, we also learned a great deal from each other and from the couples who critiqued our dialogue.

In chapter one we began with the premise that Christian marriage means being disciples of Jesus together. In fact, it entails all the virtues that comprise a truly Christian life, such as love, repentance, forgiveness—one might say, even more so than in normal daily Christian living since marriage is a 24-7 commitment.

Certainly, we agreed once more that loyalty to Jesus supersedes all other commitments, even the one to our spouse. At the same time, we realized a truly Christian marriage does not need to be a competition between Jesus our Lord and our spouse. Why not? Because we are *one flesh* together, and husband and wife should be striving to be of one mind (as Jesus prayed for the church in John 17) and that one mind is to serve Christ's kingdom as a unified team. As we will see shortly, our responders were to expand the dimension of this issue even wider as they took into consideration the wider family.

In our discussion, we discerned that God has provided us mates to help us develop our spiritual gifts and graces, to help us bear fruit under the Holy Spirit's empowerment and to please God by, in turn, building our spouse up in each of these areas. Marriage is about sacrificing one's self to gain a pearl of great price—a godly companion. It is, thus, a teaching tool God employs to encourage us to seek the greatest and most priceless pearl of all: God's complete rule in our lives.

Chapter two was the test of how well we reached our irenic goals and readers can judge if we successfully achieved them. Here we confronted the explosive topics of head and submission and were delighted to discover that even here we had profound areas of agreement. The bridge between our viewpoints was love. For a husband to be a wife's head, whether that means source or leader/protector, means that he loves, honors, nurtures, and sacrifices for her. Such love mirrors the great love within the Trinity, the paradigm for all that can truly be called love on earth. Both couples affirmed a mutual submission in marriage that never involves forced subjection, but is motivated by respect and a desire to cooperate with each other and to obey Christ. Again, Jesus was the model. The gain was to become more Christlike, receive love and respect back, and witness for Jesus through displaying love to the watching world—a phenomenal payoff.

Differences we discovered were just as profound. Most notable was a difference in our understanding of the relationship between gender and God. The Tracys began their discussion with a study of 1 Corinthians 11:3 and focused on headship, believing that male/female relationships are patterned after the Father/Son relationship in which the Father is shown to initiate, protect, honor, and empower the Son. Their study of *head* causes them to conclude that Scripture deemphasizes and significantly qualifies a husband's authority. Thus, the essence of a husband's biblical *headship* is not power and authority over his wife but a responsibility to serve her. So in marriage a husband is to use his headship to lift up and empower his wife so that they might work together as one. The Spencers began their discussion with their understanding of authority and moved to Ephesians 5 and the discussion of head, seeing personhood as reflecting God in Genesis 1:27 and gender as strictly material,

God's teaching tool to instruct humans to learn to love an other in preparation for loving the Wholly Other. The Spencers emphasized the unity within the Godhead, reflected in a unity among humans that precedes diversity, so being single (independence) precedes being married (interdependence). Singles reflect the unity of God; the married image God's diversity. Personhood as the key factor assures that even someone who is hermaphroditical also reflects God's image, since personhood precedes the apparatuses of gender. The Tracys' model also emphasizes intimacy and mutuality yet acknowledges that in the Trinity as well as in marriage, there are some differing emphases and activities. They note that some of the commands in Scripture to husbands and wives are gender specific. Thus, while they affirm mutual submission and mutuality of work in marriage they also argue that husbands are to initiate, protect and lead, and wives are to yield in love. The loving agreement of husband and wife reflects the loving accord in the Trinity and the unity of God. This shared love within a soft authority structure is what they understand Paul is teaching in Ephesians 5. The Spencers, on the other hand, compared Paul's teachings in Ephesians 5 and Titus 2:4 to conclude his advice was applicable to both spouses. They saw this as indicative of the way power is distributed in shifting patterns in the Trinity (for example, the self-humbling of the Son during the salvific task of the incarnation) and in humanity in authority being distributed according to giftedness, abilities and mutually agreed upon responsibilities when addressing tasks in the home and the larger church.

As might be expected, we discovered we were viewing this issue in nearly opposite ways. For example, the Tracys used *headship* as a lens to view mutual submission, the Spencers mutual submission to understand *head*. Though both couples assumed the highest view of the authority of Scripture, our interpretive methodologies and premises differed. Ironically, each thought the other couple used texts more broadly and they themselves focused more narrowly!

But, at the end of the discussion, we realized together that the key in both marriage and in our relationship in the greater church was unified in the essentials: that love is key and authority should never overpower another.

Chapter three was enlightening. Although roles in marriage is the wrestling ring of the egalitarian-complementarian debate, we were amazed to find over a dozen points of agreement, which certainly shows that the unifying bond of Christ is stronger than the variety of differing interpretations. In a time when a "multitude of Christianities" are posited by many scholars for the Bible as well as the church, we are heartened to see emerging in our dialogue a single, solid faith with universal standards that lies at the heart of our faith in Jesus Christ. Some of these standards include giftedness of both women and men by God, marriage as an end of singleness and a beginning of the new *one-flesh* entity, a joint "marital mission," as well as many others.

Further, both couples are against separate spheres for husband and wife. Both are agreed the husband alone is not the priest of the household, even though for the Tracys he initiates, protects, and empowers others in family devotions, whereas the Spencers believe either husband or wife can initiate, protect and empower others in family devotions, another example of sharing the same values but holding a different understanding of which spouse should lead them. We all agree, however, that *head* and *submission* need nuanced descriptions, and couples must watch out for the dangerous use of power and control. We agree wholeheartedly we must all follow Jesus' example as he modeled servant leadership and never overpowered or usurped power over another (not even over the high priest or procurator who condemned him). In fact, even in a controversial passage like Ephesians 5 we agreed the emphasis in *head* is on Christ as servant, so both couples are against power-intensive top-down authority. The Tracys stressed authority as an authority of love not power. And we both agree that men need respect, women need love (and vice versa) and couples should minister and parent together using their gifts jointly. Husbands and wives need each other's input. We all differ with Aristotle's view that women are inferior. Everyone should be empowered and each couple should clarify their own roles and goals and make joint decisions, even if for the Tracys the husband might prayerfully have to decide (every rare while) where there is no consensus, and the Spencers would hold out (after 36 years and counting) that they would jointly seek Jesus' leading in prayer and not advance until consensus is reached. However, even this difference is more philosophical than real, since in practice most of the time decision making is done together by both couples.

Disagreement continued to flow from our differing views on male/female distinctives and their relationship, if such distinctives exist, to marital roles. The Tracys saw specific differences built in by God "to more fully and distinctly image him." These differences were present at creation (they see significance in man being created before woman) and illustrated throughout the biblical data on fathers, mothers, husbands and wives. They also devoted considerable attention to science and social science research which they saw supporting their viewpoint. Particularly, they cited studies that they felt documented innate biological gender differences, such as male assertiveness/aggression, power and status orientation, and female intimacy/relationship orientation and heightened emotional/relational sensitivity. Gender differences, they concluded, were part of a couple's "corporate responsibilities and mutual mission." In summary, the Tracys observed that "form follows function" in marriage in a "beneficial complementation."

The Spencers also recognized biological differences, but saw these differences as belonging to the material not the spiritual dimension of humanity, neither dictating tasks nor leadership. Basing their view on the pre-Fall command jointly to man and woman to rule, they saw God's present intention for redeemed humanity to reach back to that primal model and embrace complete equality of role and function based on giftedness, education, and godly characteristics. The Spencers suspect fallen, corrupted and biased societies and cultures and doubt that their research often does much more than bolster their prejudices and "conform" us to their fallen world perspectives. Therefore, while they certainly value rigorous research, they approach its data and interpretations with great caution. In their home, they make decisions based on what they discern are the biblical criteria of spiritual gifts, natural and learned abilities, equal division of labor, accepted responsibility, time factors, and will only move forward with consensus.

Chapter four, both couples agreed, was the most unified in perspective, showing, as the Tracys expressed it, "that Spirit-empowered love looks very similar in Christian marriage regardless of differing convictions regarding women's roles," "for it suggests that walking with God and loving your spouse for several decades reveals common truths about intimacy." The Spencers agreed that "much of this chapter may have uncovered what was foundational to all Christian marriage, independent of perspective." Particularly strong were our joint emphases on tenderness, marital fidelity and the sacredness of the marriage bond. We jointly agreed that marriage and sex belong to God and are "not subject to human whim or redefinition." Sex, particularly, expresses the *one-flesh* relationship of marriage and is holy. Intimacy begins with God, who is in relationship, so our relationship with each other is informed by deepening our relationship with God. Deepening the love, trust, emotional closeness, empathy, respect, honesty, sexual fidelity and relational intimacy with each other causes a more healthy, mutually satisfying sexual relationship as the natural result.

So, chapter four we all found most encouraging, since we discovered that, despite our fallenness, we had all ended up by God's grace in marriages that imaged something of Christ's love and intimacy. We were also able to see in each other's marriage a Christlike spirit of sacrificial love, a glimpse of the profound love with which Christ loves the church. In that regard, our marriages do look very similar, as we have been blessed with intimate, joyful marriages.

The differences that we recognized in this chapter were fewer than in previous ones and they flowed from our earlier perspectives, but the final sense we were left with was appreciation for the other couple's wholesomeness, godliness and exemplary love for each other and the blessing of the enrichment of having shared this dialogue together.

At this point our responders entered into the discussion and expanded our perspectives considerably.

Bob and Wanda Pazmiño immediately added a dimension both of us couples were missing, an emphasis on the extended family's participation in the relationship and the added blessings and tensions that participation brings. Particularly striking is such active participation's effect on the leaving and cleaving aspect present in Genesis 2:24 and on what we assumed to be a straightforward commitment for Christians: choosing Jesus over the family. Both of these issues take on a whole different cast in the attitude of Hispanic and other Two-Thirds World cultures. Strong in their communal perspective, Bob and Wanda underscored mutual submission, acknowledging that Hispanic families can be either patriarchal or matriarchal, but the model enacted is due more to economics than philosophy. At the core, prayer, patience, love and respect reside at the heart of every truly Christian Hispanic marriage.

The Kims also acknowledged and stressed family involvement, sometimes in the form of pressure to please parents, make money and rear successful children that mixes old world values with the American Dream. Such pressure, they explain, can cause a wife to feel so abandoned that she leaves the marriage, since, in the old Confucian style, so much emphasis has been traditionally placed on a husband choosing his parents' wishes over any others', including his wife's. As a Korean American husband, Matt finds emphasizing advancing God's rule along with the biblical principle of leaving and cleaving as necessary survival tools in the American environment, where shared leadership along with becoming *one flesh* are healthy antidotes for treating beleaguered bicultural Asian-Christian marriages, as they are strained to the breaking by the pull of each culture, both the present and the past.

The Poullards, like the Kims, come from the frontlines of pastoral ministry. They particularly stress faithfulness to God and spouse that fosters loving and honoring intimacy as a crucial need today, and they appreciate its central place in the book. As well they stress as absolutely necessary for marriages to succeed the principal virtues of unselfishness, forgiveness, resolving anger constructively, learning to communicate effectively, and putting Jesus first, that can only be realized consistently when the Holy Spirit transforms our lives.

At the same time, they felt more emphasis was needed on eliminating the barriers to effective communication, which they then listed for readers. They also cautioned us that some African American males will possibly feel threatened by our joint emphasis on mutual submission, feeling that the last refuges for leadership of the black male in our oppressive society, the church and the home, are being taken away. The

Poullards assure us, however, that the mature black Christian male will instead feel empowered by discovering Christ's true model of power, a model that will lift up both black men and black women together, empowering couples to be full leaders together, a deeper and higher goal.

THE SPENCERS' CONCLUDING REFLECTIONS

What a delight to have gotten to know the Tracys through working on this project together. We so appreciated their hearts of love for God and one another. As the dialogue progressed, we realized that even though we tried to be completely open at the outset, we began with some distrust and progressively discovered that some of the things we thought true about the other view were misunderstandings. We learned that there are many nuanced positions, such as hierarchalist, complementarian, soft complementarian. This makes us reflect on what types of nuances exist among egalitarians.

True, we were all committed to irenic dialogue, but we did not consciously structure the resultant *Marriage at the Crossroads* to look like a positive sandwich. It simply began and ended with the first and last chapters as the ones in which we had most agreement and the second and third chapters as the ones in which we most disagreed. We found it affirming that what emerged as central among our agreements was that the scriptural affirmation "God is love" (1 Jn 4:8, 16) revealed itself as the basis of both of our theologies of marriage. This may seem obvious to some, but in a culture where "God is power" appears to be the central conviction, "God is love" is a healthy therapeutic. Since God is love was our basis, it is no surprise we saw love affecting both our ideas and practice. It recalled to our minds the time when a teacher of the law asked Jesus which is the most important commandment and Jesus answered that the greatest commandment is to love God and the second is to love our neighbor as ourself (Mk 12:29-31).

Consequently, forgiveness and humility also showed themselves as important and the basis for intimacy. We appreciated the accord in chapter four as we all agreed that intimacy thrives on trust and that "knowing" our spouse is a fully orbed description of mature intimacy. We also agreed, if the Lord is indeed first, then "Me first" is a poor approach to marriage. We need to steward our marriage relationships by keeping our commitments to God and our spouse and practicing a biblical sexual morality with conviction. Such measures, we all agreed, nurture the *one-flesh* relationship.

With all this accord, are we left, then, with any differences? Yes, but also a more informed understanding that these perspectives vary after having agreed on the basics. What differences do we still recognize? When Jesus answered the teacher of the law in Mark 12:29-31, he quoted Deuteronomy 6:4-5 and Leviticus 19:18. Thus, he introduced his answer with "Hear, O Israel: the Lord our God, the Lord is one" (Mk 12:29). We wholeheartedly agree our God is Lord, and the Lord is "one." We all agree that God as a Trinity informs marriage, but we differ in our understanding of how that applies.

Another key difference in practice was that, for the Tracys, the wife needs to yield to the husband's leadership, whereas for us the husband and wife need to yield to and cooperate with each other's leadership, since Christ is the only final authority. We see a heavier burden on the husband for the Tracys, but an equal burden on husband and wife for us. We still do not see any clear sex-based or gender-differentiated traits, or tasks, or spiritual strengths that are prescriptive for believers in assigning authority or roles. This, perhaps, remains as a defining difference between us: for the Tracys, *role* is defined as "the unique part a male or female plays in joint tasks of marriage," while for us *role* is simply a "task or function."

However, despite these differences, and along with our basic agreements, we were edified by the Tracys' life of faith together and blessed by their obvious devotion to one another.

THE TRACYS' CONCLUDING REFLECTIONS

We loved this project and thoroughly enjoyed and were blessed by co-authoring *Marriage at the Crossroads*. It required of us an even deeper reflection into our own marriage and a determined and sensitive willingness to listen to numerous divergent voices outside of ourselves. Working with the Spencers was both stimulating and encouraging. As we wrote and reviewed each chapter, we were frequently surprised and consistently delighted in the marital convictions and practices we passionately shared as couples. Historically, we have appreciated much about egalitarianism, particularly the emphases on empowering and developing women, acknowledging and condemning the widespread abuse of male power and marital complementation being reflected not in wives serving husbands but in husbands and wives serving each other. The Spencers affirm these principles and many others which we heartily endorse. At the same time, we have come away from this project with an even deeper commitment to an "incarnational" model of male headship as defined by an *authority of love* and not an authority of power. We are also convinced that the explicit biblical data on marriage and family, as well as the scientific research, reveal beautiful gender differences purposefully designed by God. For us, this is an elegant part of the mystery of bonding and complementation. The deeper we dived into the social science research, the more we saw profound and exquisite gender-based complementation that we desire other married couples to embrace and enjoy.

Conversely, neither does our model conform to a hierarchical "complementarian" marriage model in which gender roles are broadly and rigidly distinct. Our failure to conform to either of the dominant two evangelical gender camps made writing this book a challenge, for we often needed to distance ourselves not just from one alternative model but from two. Yet this also had a positive aspect, for it stimulated us to deemphasize preconceived labels and focus on the data before us, drawing conclusions from the data regardless of how they harmonized with other models. This process was helpful in strengthening and articulating our marital convictions. At the same time, we came away from this project deeply humbled by the reminder that equally godly scholars with strong, loving marriages can and do draw contradictory conclusions from the same biblical data. This observation has a very positive underpinning, for though various significant differences are evident between us and the Spencers, we found far more common ground, especially in the daily practices of married life, than we had anticipated. This was one of the most encouraging findings of our project.

Finally, this book project deepened our commitment to work together with evangelicals of varied theological persuasions to advance the cause of Christ. In spite of the largely Christian trappings of our culture, we are living in a post-Christian society. Seismic shifts are rapidly changing the social landscape. For the first time in American history more adults are single than married. We live in a culture where fear of intimacy is the norm, not the exception. Young couples vainly search for marital scripts to guide them; few have seen marriages they want to emulate. Pornography is utterly transforming the relational fabric of our culture, distorting our moral values, and shattering our capacity for genuine intimacy. We now have the first generation of young adults who throughout their entire sexual and relational development have been educated on porn. This pornified culture has stamped their beliefs and conceptualizations of gender, relationships and marriage. With unprecedentedly high levels of sexual, relational and marital brokenness around us, it is time we evangelicals quit fixating on the "in-house" gender debates. We are already late in making this shift. As Christian leaders we must focus on the bigger picture. Together with the Spencers, we are calling for a dramatic shift of emphasis. Let's make the main things the main things—loving our spouses and fellow evangelicals with the sacrificial love of Christ, practicing sexual purity and living out the gospel in our marriages. For Christ's sake, let us move beyond the strident role debates, combining instead, our energy into addressing the questions and needs of today and modeling together godly and radical intimate Christian marriages.

CONTRIBUTORS

Wanda R. Pazmiño is of Puerto Rican descent and has lived in New York City, Puerto Rico and Massachusetts. She serves as the Liaison for Hispanic Families in the Public Schools of Newton, Massachusetts, supporting numerous first-generation families navigating through school and community services. She is an avid reader who delights all with her stories and caring presence. Wanda and her husband Bob have two grown children, David, a writer and professor of the culinary arts, and Rebekah, a law student, and one grandson, Oliver, who attends the Newton Schools.

Robert W. Pazmiño is of Ecuadorian, Dutch and German descent from Brooklyn, New York. He is Valeria Stone Professor of Christian Education at Andover Newton Theological School in Newton Centre, Massachusetts. He is the author of several books, including *Latin American Journey: Insights for Christian Education in North America; Basics of Teaching for Christians: Preparation, Instruction, and Evaluation; God Our Teacher: Theological Basics in Christian Education;* a third edition of *Foundational Issues in Christian Education;* and a book dedicated to his grandson entitled *So What Makes Our Teaching Christian? Teaching in the Name, Spirit, and Power of Jesus.* He is ordained in the American Baptist Churches.

Matthew D. Kim is senior pastor of Logos Central Chapel in Denver, Colorado. He earned his B.A. in history from Carleton College, his M.Div. from Gordon-Conwell Theological Seminary, and his M.Th. and his Ph.D. in theology and ethics (with a concentration in homiletics) from the University of Edinburgh, Scotland. He is the author of *Preaching to Second Generation Korean Americans: Towards a Possible Selves Contextual Homiletic* (New York: Peter Lang, 2007) and has contributed to various journals and books on Asian American ministry and preaching. His current book project is *My First Year in Ministry: 7 Lessons for New Pastors* (forthcoming from Chalice Press). He has also taught as an adjunct faculty member and as the Sams Visiting Professor of Preaching at Gordon-Conwell Theological Seminary. He has been married to Sarah S. Kim since 2002. They are parents of a son, Ryan, with another child on the way.

Sarah S. Kim earned her B.S. in education at Boston University and completed postgraduate studies in community education at Moray House School of Education at the University of Edinburgh, Scotland. She is currently pursuing the M.A. in counseling licensure at Denver Seminary. She worked for several years as a campus staff minister at Boston University through InterVarsity Christian Fellowship and pioneered a new Asian American chapter at Boston College. She has extensive experience in church administration, student ministry and the nonprofit sector.

Darin Vincent Poullard is the pastor of the Fort Washington Baptist Church, located in Fort Washington, Maryland, where he has served since October 2002. Pastor Poullard is a graduate of York College, the City University of New York, where he earned a B.S. in Information Systems and Gordon-Conwell Theological Seminary, the Center for Urban Ministerial Education (CUME), where he earned an M.Div. He has served as the Family Life Minister at St. John's Baptist Church, Woburn, Massachusetts and an Athanasian Teaching Scholar (CUME). Since 1990 he has been married to Vicki Delores Poullard. They are parents of two daughters and live in Waldorf, Maryland.

Vicki Delores Poullard has served in many capacities in the local church. She has served as the church clerk, chairperson of Public Relations, Sunday school secretary, a Bible study teacher for the youth, a children's church facilitator, and the editor for the church newsletter. In her professional life she has worked as a pharmaceutical research analyst and a program manager for the Mary Mcleod Bethune Institute, a nonprofit organization that addresses the various educational needs of

African American and Hispanic girls. She is a graduate of the Mass
Bay Community College in Newton, Massachusetts. Together she labors with Pastor Poullard at Fort Washington Baptist Church. They
are both natives of Queens, New York.

William David Spencer and Aída Besançon Spencer, married in Au-
gust 1972, have written and edited seven books together (including
*Global Voices on Biblical Equality: Women and Men Ministering Together
in the Church, God Through the Looking Glass: Glimpses from the Arts, The
Goddess Revival, The Prayer Life of Jesus: Shout of Agony, Revelation of
Love, A Commentary, The Global God: Multicultural Evangelical Views of
God, Joy Through the Night: Biblical Resources on Suffering, 2 Corinthians:
Bible Study Commentary),* and written and edited books and articles
separately. Bill has written *Mysterium and Mystery: The Clerical Crime
Novel, Dread Jesus,* and coedited *Chanting Down Babylon: The Rastafari
Reader.* He is editor of *Priscilla Papers* (the academic voice of Christians
for Biblical Equality). He has a Th.D. in theology and literature from
Boston University, an M.Div. and Th.M. from Princeton Theological
Seminary, and a B.A. from Rutgers University. He has served as Protestant chaplain at Rider University, adjunct professor with New York
Theological Seminary and helped establish and serve as director of personnel for the Alpha-Omega Community Theological School
(A.C.T.S.). He served as teaching coordinator of the adult literacy program for the Jefferson County (Kentucky) Board of Education and
serves as pastor of encouragement of Pilgrim Church (Beverly, Massachusetts.). He is the Ranked Adjunct Associate Professor of Theology
and the Arts at Gordon-Conwell Theological Seminary's Center for
Urban Ministerial Education (CUME) in Boston.

Aída has written *Beyond the Curse: Women Called to Ministry; Paul's
Literary Style: A Stylistic and Historical Comparison of II Corinthians
11:16–12:13, Romans 8:9–39, and Philippians 3:2–4:13; 2 Corinthians,
Daily Bible Commentary;* and coedited *The Latino Heritage Bible.* She
has a Ph.D. in New Testament from Southern Baptist Theological
Seminary and an M.Div. and Th.M. from Princeton Theological Seminary. She has served as a community organizer (Plainfield, New Jer-

sey), protestant campus minister (New Jersey State College), adjunct professor (New York Theological Seminary), academic dean (A.C.T.S.) and pastor of organization of Pilgrim Church. She is professor of New Testament at Gordon-Conwell Theological Seminary in Hamilton. The Spencers have spoken at churches, conferences and classes on different biblical, theological and experiential aspects of marriage. Both are ordained Presbyterian Church U.S.A. ministers. As ministers, they have counseled many couples before and during marriage. They are parents of Stephen, a chef, musician and filmmaker.

Steven R. and Celestia G. Tracy are high school sweethearts and have been married for thirty years. They are the proud parents of three grown children: Elizabeth, Luke and Abby. For the past decade they have enjoyed an extensive speaking ministry in the United States and Africa on sexuality, marriage and abuse. They are the founders of Mending the Soul Ministries, a Christian nonprofit organization specializing in research, curriculum and training on abuse and healthy sexuality. Celestia studied theology at Western Seminary in Portland, Oregon, and earned her M.A. in Counseling/Psychology from Lewis and Clark College. She has been a licensed professional counselor for fifteen years and is the founding partner of Professional Counseling Associates, a private Christian counseling practice in Mesa, Arizona. Clinically, she has extensive experience and expertise with trauma (particularly physical and sexual abuse), grief and loss, marriage and sexual intimacy. Celestia served as the consultant for *Mending the Soul: Understanding and Healing Abuse* (Zondervan), coauthored and edited a workbook for *Mending the Soul*, and is currently writing a book on building healthy relationships entitled *Forever and Always: The Art of Bonding*.

Steve teaches at Phoenix Seminary as professor of theology and ethics. He previously served Phoenix Seminary for eight years as vice president of academic affairs. He received an M.Div. and Th.M. from Western Baptist Seminary, and a Ph.D. in Biblical Studies from the University of Sheffield (England). Steve served as a pastor for fifteen years in three churches and has extensive marital and sexuality counseling experience. Steve serves on the Executive Committee of the

Gender Study Group for the Evangelical Theological Society and has authored ten academic book chapters and journal articles as well as numerous articles and booklets on gender, sexuality and abuse. He is the author of *Mending the Soul: Understanding and Healing Abuse* (Zondervan), and editor of the *Mending the Soul Workbook*. Steve uses his expertise, specifically on sexuality issues, extensively in the broader secular community as a conference speaker and consultant, and has served for three years on the Governor's Commission for the Prevention of Violence Against Women for the State of Arizona.

SUBJECT INDEX

abuse, 57, 59, 61, 72, 104, 134, 158, 170, 200, 216

Achsah and Othniel, 102

Adam and Eve, 27-29, 31, 102-3, 114, 119, 125-26, 139, 146, 162, 167

addiction(s), 107-8, 174

adultery. *See* sexual/sexuality, vulnerability

Africa, 59-60, 148

aggression. *See* power

Ahasuerus (Xerxes I) and Vashti, 77-78

Allender, Dan. *See* Longman, Tremper

Ananias and Sapphira, 17-18, 22, 30, 167n. 3

Anderson, Herbert, 28, 113, 115, 175-76

anger. *See* sin(s)

Antipater, 80

apostle(s), 25, 27, 81-82, 84-85, 104, 168, 178, 180

Aquila. *See* Prisca

architecture, 120, 134

Aristotle, 101, 124n. 11, 139, 210

Aron, Arthur, 173

authority, 12, 50-51, 60-66, 69, 71, 73-75, 78-79, 86-87, 94, 97, 102, 122, 124, 178, 192, 203-4, 208, 215
  defined, 79-84
  exousiazō/exousia, 81-82, 84
  of love, 66, 76, 95-96, 98, 126, 132, 208-10, 216
  of power, 66, 93-95, 98, 101, 118, 191, 210, 216
  See also leadership

Balswick, Jack, and Judith, 105, 112-13,

171, 181n. 15

black male(s), 203-4, 213-14

bonding. *See* intimacy; *one flesh*

Brouwer, Douglas, 40-41, 94

Brown, Lucy, 173

Buechner, Frederick, 148-49

Cain, 162

Caleb, son of Jephunneh, 102

call/calling, 20, 40, 47, 51, 61, 70, 84, 110-11, 134, 139, 156

Candace, 83

career. *See* call

Causey-Drake, Mischelle, 112-13

Chapman, Gary, 113, 175

Charles, Ray, 157

child rearing, 67-68, 104-5, 107, 111, 115-16, 122, 124, 127, 134-37, 139-40, 154, 165-66, 171, 193-94, 210, 213

Chrysostom, John, 101-2, 112, 168

church, 84-85, 90, 95-96, 103

Cinderella, 155

Claudius, 23

cleave to (*kollēthēsetai*), 27n. 20

cohabitation, 10, 34

Cohen, Simon-Baron, 127, 129-30

command (*epitassō/epitagē*), 83

communication, 202, 213
  nonverbal, 149
  verbal, 150-51
  See also intimacy

competition, 169-70, 179, 203, 207

complementarian, complementation, 9, 11, 61, 119, 138, 140, 155, 210, 214, 216

defined, 51
  See also gender
conflict, 34-35, 38, 43, 45, 67, 112-16,
  139, 175-76, 192, 200, 202-4
Confucian, 194, 196, 213
contraception, 177n. 11
cost of discipleship, 21-23, 25, 39, 53,
  75, 101, 110, 160
covenant commitment, 30, 33, 146, 163,
  170, 172, 190, 192
coworker(s). *See* ministering together
Darlington, Cynthia, 127, 130-31
David, King, 90
decision maker/making (*kritēs*), 89, 105,
  106n. 5, 108-12, 115, 133, 138-39, 141,
  210-11
despotēs. *See* master of house
disciple(s) of Jesus, 17-21, 32, 38-39,
  44-46, 49-50, 89, 96, 101, 190,
  192, 194, 197, 207-8, 210. *See also*
  cost of discipleship
divorce, 26, 28, 33-35, 41, 43, 77, 94,
  173, 180, 204
domineer or murder (*authenteō/authentēs*),
  80-81
dopamine, 173
egalitarian, 9, 11, 51, 62, 66, 106n. 5,
  138, 140, 191, 210, 216
'*ehād*, 28-29. *See also* one
electronic mail, 114, 117, 149, 159
Eliot, T. S., 45
Elisha, 78-79
equality, 35-37, 50, 119, 123, 181,
  194-95, 211
Eve. *See* Adam
Ezekiel, wife of, 91
faithful. *See* sexual/sexuality, integrity
family, 25, 38, 45, 49, 52, 133, 166, 175,
  189-92, 194, 212-13. *See also* parent(s)
female (*nĕqēbâ*), 119, 127. *See also* gender

feminism, 117-19, 125, 133
fiesta, 189-90, 192
first-born(s), 34, 46
Fisher, Helen, 173
Fite, Robert Cotton. *See* Anderson,
  Herbert
forgive(ness), 18-19, 41, 43-44, 51, 81,
  167-68, 200-203, 207, 213-14
Friedan, Betty, 117
Gallup, George, Jr. 18-19
Gehazi, 79
gender, 96, 208
  conformity (roles), 97
  differentiation (roles and nature), 96,
    98, 117-31, 139-41, 154-5, 157n.
    29, 185, 211, 216
  flexibility (roles), 98, 103-4, 108,
    114-15, 138, 185, 191
  role(s), 57, 60, 72-73, 92, 121, 128,
    140-41, 190-92, 195, 211, 215
gift(s), gifting, 87, 92-93, 102-4, 110,
  112, 122, 134, 138, 141, 169, 191, 203,
  208-11
God
  Elohim, 29n. 23
  image of, 37, 52, 96, 126, 140, 145-46,
    185, 199-200, 211
Gottman, John, 43-44, 93-94
grace, 41, 43, 52, 126. *See also*
  forgive(ness)
Halm, Friedrich, 17
head, headship (*kephalē*), 12, 39, 57-60,
  74-76, 97, 118, 122, 192, 194-95, 204,
  208-10, 216
  defined, 60-64, 88-95, 101, 191
  essence of (initiation, protection,
    provision), 66-70, 75-76, 123-25,
    127, 131-32, 134-36, 155, 209-10
  foundation, 65-66
  purpose of, 70-72, 92, 96, 203

See also Trinity

heart (*kardia*), 44-46, 52, 70, 91, 123, 201, 214

Hefner, Hugh, 145

helper (*ēzer kĕnegdô*), 119

heterosexual, 27

hierarchy/hierarchalist(s)/hierarchical, 51, 59, 65, 78, 106n. 5, 138, 214, 216

Hillel, 26-27, 33. *See also* rabbinic

holy, 89-91

Holy Spirit, 17, 46, 52, 58, 82, 103, 108, 182, 200, 208, 211, 213

filled by, 84-85, 89, 107, 147

See also intimacy; Trinity

Homer, 17

honesty, 34, 150, 159-60, 167, 172, 184, 199, 212. *See also* intimacy

honoring. *See* head, essence of

household management. *See* master of house

Hubbard, Gay. *See* Mathews, Alice

humility, 30-31, 46, 50, 190, 214

humor, 31, 171-72

hypotassō/hypotaxis. *See* submission

immigrant, immigration, 194

incarnational. *See* Trinity

initiation. *See* head, essence of

integrity, 20. *See also* sexual/sexuality

intimacy, 41-42, 47, 67-68, 70-72, 76, 95, 129, 131, 133, 140, 145-47, 164, 192, 199, 209, 211-13

emotional, 147-51, 154, 156, 164, 174-76, 183-84, 190, 199-200, 202

personal, 164-7, 176, 183-84

relational, 147, 154-55, 164, 167-74, 176, 183-84, 200, 202

sexual/physical, 69, 120, 145-46, 151-62, 164, 176-83, 185, 190, 199-200, 202, 212

spiritual, 147, 164-65, 176, 183, 212

See also marital counseling; sexual/ sexuality

Irenaeus, 102

Jairus, 24

Jerome, 81, 85, 92, 107

Jesus. *See* disciple(s); Trinity

join fast (*proskollaomai*), 27

Joshua, 102

Joseph, 125

Josephus, 33, 35, 80

Joy, Donald, 145

Junia, 82

kingdom (reign) of God, 19, 25, 37-38, 50, 109-10, 121, 136, 139, 193-94, 207, 213. *See also* disciple(s)

know (*yāda'*), 146-47, 150, 162, 166, 176, 183, 214

Lamaze, 165

lead (*hēgeomai/hēgemōn*), 83-84

leadership, 24, 74, 82, 84, 87, 95, 101, 103, 115-16, 132, 140-41, 203, 213, 215

Loder, James, 192

Longman, Tremper, III, 73, 123, 126, 131

lord (*kyrios*), 84

love, 9, 18-19, 22, 24, 29-30, 37, 41, 43, 50, 67-68, 70, 72, 74-75, 84, 87, 89-93, 95-98, 114-15, 118, 125, 131, 133, 147, 151-52, 154-55, 159, 171-73, 182, 184-85, 192, 201, 204, 207-10, 212-14, 217

Luther, Martin, 121

Madeson, Amber, 176-78

Malcolm, Kari Torjesen, 19, 175

male (*zākār*), 120, 127

Marazziti, Donatella, 173

marital counseling, 41, 43-45, 93-94, 113, 115, 153, 175-76

issues, 198-202

methodology, 46, 199
  See also intimacy; sexual/sexuality;
    sin(s); vent(ing)
marriage, 77, 138
  consensus, 10-11, 13
  defined, 9, 17
  rule(s), 34-35, 43
  teaching tool, 29-30, 41-42, 47, 50, 52,
    70, 96, 208-9
  youth, 10
  See also rule(s)
Mary Magdalene, 82
master of house (oikodespoteō/oikodes-
  potēs/despotēs), 82-84, 107, 114-15,
  121-22, 125, 134-35, 139
Mathews, Alice, 18, 41-42, 47, 115, 200
matriarchy, 190, 213
Mending the Soul Ministries (MTS),
  40, 70, 221
Millennium Mission, 136-37
mind (nous), 89
  ministering together, 19-23, 47-48, 70.
    See also one
Mistinguett, 151
monogamy, 27, 41, 177-78, 181. See also
  sexual/sexuality, integrity
Moses, 103, 133
mutual(ity), 71-72, 76, 98, 123, 209
  attraction, 28
Neruda, Pablo, 154
Norton, A. Edward, 207
nourish/nurture/nurturing (ektrephō),
  91-92, 124-27, 129-30, 134-35, 141,
  153, 168
one/unity ('eḥād), 217
  couple, 19, 28-29, 52, 98, 114, 146-47
  See also ministering together; Trinity.
one flesh, 25-33, 35, 42, 47, 50-53, 72,
  76, 91, 95, 101, 122, 131, 133, 146,
  154, 162-64, 166-67, 172, 174-76, 178,

180, 183-84, 195-96, 199-200, 202,
  205, 207, 210, 212-13, 215
oversee (episkopeō/episkopē/episkopos),
  83-84
oxytocin, 127, 130, 152, 173
parent(s), 24, 26-28, 174, 190, 193,
  195-96, 212-13. See also family
parenting. See child rearing
pastor(al), 10, 19, 21, 44, 51, 59-60, 81,
  88, 134, 159, 175, 194-95, 198, 213
paterfamilias, 106
Patermouthis, Aurelius, 24
patriarchy, 39, 74, 79, 118, 190-91,
  213. See also hierarchy
phalanx, 86
Philo, 33, 80
Phoebe, 82
physical strength, 68, 104, 108, 141, 170
politeness, 24, 168-69
Poloma, Margaret, 18-19
pornography. See sexual/sexuality
power, 80-81, 88-89, 94, 114-15,
  128-29, 140, 164, 175, 181, 191, 204-5,
  209-11, 214, 216.
  to have power over (hyperochē/
    hyperechō), 83. See also authority, of
    power
prayer, 37, 46, 48, 67-69, 81, 88, 98,
  107, 109-12, 131-32, 134-35, 154,
  157, 159-60, 164, 175, 178, 192,
  199, 203, 207, 210, 213. See also
  intimacy, spiritual
priest of family, 39-40, 98, 103, 106-7,
  131, 138, 141, 194-95, 210
priesthood, 90-91, 102, 106-7, 115, 204
prophet(s), 73, 78-79, 86, 103, 125
Prisca (Priscilla) and Aquila, 22-23, 30,
  102
protection. See head, essence of
pursue (dābaq), 27n. 21

rabbinic logic, 26-27
rabbinic teachings, 30-31, 35-36,
    164-65, 172. *See also* Hillel;
    Shammai
repentance, 18, 207. *See also* sin(s)
respect (*phobeomai/phobos*), 66, 68, 74,
    83, 86-88, 92, 95-97, 137, 150, 155,
    157, 160, 168-69, 171, 176, 181, 184,
    196, 200, 208, 210, 212-13
rest, 25, 45
Roberts, Wes, 173-74
role. *See* gender
Rosenau, Douglas, 156n. 26, 157n. 30,
    181n. 14, 184
rule
    archō/archōn, 83-84, 89
    basileuō/basileus/basilissa, 83-84
    proistēmi, prostatis, 82
    See also rule(s)
rule(s)/ruler(s), 85-86, 102-3, 107, 115,
    119, 123, 140, 174-75, 178-79, 184-85.
    See also marriage; to rule
sabbath. *See* rest
    sacrifice, 22-23, 40, 47, 53, 70, 75, 84,
        89-95, 97-98, 106, 161, 191, 204,
        208, 212. *See also* cost
Salome, 82
Sarah and Abraham, 83, 91-92, 97
savior, 89, 91, 96
sensate hour, 152, 155-57, 159, 184-85.
    See also intimacy; sexual/sexuality
service/servanthood, 24-25, 39, 44,
    46-47, 50, 59, 64, 72, 74, 79, 92, 95,
    119, 190, 210. *See also* disciple(s);
    submission, mutual
sexual/sexuality, 57, 145, 149-50,
    175-76, 178, 183
    integrity, purity, 47, 69, 135, 158-59,
        180, 183, 199-200, 212-13, 215
    intercourse, 30n. 24, 57, 120, 146-47,

151-53, 160-61, 183-84, 199
    pornography, 120, 152-53, 158, 160,
        174, 179-80, 183, 217
    vulnerability, 45, 159, 163, 174,
        177-78, 180-83
    See also intimacy
Shammai, 26. *See also* rabbinic
    teaching
Shaw, George Bernard, 43
shepherd (*poimainō/poimēn*), 83-84
Shunammite, 77-79, 102
sin(s)/sinner(s), 42-46, 58-59, 61, 67-68,
    71, 74, 91, 113, 126, 167, 174-75, 192,
    200-202
Slater, Lauren, 173
Solomon, 90, 115
source, 28, 52, 59-62, 79, 80, 89,
    97-98, 101, 208. *See also* head
sovereign (*dynastēs*), 84
Stephana(s), 86-87, 102
Storkey, Elaine, 166
stress, 87, 118, 129, 174
submission, submit (*hypotassō*), 12, 24,
    57-60, 66, 73-75, 85-87, 92, 118, 124,
    191, 203, 208, 210
    mutual, 72-73, 84-88, 91-92, 94-95,
        97-98, 101-2, 192, 203-4, 208-9,
        213
Syrophoenician mother, 24
Taylor, Shelley, 127, 129-30
temptation(s), 21-22, 45, 179
Tertullian, 23, 27
thankful(ness), 87-88, 94, 98
Tkako, Aurelia, 24
Trinity
    one, unity, 29-30, 71-72, 76, 95-96,
        114n. 18, 140, 146, 149, 167, 180,
        183-85, 191, 202n. 4, 208-9, 215
    diversity, 58-60, 65-69, 74, 76, 89n.
        35, 96, 122, 208-9

incarnational, 64-66, 72-76, 96-97,
   202n. 4
unblemished (*amōmos*), 90
unity. *See* one
Van Leeuwen, Mary Stewart, 105, 111,
   114-15, 179
vent(ing), 114, 150, 202

wealth, 25, 68, 108, 133-34, 139, 141,
   146, 154, 193-94, 213. *See also* cost
widow(s), 163, 166
wonderful (*endoxos*), 89-90
Wright, H. Norman, 173-74
wrinkle (*rhytis*), 90n. 36

Scripture Index

Genesis
1–15, *119*
1:5, *28*
1:26, *29, 58, 119, 123, 126*
1:26-27, *114*
1:26-28, *29, 103, 145, 202*
1:27, *27, 29, 208*
1:28, *31, 134, 204*
1:29-30, *204*
1:31, *120*
2:2-3, *91*
2:18, *51, 119*
2:21-22, *28*
2:22, *31*
2:23, *28*
2:24, *9, 27, 28, 30, 133, 162, 180, 212*
2:24-25, *146*
3:1-6, *126*
3:1-13, *67*
3:5, *162*
3:16, *204*
3:17-19, *125*
4:1, *146, 162*
5:1-2, *114*
5:2, *114*
5:5, *167*
8, *31*
11:1, *29*
11:6, *29*
12:11-20, *92*
14:1-16, *125*
24:23, *124*
24:58, *28*
24:67, *28*
31:23, *27*
45:7, *91*
45:11, *91*

Exodus
1:17-20, *125*
4:27, *151*
13:2, *91*
13:12, *91*
17:9, *125*
18:13-26, *103*
19:6, *107*
20:8, *91*
20:11, *91*
20:12, *124*
20:14, *180*
21:15, *124*
22:17, *124*
28:2-8, *90*
29:1, *90*
29:4, *90*
29:10, *91*
29:15, *91*
29:21, *90*
29:24, *91*
29:36-37, *90*
29:38, *90*
29:44-45, *90*
34:10, *90*

Leviticus
1:3-17, *106*
6:12, *106*
6:16-18, *106*
13:1-44, *106*
19:3, *124*
19:18, *215*
21:17-20, *91*
24:5-9, *106*
27:8, *106*

Numbers
11:11-17, *103*
11:24-28, *103*
11:29, *103*
14:30, *102*
23:21, *90*
30:3-5, *124*

Deuteronomy
6:4, *29, 96*
6:4-5, *215*
20:2-4, *106*

21:19-20, *124*
22:6, *91*
22:15, *124*
22:16, *124*
24:1, *26, 30*
24:5, *126*
25:5-10, *68*
32:3-43, *126*

Joshua
4:4, *90*
4:15-17, *106*
15:13-19, *102*
23:8, *27*

Judges
1:1-9, *125*
1:11-15, *102*
4:9, *125*
6:1-6, *125*
7:1-25, *125*

Ruth
1:9, *151*
1:14, *27, 151*
2:21, *27*
2:23, *27*

1 Samuel
2:12-17, *10*
8:4-20, *103*
17:9-58, *125*
20:41, *151*
31:2, *27*

1 Kings
9:6, *90*
11:20, *91*
12:8, *91*
12:10, *91*
18:23, *90*

2 Kings
4:8-10, *78*
4:12, *79*

4:13-37, *79*
4:19, *125*
8:1, *79*
12:9-10, *106*

2 Chronicles
2:9, *90*

Nehemiah
4:13-14, *124*
10:38, *106*

Esther
1:1-9, *77*
1:10-12, *78*
1:17-18, *78*
1:20, *78*

Job
39:14, *91*
41:16-17, *27*

Psalms
8:6, *86*
10:1, *151*
13:1-5, *151*
22:1-3, *151*
22:2, *91*
22:9, *126*
22:19-22, *151*
35:17-22, *151*
37:4, *38*
38:1-22, *151*
42:1-11, *151*
55:1-5, *151*
60:1-12, *151*
73, *27*
74:1-2, *151*
74:10-12, *151*
79:1-13, *151*
84:11, *38*
88:1-13, *151*
103:13, *124, 125*
127, *134*
131:2, *125*

Proverbs
1:8, *116, 124*
3:12, *71*
5:15-20, *200*
5:18-19, *178*
7:5-27, *180*
10:12, *202*
12:15, *109*
12:16-18, *150*
12:18, *113*
15:23, *113*
15:28, *150*
15:31, *109*
16:3, *109*
16:9, *109*
16:33, *112*
17:17, *114*
18:4-7, *150*
18:18, *112*
18:24, *27*
19:20, *109*
19:21, *109*
20:5, *148*
21:23, *150*
23:24, *91*
27:17, *109*
29:22, *201*
30:11, *124*
30:17, *124*
31, *83*
31:10-31, *125*

Ecclesiastes
4:9-10, *114*
5:2, *150*
9:9, *178*
12:10-11, *150*

Song of Solomon
1:2, *154*
8:1, *126*

Isaiah
23:4, *91*
49:13-15, *125*
49:14-15, *126*
49:15, *126*
49:21, *91*
53, *149*
61:6, *107*
66:10-13, *126*
66:13, *125*

Jeremiah
22:1-3, *68, 125*
22:15-16, *68*
22:15-17, *125*
31:9, *124*
31:25, *71*
41:7-16, *125*

Lamentations
2:11-12, *125*

Ezekiel
24:16, *91*
24:21, *91*
24:25, *91*
31:4, *91*

Hosea
9:12, *91*

Joel
2:16, *126*

Micah
2:8-9, *68*
3:1-12, *68*

Zechariah
10:9, *91*
13:3, *124*

Malachi
2:16, *170*

Matthew
1, *125*
1:6, *83*
1:23, *84*
2:1, *83*
2:6, *84*
2:13-14, *125*
2:22, *83*
3:16-17, *203*
3:17, *71*
5:21-24, *175*
5:28, *44, 179*
5:31-32, *26, 180*
6:1-18, *44*
6:9-10, *65*
7:5, *113*
7:28-8:1, *26*
7:29, *81*

8:6, *83*
9:2-6, *26*
9:6, *81*
9:8, *26*
9:9-13, *41*
9:18, *83*
9:23, *83*
9:26, *26*
9:31, *26*
9:33-34, *26*
10:1, *81*
10:2-4, *22*
10:34-39, *38*
10:37-38, *38*
11:28-29, *71*
12:6, *26*
12:42, *83*
13:2, *26*
14:13, *26, 203*
14:23, *203*
15:19, *44*
15:30-31, *26*
18:4, *31*
18:15, *114*
18:21-35, *41*
18:35, *41, 44*
19, *31*
19:1-10, *26*
19:2, *26*
19:3-9, *33, 35, 180*
19:3-12, *26*
19:4, *27*
19:5, *26, 27, 30, 35, 203*
19:5-6, *28*
19:6, *27, 30*
19:9, *35*
19:13-14, *31*
19:29, *38*
20:25, *80*
20:25-28, *205*
21:6, *69*
21:23, *81*
22:30, *33*
22:37, *44*
22:37-39, *18*
23:15, *44*
23:37, *125*
25:21, *19*
25:23, *19*
26:31, *84*
26:36, *203*

27:2, *83*
28:1-10, *36*
28:10, *82*
28:18, *65, 69, 81, 84*
28:19, *29, 114*

Mark
1:4-5, *18*
1:15, *18*
1:17, *19*
1:27, *81, 83*
1:30, *24*
2:15-17, *21*
2:27-28, *25*
3:31-35, *22*
6:12, *18*
6:31-32, *25*
7:20-23, *18*
7:25-30, *24*
8:34-35, *21*
9:25, *83*
9:33-37, *20*
9:35, *46*
10, *26, 31*
10:1-12, *26*
10:2-12, *26*
10:6-9, *27*
10:7, *26*
10:7-8, *26*
10:8, *28, 30*
10:29-30, *38*
10:42-45, *24*
10:45, *20, 84*
12:18-27, *33*
12:29, *215*
12:29-31, *18, 214, 215*
12:31, *24*
13:32-37, *19*
13:34, *81*
14:14, *83*

Luke
1:32-33, *65*
4:6, *81*
6:36-38, *18*
7:36-50, *41*
7:38, *151*
8:1-3, *36*
8:21, *22*
8:25, *83*
8:41, *83*

8:41-42, *24*
9:23, *22*
10:1, *22*
10:9, *19*
10:27, *18*
10:29-37, *18*
10:38-42, *36*
11:1, *203*
11:4, *18*
11:27, *126*
12:5, *81*
12:11, *81*
12:51-53, *22*
13:17, *90*
14:1, *83*
14:22, *83*
14:26, *22, 38*
15:12, *124*
17:26, *69*
18:8, *95*
18:20, *24*
18:29, *38*
18:29-30, *22*
18:32-33, *21*
19:1-9, *41*
20:20, *81*
20:27-40, *33*
21:16, *22*
22:25-26, *59*
22:25-27, *24*
22:26, *83, 84*
22:53, *81*
23:7, *81*
23:35-39, *89*
24:26, *21*
24:47, *18*

John
1:14, *150*
3:1, *83*
3:35, *65, 71*
4, *36*
4:46-47, *24*
5:23, *69*
5:27, *81*
6:38, *65*
8:28-29, *65*
8:42, *67*
10:11, *84*
10:14, *84*
10:18, *81*
10:36, *67, 91*

10:36-38, *65*
12:21, *83*
12:42-43, *21*
13:1-17, *46*
13:3-17, *84*
13:34-35, *19, 96*
14:10, *71*
14:15, *19*
14:16, *67, 203*
14:21, *19*
14:23, *203*
14:23-24, *19*
14:26, *67, 203*
15:1-2, *67*
15:10, *65*
15:18-21, *21*
16:13, *203*
16:15, *65*
16:32, *71*
17, *207*
17:2, *65, 81*
17:10, *65*
17:11, *71*
17:17, *67*
17:21-23, *71, 98*
19:10-11, *81*
19:26-27, *24*
20:15, *83*
20:17, *82*

Acts
1:7, *81*
2:4, *103*
2:17-18, *103*
3:15, *84*
5:2-3, *17*
5:3-4, *17*
5:8-9, *17*
5:9, *17*
5:31, *84*
7:10, *83*
8:27, *83*
9:14, *81*
11:29, *69*
15:11, *71*
15:22, *83*
18:2, *23*
18:3, *23*
18:18, *23*
18:26, *23*
19:16, *80*
20:28, *83*

20:37, *151*
23:24, *83*
26:2, *83*
26:18, *81*
26:25, *83*
26:30, *83*

Romans
5:12-19, *126*
8:7, *85*
8:27, *203*
8:31-32, *38*
8:34, *203*
9:21, *81*
10:3, *85*
10:9, *203*
12:1, *90*
12:2, *103, 180*
12:8, *21, 82*
12:10, *92*
12:15, *148*
13, *81*
13:1, *73, 81, 83, 86*
13:1-3, *83*
13:1-7, *81*
15:16, *90*
16:1-2, *82*
16:3, *23*
16:3-5, *23*
16:4, *23*
16:7, *82*
16:16, *151*

1 Corinthians
1:12-13, *95*
5:1-2, *158*
6:7-8, *160*
6:15, *158*
6:15-20, *180*
6:16, *30*
7:1-5, *184*
7:3, *160*
7:3-5, *178*
7:4, *72, 81*
7:5, *160, 179*
8:6, *67*
11:3, *58, 60, 64, 96, 97, 208*
11:10, *81*
12:4-6, *71*
12:4-11, *204*
12:11, *69*

12:26, *92, 184*
13:4, *172*
13:7, *114*
14:29-31, *86*
14:32, *73, 86*
15:6-7, *82*
15:21-22, *126*
15:28, *73*
16:15-18, *87*
16:16, *74*
16:19, *23*

2 Corinthians
1:5, *69*
1:24, *84*
2:12, *30*
5:11-13, *150*
6:6-7, *150*

Galatians
1:1, *71*
3:28, *204*
4:2, *124*
5:13, *72*
5:22, *38*
6:2, *72*

Ephesians
1:4, *67, 90*
1:5, *84*
1:18, *84*
1:21, *81*
1:22, *63*
1:22-23, *89*
2:2, *81*
3:10, *81*
4:1, *84*
4:2, *72*
4:7-8, *64*
4:11-16, *64*
4:14, *89*
4:15, *63, 64, 150*
4:15-16, *89*
4:25, *34, 150*
4:25-32, *202*
4:26, *34, 175, 202*
4:26-27, *113*
4:29, *150*
4:31, *87*
5, *79, 92, 97, 112, 208, 209, 210*
5:1-2, *84, 89*

5:2, *89, 90, 91*
5:4, *87*
5:15-18, *84*
5:18, *89, 107*
5:19-21, *85*
5:20, *87*
5:21, *74, 86, 87, 88, 92*
5:21-24, *88*
5:21-33, *12, 72, 75, 84, 97*
5:22, *74, 85*
5:22-24, *85, 203*
5:22-31, *126*
5:23, *63, 88, 95*
5:23-29, *64*
5:24, *85*
5:25, *89, 90, 114, 125*
5:25-26, *89, 90*
5:25-27, *89, 90*
5:25-32, *131*
5:25-33, *70, 85, 88*
5:26, *90*
5:27, *90*
5:28-30, *89, 91*
5:31, *27, 91*
5:33, *66, 85, 87, 89, 101, 107, 168*
6:1, *74*
6:5, *74, 83*
6:9, *83*
6:12, *81*

Philippians
1:1, *83*
2:1-4, *72*
2:3, *83*
2:8-11, *65*
2:9-11, *69*
4:7, *110*

Colossians
1:13, *81*
1:15-20, *63*
1:16, *63*
2:10, *63*
2:14-15, *64*

2:15, *81*
2:16-23, *64*
2:19, *63, 64*
3:15, *110*
3:17, *110*
3:18, *73*
3:20, *74, 124*
3:22, *74*
4:1, *83*
4:3, *110*

1 Thessalonians
1:1, *71, 91*
2:7, *91, 124*
4:4, *180*
5:12, *82*

2 Thessalonians
2:13-14, *67*
2:16-17, *71*
3:7-13, *108*

1 Timothy
2:2, *83*
2:8-10, *81*
2:12, *80, 81, 83*
3:1, *83*
3:2, *83*
3:4, *115*
3:4-5, *82*
3:12, *82*
5:8, *68*
5:10, *125*
5:13-14, *108*
5:14, *83, 115, 125, 163*
5:17, *82*
6:1, *83*
6:15, *84*

2 Timothy
2:15, *180*
4:19, *23*

Titus
1:7, *83*
2, *121*
2:4, *92, 97, 114, 209*
2:4-5, *125*

2:5, *73, 115*
2:9, *83*
2:11, *71*
2:13-14, *90*
2:15, *83*

Philemon
8, *83*

Hebrews
2:5-8, *73*
2:8, *86*
2:10, *84*
6:20, *84*
7:26-27, *106*
10:11, *106*
12:2, *84*
12:9, *85*
13:4, *180*
13:7, *83*
13:17, *83*
13:20, *84*
13:24, *83*

James
1:17, *38*
1:20, *202*
3:6, *90*
3:9, *30*
4:7, *85*
4:8, *165*
4:13-15, *109*
5:13-18, *203*
5:16, *148, 175*

1 Peter
1, *74*
1:2, *67, 71*
2:9, *91, 204*
2:13, *83, 87*
2:13-14, *83, 86*
2:17, *87, 92*
2:18, *83*
2:20-24, *92*
3:1-2, *73*
3:1-4, *107*
3:5, *73*
3:6, *83, 92*
3:7, *69, 92, 97, 104, 170*

4:8, *168*
4:10, *69*
5:2, *83*
5:3, *84*
5:4, *84*
5:5, *74*

2 Peter
1:2, *71*
2:19, *107*

1 John
1:9, *203*
2:1, *203*
4:8, *95, 214*
4:16, *214*
4:20, *30*

2 John
1, *83*
1:5, *83*

Jude
4, *84*
20-21, *71*
23, *90*
25, *81*

Revelation
1:5, *84, 204*
1:6, *91, 107*
1:8, *69*
2:26-27, *81*
3:19, *71*
5:10, *83, 91, 107*
6:8, *81*
7:17, *84*
11:6, *81*
12:10, *81*
13:2, *81*
13:4, *81*
13:5, *81*
13:7, *81*
15:3, *69*
16:9, *81*
16:14, *69*
18:1, *81*
19:15, *84*